Lyn Elizabeth M. Martin
Editor

The Challenge of Internet Literacy: The Instruction-Web Convergence

Pre-publication
REVIEWS,
COMMENTARIES,
EVALUATIONS . . .

E ditor Lyn Martin brings together in this welcome volume the words and experiences of a number of diverse librarians at many levels of higher education and from a variety of geographical perspectives. Helpful inclusions for the readers are concise abstracts, keyword listings, and up-to-date bibliographies for each chapter.

"Students must learn to embrace future possibilities without disregarding traditional avenues for information." A strength of this book is its demonstrated theory and practice of students taking responsibility for their own learning; developing critical thinking skills; and becoming empowered as they learn Internet navigation as an enhancement to accessing more traditional resources.

Nancy Seale Osborne, MS, MLS, Certified Archivist
Librarian, Coordinator of Library Instruction and Special Collections, SUNY College at Oswego, NY

The authors of this volume offer many diverse methods of presenting online research strategies and making sense of the exploding information superhighway called the Internet and/or the World Wide Web. In addition to a discussion of affective and cognitive information behavior of library users and trying to help some overcome their technophobia while counseling others not to depend solely on the electronic information for all of their research needs, the authors focus on teaching users conceptual frameworks, similar to that offered in the pre-technology bibliographic instruction environment.

The strengths of this book include the coverage of the challenges in teaching an uncontrollable maze of information in an electronic environment. The highlights are the variety of teaching methodologies presented. There are beneficial tips for anyone getting started in an effective library-user-education program for information technology literacy.

Maureen Pastine, MLS
Central University Librarian, Southern Methodist University, Dallas, TX

This book is a collection of articles that highlight various issues about bibliographic instruction and the Internet. This book describes many examples of research strategies on the Web and possible problems when teaching the Web. Student learning styles in relation to information literacy are discussed and many helpful Internet Web Site addresses are included. In addition, the book examines using the Web as a teaching tool.

This book fills a gap in library literature about a topic many librarians are trying to grasp. The bibliography of further resources to train librarians to train others is a definite plus. This is a timely source for library managers, reference librarians, and instruction librarians. Highly recommended!

Mary F. Salony, MLS
Director of Learning Resources, West Virginia Northern Community College

More pre-publication
REVIEWS, COMMENTARIES, EVALUATIONS . . .

Like the Web itself, techniques and theories spin out in all directions, detailing the host of teaching, reference, and serendipitous functions of the WWW. Librarians should read with pen and paper at hand to jot down the many ideas this book sparks for planning class sessions or faculty workshops; for creating Web-based tutorials, pathfinders, and interactive assignments; and to note the quality Web sites identified and described.

Instruction and the Web truly converge in these chapters that describe how proven teaching methods can be effectively applied by librarians to this ever-changing resource while, at the same time, offering suggestions for incorporating the Web into traditional library instruction sessions.

Librarians who are feeling bombarded by the plethora of resources available on the Web will find in these chapters welcome suggestions, pertinent questions to ask, and pitfalls to avoid, when using the Web as part of their instruction.

Beth L. Mark, MSLS
Library Instruction Coordinator,
Messiah College, Grantham, PA

Who isn't trying to integrate the Web effectively into instruction, whether in the classroom or at the reference desk? This book offers a great range of resources for librarians in any environment who are faced with the challenge of making sense out of Web chaos for many different levels and types of users. Chapters cover theoretical as well as practical instruction issues. Adaptable models are offered for structuring the research process, instruction programming and content, as well as for site construction, use, and promotion. Useful resources for training trainers, for reaching special groups, and for finding information in specific subjects are also presented.

The result is a multifaceted look into the many instruction opportunities and challenges that face libraries as the Web becomes an increasingly prominent information tool. *The Challenge of Internet Literacy* provides ideas that can help you find new solutions to the puzzle of Web instruction.

Janelle M. Zauha, MA, MLS
Electronic Information Coordinator,
The Libraries, Montana State University–Bozeman

The Haworth Press, Inc.

The Challenge
of Internet Literacy:
The Instruction-Web
Convergence

The Challenge
of Internet Literacy:
The Instruction-Web
Convergence

Lyn Elizabeth M. Martin
Editor

The Haworth Press, Inc.
New York · London

The Challenge of Internet Literacy: The Instruction-Web Convergence has also been published as *Internet Reference Services Quarterly,* Volume 2, Numbers 2/3 and 4 1997.

The development, preparation, and publication of this work has been undertaken with great care. However, the publisher, employees, editors, and agents of The Haworth Press and all imprints of The Haworth Press, Inc., including The Haworth Medical Press and Pharmaceutical Products Press, are not responsible for any errors contained herein or for consequences that may ensue from use of materials or information contained in this work. Opinions expressed by the author(s) are not necessarily those of The Haworth Press, Inc.

Cover design by Thomas J. Mayshock Jr.

The Haworth Press, Inc., 10 Alice Street, Binghamton, NY 13904-1580 USA

Library of Congress Cataloging-in-Publication Data

The challenge of Internet literacy : the instruction-Web convergence / Lyn Elizabeth M. Martin, editor.
    p. cm.
    Includes bibliographical references (p.   ) and index.
    ISBN 0-7890-0346-5 (alk. paper) – ISBN 0-7890-0347-3 (pbk. : alk. paper)
    1. Internet (Computer network)–United States. 2. Library information networks–United States. 3. Library orientation–United States–Data processing. I. Martin, Lyn Elizabeth M.
Z674.75.I58C48 1997
025.04 dc21   97-22247
                                                                  CIP

INDEXING & ABSTRACTING

Contributions to this publication are selectively indexed or abstracted in print, electronic, online, or CD-ROM version(s) of the reference tools and information services listed below. This list is current as of the copyright date of this publication. See the end of this section for additional notes.

- *Applied Social Sciences Index & Abstracts (ASSIA) (Online: ASSI via Data-Star) CDRom: ASSIA Plus),* Bowker-Saur Limited, Maypole House, Maypole Road, East Grinstead, West Sussex RH19 1HH England

- *CINAHL (Cumulative Index to Nursing & Allied Health Literature),* in print, also on CD-ROM from CD-PLUS, EBSCO, and SilverPlatter, and online from CDP Online (formerly BRS), Data-Star, and PaperChase (Support materials include Subject Heading List, Database Search Guide, and instructional video), CINAHL Information Systems, P.O. Box 871, 1509 Wilson Terrace, Glendale, CA 91209-0871.

- *CNPIEC Reference Guide: Chinese National Directory of Foreign Periodicals*, P.O. Box 88, Beijing, People's Republic of China

- *Computer Literature Index,* Applied Computer Research, Inc., P.O. Box 82266, Phoenix, AZ 85071-2266

- *Computing Reviews,* Association for Computing Machinery, 1515 Broadway, 17th Floor, New York, NY 10036

- *Current Index to Journals in Education,* Syracuse University, 4-194 Center for Science & Technology, Syracuse, NY 13244-4100

- *European Association for Health Information & Libraries: selected abstracts in newsletter "Publications" section,* EAHIL Newsletter, Mohrhaldenstr. 166A, ch-4125 Riehen, Switzerland

- *Index to Periodical Articles Related to Law,* University of Texas, 727 East 26th Street, Austin, TX 78705

(continued)

94076

- *Information Science Abstracts,* Plenum Publishing Company, 233 Spring Street, New York, NY 10013-1578

- *Informed Librarian, The,* Infosources Publishing, 140 Norma Road, Teaneck, NJ 07666

- *INSPEC Information Services,* Institution of Electrical Engineers, Michael Faraday House, Six Hills Way, Stevenage, Herts SG1 2AY England

- *INTERNET ACCESS (& additional networks) Bulletin Board for Libraries ("BUBL"), coverage of information resources on INTERNET, JANET, and other networks.*
  - JANET X.29: UK.AC.BATH.BUBL or 00006012101300
  - TELNET: BUBL.BATH.AC.UK or 138.38.32.45 login 'bubl'
  - Gopher: BUBL.BATH.AC.UK (138.32.32.45). Port 7070
  - World Wide Web: http://www.bubl.bath.ac.uk./BUBL/home.html
  - NISSWAIS: telnetniss.ac.uk (for the NISS gateway)
  The Andersonian Library, Curran Building, 101 St. James Road, Glasgow G4 ONS, Scotland

- *Journal of Academic Librarianship: Guide to Professional Literature, The,* Grad School of Library & Information Science/Simmons College, 300 The Fenway, Boston, MA 02115-5898

- *Konyvtari Figyelo-Library Review,* National Szechenyi Library, Centre for Library and Information Science, H-1827 Budapest, Hungary

- *Library & Information Science Abstracts (LISA),* Bowker-Saur Limited, Maypole House, Maypole Road, East Grinstead, West Sussex, RH19 1HH, England

- *Microcomputer Abstracts,* Information Today, Inc., 143 Old Marlton Pike, Medford, NJ 08055-8750

- *National Clearinghouse on Child Abuse & Neglect,* 10530 Rosehaven Street, Suite 400, Fairfax, VA 22030-2804

- *Referativnyi Zhurnal (Abstracts Journal of the Institute of Scientific Information of the Republic of Russia),* The Institute of Scientific Information, Baltijskaja ul., 14, Moscow, A-219, Republic of Russia

(continued)

SPECIAL BIBLIOGRAPHIC NOTES

related to special journal issues (separates)
and indexing/abstracting

☐ indexing/abstracting services in this list will also cover material in any "separate" that is co-published simultaneously with Haworth's special thematic journal issue or DocuSerial. Indexing/abstracting usually covers material at the article/chapter level.

☐ monographic co-editions are intended for either non-subscribers or libraries which intend to purchase a second copy for their circulating collections.

☐ monographic co-editions are reported to all jobbers/wholesalers/approval plans. The source journal is listed as the "series" to assist the prevention of duplicate purchasing in the same manner utilized for books-in-series.

☐ to facilitate user/access services all indexing/abstracting services are encouraged to utilize the co-indexing entry note indicated at the bottom of the first page of each article/chapter/contribution.

☐ this is intended to assist a library user of any reference tool (whether print, electronic, online, or CD-ROM) to locate the monographic version if the library has purchased this version but not a subscription to the source journal.

☐ individual articles/chapters in any Haworth publication are also available through the Haworth Document Delivery Services (HDDS).

The Challenge of Internet Literacy: The Instruction-Web Convergence

CONTENTS

"HOT" BIBLIOGRAPHIES

ABOUT THE EDITOR

Lyn Elizabeth M. Martin holds a BA in English (Cum Laude) from the College of St. Rose, Albany, New York and an MLS from the University at Albany, State University of New York, Albany, New York. She is Head of Technical Services and Associate Librarian, A.A. Lemieux Library, Seattle University, Seattle, Washington, where she manages acquisitions and approvals, accounting, cataloging, serials, and physical processing. Ms. Martin is a patient and enthusiastic teacher and mentor of library and information science graduate interns, as well as both fledgling and seasoned catalogers. She also serves on the Editorial Boards of the e-journal *MCJournal*, and the *PNLA (Pacific Northwest Library Association) Quarterly* and has written numerous articles and spoken and taught widely on a broad range of library topics, covering and bridging technical and public services, including the Internet. In addition, Ms. Martin is a freelance book editor and prior to receiving her MLS worked as a newswriter and for an advertising agency.

How Some Web Pages Came About

Katharine A. Waugh

The illustrator, Katharine A. Waugh (kawaugh@vaxsar.vassar.edu), is Reference Librarian, Vassar College Library, Poughkeepsie, NY 12601.

[Haworth co-indexing entry note]: "How Some Web Pages Came About." Waugh, Katharine A. Co-published simultaneously in *Internet Reference Services Quarterly* (The Haworth Press, Inc.) Vol. 2, No. 2/3, 1997, p. 1; and: *The Challenge of Internet Literacy: The Instruction-Web Convergence* (ed: Lyn Elizabeth M. Martin) The Haworth Press, Inc., 1997, p. 1. Single or multiple copies of this article are available for a fee from The Haworth Document Delivery Service [1-800-342-9678, 9:00 a.m. - 5:00 p.m. (EST). E-mail address: getinfo@haworth.com].

INTRODUCTION

Endings/Beginnings:
Some Convergent Thoughts
About Cyberinstruction

Susan Griswold Blandy

SUMMARY. The author uses the analog/digital phenomenon to explore the responsibility of the librarian to train students in lifetime critical thinking skills, even as the students are assisted in learning to navigate the Internet for the moment's ephemeral answer. *[Article copies available for a fee from The Haworth Document Delivery Service: 1-800-342-9678. E-mail address: getinfo@haworth.com]*

KEYWORDS. Critical thinking, bibliographic instruction, analog/digital phenomenon

Here in upstate New York it is snowing . . . snowing and snowing . . . snowing and snowing. . . .

Susan Griswold Blandy (blandsus@hvcc.edu) is Professor and Assistant Librarian at Hudson Valley Community College, Troy, NY 12180.

[Haworth co-indexing entry note]: "Endings/Beginnings: Some Convergent Thoughts About Cyberinstruction." Blandy, Susan Griswold. Co-published simultaneously in *Internet Reference Services Quarterly* (The Haworth Press, Inc.) Vol. 2, No. 2/3, 1997, pp. 3-7; and: *The Challenge of Internet Literacy: The Instruction-Web Convergence* (ed: Lyn Elizabeth M. Martin) The Haworth Press, Inc., 1997, pp. 3-7. Single or multiple copies of this article are available for a fee from The Haworth Document Delivery Service [1-800-342-9678, 9:00 a.m. - 5:00 p.m. (EST). E-mail address: getinfo@haworth.com].

3

Well, your Editor has asked me for an opinion piece to accompany this volume on bibliographic instruction and the Internet. And, while it is easy to sit around a table and be opinionated among friends who will not hold you to it the next day, it is more dangerous to be opinionated in print.

For one thing, those of us who teach critical thinking skills are always reminding our students to be wary of opinions, a string of assertions. Assertions, no matter how loudly or eloquently expressed, are not fact statements, but rather very personal windows into the psyche of the speaker and the culture. Their validity for guiding our behavior is very limited. When we yield up to the demands, it is a surrender to power, rather than to reason. However, the power may not be in the cohesiveness of the speaker's position, but rather in the speaker's ability to describe and give shape to a world that we recognize. To paraphrase T.S. Eliot: we return and recognize the place for the first time.

On these pages I plan to be opinionated about the teaching librarian's (now . . . teaching cybrarian's?) responsibility to help students come to understand that they are not in school to deny or accept uncritically what an expert states. Our responsibility is to the questions: "How do we imagine? How do we structure? How do we search? How do we evaluate? How do we respond?"

For a moment, let's go back a bit in time. It is December 20, 1996–the end of the semester for the students on my campus–on many of our campuses. "Done," says Howard, smiling as he strides across campus.

Done? Done! Done!!!??? I know the feeling well. I just finished the last hour of the semester. Like the students, I'd like to crash, sleep 21 hours, and, no matter how well I did this fall, get a fresh start in January. That's part of the appeal of education and gardening and music. There are always what seem to be endings and new beginnings–again and again and again.

The problem, of course, is that the last class should mark a beginning, the point where students are ready to take on the responsibility for their own learning in that subject. No professor wants the last class to be the end of the matter. No librarian wants today's reference interview to be the last time that a student asks for help. For all the hype about independent, asynchronous, geographically-liberated students, we really still want to maintain human-to-human interaction at the core of the process. That is, live with humans in real time, if possible–all that, even in the ever-evolving cyberworld.

So, the core question for librarians (particularly instruction librarians) is, within the confines of our collections of resources and services, within the possibilities of the courses, given those students in these classes: "What are we teaching? What can we communicate? What is the student supposed to do with it?" The better and more experience we get, the more we realize that the answer cannot be expressed solely in terms of content, facts, and formula.

Xerox ran an ad around the end of December 1996/beginning of January 1997 in *The Chronicle of Higher Education,* banner headline, to the effect of: "Most College Textbooks are out of Date in 18 Months." Everyday, we are bombarded with messages like this: rapid fire changes, the inevitability of change (which we no longer equate with progress). The appropriate student reaction to the Xerox message is, "Why buy or read a textbook that will be worthless? Why study hard, since there's no point in learning what I'll only have to forget in 18 months? Hey—by the time I graduate from college, about 65% of what I learned will be out of date—where does that get me?"

For the teaching faculty and librarians, if we are concentrating on teaching the ever-changing specifics, how do we keep sight of the basics? It can be very hard to teach the foundation of philosophy of a course to students who arrive, as one professor put it, "So needy." They need to be taught how to be college students—educated people. Most of our students arrive unfamiliar with the intellectual process of research, evaluation, reflection . . . unfamiliar with the idea of a *foundation* of knowledge, ignorant that the subject areas are called disciplines because they require discipline of thought.

The fact and reality is: students arrive inexperienced in thinking itself. Students come to us used to getting their information easily in pre-packaged units of "truth." They arrive with a tremendous will to believe in "THE ANSWER." We have to teach them to think and study and reflect the old-fashioned way: through researching the possibilities, evaluating the probabilities, weighing the conflicting values, and choosing action in uncertainty. We need to teach them the "AHA!" of being in balance—the convergence of conflict and uncertainty with knowing and understanding.

Well . . . time for a little motivational reporting from one of the best human resource tanks. At Charles River Consulting, George Klemp noted that the most consistent finding has been that the amount of formal knowledge one acquired about a content area is generally unrelated to superior performance in an occupation. While colleges traditionally emphasize formal cognitive skills, employers also look for *inter*-personal and *intra*-personal skills, such as sensitivity, initiative, and persistence—a sense of how the work at hand fits into the large picture—a familiarity with values and ethical dimensions.

I tend to see this tension between teaching the data and teaching the wisdom, between the know-how and the know-why, as the tension between the digital and the analog universes.

As faculty, we tend to test for the digital universe (the precise facts about terminology) because it is so difficult to *test* for the analog universe (when would it be appropriate to . . .). You will see this tension in the discussions about library instruction methods and content.

Some things are vastly improved in the digital universe: sound recordings, nuclear power plant controls, drug prescriptions. Some things aren't improved by being exactly the same each time: leaves, flowers, clouds, hugs. A term paper just turned in, which is exactly like the one you saw last year . . . well, OK, that's fraud and plagiarism. We are all analogies of each other, of who we were yesterday, of other students, other customers, other friends, other colleagues.

From our own education, most of us will remember pale shadows of the information communicated in class, found in the library. We will know where to look when we need it. We will respect people who specialize in that. We *do* remember digitally what is most personal, most useful and most reliable—the digital memory of one's street address, for instance, but this information is least useful for transfer to other situations. For that transfer we need to generalize about the useful characteristics or patterns in the digital information, so that the analogy will guide us in how and when to apply the digital. For a flagrant example of the analog of scholarship run amok, try looking up the wildly popular Illuminati Web page.

This tension between answering the specific question and structuring the search, between teaching the mechanical skills and helping frame the question . . . this tension between having and being, as Eric Fromm might put it, is at the heart of electronic-virtual-cyber-librarianship. Usually we try to make it an "AND" situation, where we use the specific search "AND" model what other searches might be like. We try to push the student from the precise digital mind-set to the generalized structure. We try to leave them with something worth knowing in 18 months.

This is the thinking: how do we get from digital to analog, from current data to long-lived basics, that prompted me to give my American Architecture students their final exam questions the first day of class? Those questions become organizers for the data in the class. I intended to mess up my students' sense of beginning and endings, of digital and analog, of what changes and what endures. Why identify Rockefeller Center and the Northwest Ordinance of 1787, if you don't know why they are important? If you know why they are important, you can analyze the proposed development of a the new interstate interchange in what is now rural East Greenbush in upstate New York.

So . . . respectfully, I must disagree with Xerox. Through our actions and assumptions, we must nurture our students in their discovery of their own confidence, initiative, and vision. We must feel it is as appropriate to intervene with a "'Net wanderer" as we did with a "card thumber." It is as appropriate to give students Machiavelli as Gingrich's Web page. And, it is essential to teach the student why we acted as we did, why it matters.

Do we always succeed? No! Is it worth doing? Yes!

Wasn't it Frederick Douglass who said: "If there is no struggle, there is no progress. Those of us who profess to favor freedom, yet depreciate agitation are men who want the crops without plowing up the ground. They want rain without thunder. They want ocean without the awful roar of its many waters"?

Imagine this: our students sitting today for hours at the computer terminals examining other people's ideas, no flakes of flint, no fist-size cobbles to mark their work or their thought, to define their intentions, to measure their progress . . . no physical presence in the Olduvai Gorges of the 21st century. Our challenge is the convergence of the ephemeral and the historical, the digital and the analog—the electronic current and the brain wave.

And, here in upstate New York, it's still snowing and snowing . . . snowing and snowing . . . a challenge and a convergence of water and temperature. So, I invite you to read on. The information and insights so quaintly compiled into an ergonomically appropriate print volume may well challenge your assumptions about library skills instruction and the Internet. Perhaps this volume will persuade you to join in the search for ways to guide our students into the rushing flow of online and Internet research. I invite you to explore the convergence of the Internet, a stream constantly reinventing itself, and the old river, the old ways of thinking essential to our students: the timeless abilities to analyze, evaluate, and respond.

THE CHALLENGE OF THE INTERNET-TAXONOMY CONVERGENCE

The Internet Response Meter

Katharine A. Waugh

The illustrator, Katharine A. Waugh (kawaugh@vaxsar.vassar.edu), is Reference Librarian, Vassar College Library, Poughkeepsie, NY 12601.

[Haworth co-indexing entry note]: "The Internet Response Meter." Waugh, Katharine A. Co-published simultaneously in *Internet Reference Services Quarterly* (The Haworth Press, Inc.) Vol. 2, No. 2/3, 1997, p. 9; and: *The Challenge of Internet Literacy: The Instruction-Web Convergence* (ed: Lyn Elizabeth M. Martin) The Haworth Press, Inc., 1997, p. 9. Single or multiple copies of this article are available for a fee from The Haworth Document Delivery Service [1-800-342-9678, 9:00 a.m. - 5:00 p.m. (EST). E-mail address: getinfo@haworth.com].

Information Counseling Inventory of Affective and Cognitive Reactions While Learning the Internet

Diane Nahl

SUMMARY. Library professionals in the information age are called upon to provide user-friendly information environments. To accomplish this, more detailed knowledge is needed about the information behavior of users. The concept "information counseling" reflects this new orientation and involves instruction activities such as: orienting, advising, and reassuring novice learners. The taxonomic approach transforms self-witnessing reports into classified segments of information behaviors at three levels of internalization and in three behavioral domains, including: affective, cognitive, and sensorimotor behavior. Reference librarians and instructors are invited to contribute to the taxonomy and make use of it in planning and designing programs and facilities. This behavioral inventory of information behaviors learning the Internet is presented with illustrative entries under each category for affective and cognitive behavior. Suggested uses for the inventory include promoting information self-counseling skills, helping learners overcome technophobia through generational self-witnessing reports, and creating better point-of-use instructions for novices using complex information systems. *[Article copies available for a fee from The Haworth Document Delivery Service: 1-800-342-9678. E-mail address: getinfo@haworth.com]*

Diane Nahl (nahl@hawaii.edu) is Assistant Professor, School of Library and Information Studies, University of Hawaii, 2550 The Mall, Honolulu, HI 96822.

[Haworth co-indexing entry note]: "Information Counseling Inventory of Affective and Cognitive Reactions While Learning the Internet." Nahl, Diane. Co-published simultaneously in *Internet Reference Services Quarterly* (The Haworth Press, Inc.) Vol. 2, No. 2/3, 1997, pp. 11-33; and: *The Challenge of Internet Literacy: The Instruction-Web Convergence* (ed: Lyn Elizabeth M. Martin) The Haworth Press, Inc., 1997, pp. 11-33. Single or multiple copies of this article are available for a fee from The Haworth Document Delivery Service [1-800-342-9678, 9:00 a.m. - 5:00 p.m. (EST). E-mail address: getinfo@haworth.com].

KEYWORDS. User-centered, user studies, behavioral inventories, information literacy, information-seeking behavior, self-counseling, taxonomy

IMPLICATIONS OF A USER-FRIENDLY PARADIGM

Reference services in "user-centered information environments" can be facilitated through detailed knowledge of the information behaviors of users.[1] Carol Kuhlthau has proposed that library professionals in the information age have a new mission since the spread of technology in the workplace, bringing with it new user issues.[2] As the amount of information continues to increase and the changes in the information environment accelerate, users are faced with "unpredictability in all aspects of life" and thus, "there is a critical need for professional counseling in seeking meaning and in understanding information."[3]

Kuhlthau elaborates somewhat on the form information counseling could take. Reference and instruction librarians, acting as information counselors, would conduct appropriate interviews to allow them to diagnose users' needs at five levels of mediation or intervention. For example, level 2 intervention merely involves identifying a specific location or source, while level 3 mediation identifies a group of sources related to a topic. Level 4 mediation, or "pattern intervention," recommends a strategic sequence for processing the recommended sources. At level 5, information counselors use dialog to act as a term paper advisor, addressing the search process as a "holistic experience" involving interpretation and personal growth.

This counseling orientation represents a new emphasis for reference service in the coming years. Granted that the user-centered revolution has become the perspective in ascendancy; however, there are basic issues still to be resolved. For instance, how much information about users do we need to have? What kinds of user information are needed to manage information environments? How much is involved in being an information counselor, and how do we keep our services at the information consultation level rather than at the psychological counseling level?

Kuhlthau presents no specific tools for implementing this new mission for reference librarians and instructors. However, research and theory on the taxonomic approach to understanding information behavior may provide a useful tool in the future repertoire of reference librarians.[4] Information counseling is a set of techniques librarians can use to assist novices with their affective information needs. The purpose of this discussion is to share some empirical methods that can be used to transform comments in user self-reports into a *taxonomy of information behaviors* librarians can expect to deal with when novices are learning the Internet. In customer-oriented models of service, managers of information environments, such as academic and public reference service departments, need new forms of user-based data with which to make informed decisions about types and levels of service. Managers need methods that will provide information and insight from the users' point of view in order to develop accurate customer satisfaction measures.

One of the products of the taxonomic or matrix approach has been an inventory that is classified into behavioral domains and levels of internalization, with sample entries for affective and cognitive information seeking behaviors. The inventory (presented in Table 2) is illustrative and not comprehensive in its examples, and thus can be added to and used as a prototype for gathering data about experiences of people in information environments. The "Behavioral Inventory of Internet Learning" provides information counselors and reference librarians with a map of what behaviors to expect from novice learners, and possibly, how to intervene at an appropriate level, to facilitate and promote the user's needs and goals.

ACS CLASSIFICATION FOR FEELINGS, THOUGHTS, AND ACTIONS

The analysis of the behavior of users in information environments has led to the development of a matrix system that is intended to be exhaustive and applicable to any user environment. Table 1 depicts three domains and three levels of information behavior, yielding nine zones within which to classify types of user problems and solutions. The three *columns* are the three behavioral domains: affective, cognitive, sensorimotor. The order of the ACS domains, from left to right, indicates that to begin with, there are intentions or information needs (A), which lead one to thoughts about solutions (C), which finally eventuate in some related overt action (S). The three *levels*, arranged from the bottom up, indicate that novices begin at the lowest level, and move up in focus and development of information skill.

In popular psychology, whatever people do always falls in three exhaustive categories of behaving, following in a sequence: intention–plan–execution. In scientific psychology, the sequence is rendered as motivation–cognition–behavior. In education, it is value–understanding–performance.

1. The *affective domain (A)* includes behavioral acts that relate to feelings, i.e., interests, values, motivation, purposes, and goals.
2. The *cognitive domain (C)* includes behavioral acts that relate to cognitions, i.e., knowledge, comprehension, problem solving, and critical interpretation.

3. The *sensorimotor domain (S)* includes behavioral acts that are externally observable, i.e., visual perception, speaking, and navigating. (Sometimes this is called the "psychomotor" domain.)

The three behavioral domains shown in Table 1 are involved in every human act, no matter how small.[5] For example, at the macro level, students engage in daily studying because they are continuously motivated to pass (affective domain), and they memorize or process information (cognitive domain), while listening, reading, and note taking (sensorimotor domain). Or, at the micro level, a user wants to select a particular database from a menu (goal–affective domain), knowing that it contains relevant material (memory–cognitive domain), and so highlights the item with the arrow key and presses the return key (sensorimotor domain).

In this approach, everything that a searcher can feel or choose (A), think or infer (C), and overtly see or do (S), is termed "information behavior," as long as our focus is the information environment and how it dynamically influences searchers. It is important to maintain this objective focus, especially since the reference relationship is being expanded to include users' feelings, thoughts, and perceptions. We need a classified inventory of information behaviors which lists, in an objective language, what feelings and thoughts of searchers are an ordinary aspect of the information world.

TABLE 1. Generic ACS Taxonomy for Developing Lifelong Information Behavior

LEVELS	AFFECTIVE DOMAIN A	COGNITIVE DOMAIN C	SENSORIMOTOR DOMAIN S
3 *Internalization Level* Identifying with & Personalizing	affective internalization	cognitive internalization	sensorimotor internalization
2 *Interaction Level* Searching & Navigating	affective interaction	cognitive interaction	sensorimotor interaction
1 *Adjustment Level* Orienting & Adjusting	affective adjustment	cognitive adjustment	sensorimotor adjustment

TABLE 2. Information Counseling Taxonomy of Solutions to Users' Affective Information Needs

Affective Function	Affective Information Needs	Information Counseling Solutions
3 REASSURING CONSOLING (to encourage acceptance and support)	Feeling enthusiasm vs. displeasure	Affirming to users the eventual outcome will be successful
	Feeling empowered vs. helpless	Affirming the principle that "users are never at fault"
	Accepting vs. rejecting	Presenting lifelong information literacy as an attainable goal
2 ADVISING COACHING (to strengthen information intentionality)	Experiencing fun vs. tedium	Sharing convenient tips & information with users
	Feeling confident vs. anxious	Giving feedback (what will happen if...)
	Experiencing clarity vs. confusion	Identifying something on a diagram or analyzing an example
1 ORIENTING ADJUSTING (to overcome resistance to information seeking)	Being patient vs. impatient	Telling users how long things take (secs., mins., hours)
	Feeling guided vs. lost	Telling users about common errors from generational lists
	Being thankful vs. complaining	Showing concern for users' technical difficulty
	Being realistic vs. disappointed	Telling what is reasonable to expect
	Feeling cared for vs. neglected	Showing where something needed can be found

The Three Levels: Orientation, Interaction, Internalization

Level 1 information behaviors occur within all three domains and revolve around users' initial needs to *orient* and *adapt* to information situations. For example, level 1 information behavior in the cognitive domain takes place when a user attempts to *identify* some element in the environment (cognitive). This information is obtained from the user's own self-witnessing report describing the orienting and adapting efforts made:

> I was unaware that the introduction to Mosaic was a type of menu that one is able to highlight certain words and ultimately get into that particular topic. Through this discovery, I found that my frustration when I first attempted to use Mosaic soon turned into feelings of confidence and especially accomplishment.

This self-witnessing segment reveals aspects of the user's affective and cognitive behaviors. Sentence 1 describes the individual's *cognitive* activities of (i) becoming aware of a new element in the information environment, and (ii) finding out or discovering a relation between a screen menu and a link function. Sentence 2 describes the individual's *affective* activities of (i) feeling frustrated while exploring a Web browser for the first time, (ii) feeling a sense of accomplishment with progress in small steps, and (iii) experiencing greater self-esteem, achieved through entering into the process of mastery. The affective and cognitive information behaviors in this example concern basic skills in learning new software and keeping one's motivation going throughout a task.

Level 2 information behaviors go beyond orientation and adaptation to include some form of self-directed *interaction* with the information environment. Consider the following self-witnessing segment:

> I also discovered that a computer mouse may work differently in different programs. Most of the time I could only get the mouse to highlight some of the words I wanted highlighted. I felt very frustrated as I had to use the mouse to travel from menu to menu. My clumsiness and slowness with the mouse made the extensive menu lists seem endless.

In sentence 1, the witness describes having a human-computer interaction, in which the discovery is made (C2) of the mouse's variable potential or performance across different applications. In sentence 2, the witness describes variable highlighting techniques on different platforms (S2), while sentence 4 shows the presence of intense frustration from being impeded in her progress (A2) which is further described by the witness as *feeling clumsy* and *having something seem to take too long.*

Learning is impeded when various types of negative affect in level 2 interfere with desired or positive outcomes of information behavior (e.g., frustration, clumsiness, boredom, confusion, endlessness, hopelessness, etc.).

A conditioned form of lack of self-confidence may develop; a type of learned helplessness that has deleterious effects on both search efficiency and comprehension of instructions.[6]

It is important to note that the three levels are both sequential and continuous, and that individuals operate at all three levels in any information situation. Level 1 activities are orientational and adaptive. Since the information environment is very complex and ever changing, all of us are lifelong novices.[7] As new systems such as the Internet arrive on the scene, we never seem to be able to get out of level 1 completely, and we have to continue our adapting process as the information environment changes.[8] We must assume that new systems will always come into existence, continuously pressuring the population to acquire new skills with systems. Thus, level 1 activity continues to develop even as level 2 continues ceaselessly, in the sense that we are lifelong interactors with new forms of information systems. While level 1 and 2 activities proceed and prosper, level 3 activities slowly begin to develop. Typically, an individual in an information situation performs activities in all nine zones of the matrix, at all three levels and in all three domains, experiencing varying degrees of difficulty and success, depending on their familiarity with the system and the task.

Level 3 information behaviors relate to *personalizing* or *internalizing* information activities. In the strict sense, at the beginning of the orientation process, new learners are not yet users. Using an information system presupposes having a personal need or interest, whether intrinsic or extrinsic in nature. At the beginning stages, learners may recognize and learn some of the mechanics involved but it takes another stage to begin to see themselves as actual users. This activity of personalizing an information behavior constitutes an act of internalization.[9] Consider this report:

> I was surprised to find the topic Aviation right under subjects in the WWW. This had so much helpful stuff in it, I was very ecstatic. I began then to really love Lynx. Wow, I came a long way from just being able to wordprocess to now being able to find info from home on just about any topic that I want. I'm very pleased with my improvement on the computer and on the Internet.

This self-report segment is classified as level 3 affective information behavior because this student refers to seven *affective information behaviors* that show this student's discovery of personal interest and how she values Internet use for personal reasons:

- feeling surprised at the prominent location of a topic
- feeling information is helpful

- feeling enthusiasm (ecstasy) over the information found
- loving information systems
- gaining self-confidence, self-efficacy, and self-esteem
- feeling empowered by information skills
- experiencing mastery of information systems

The key to identifying the level of these behaviors is sentence 2: "This had so much helpful stuff in it, I was very ecstatic." For this user, in this brief episode, the World Wide Web suddenly became an entirely new kind of thing to relate to, something personal, vivid, passionately cared for, leading even to ecstasy. For this novice, the process of internalizing the Internet is now underway, as the student begins to experience level 3 information behavior.

THE DIMENSIONS OF INFORMATION COUNSELING

The taxonomic approach outlined here is *behavioral* or objective, in the sense that feelings and thoughts are treated as measurable mental behavior units that can be identified, described, learned and unlearned under appropriate instructional conditions. Individuals, acting as "witnesses" to themselves, can report what emotions they are feeling at a particular moment, how intensely they are motivated to do some task, what they think something means, or what they are afraid to try. These self-witnessing reports may not be completely accurate or valid in any one situation or case history. They cannot be used to determine someone's personality or learning style; however, self-witnessing reports can be used to identify in an empirical way the range or repertoire of information behaviors that can and do occur in the information environment on a routine basis. The inventory goes no further than identifying information behaviors that regularly occur in information environments and organizing them according to their behavioral and developmental functions.

This study took place in a learning context known as a social generational classroom that facilitates group loyalty and identification, which in turn promotes accuracy in self-witnessing reports. Ericsson and Simon review the validity and reliability issues involved in self-reports, concluding that we can rely on self-reports under controlled conditions, especially if they are gathered concurrent with the task.[10] Self-witnessing reports of searchers can be directed at various levels of detail. For instance, one can capture affective information from users at the very moment they see and react to the results of a search query.[11]

The classified inventory, presented in the next section, is generic in the sense that each class or zone of information behavior is defined by its marginal titles. Plus (+) and minus (−) signs indicate positive and negative aspects of Internet learning experiences. In general, plus signs represent skills while minus signs indicate errors, misjudgments, incorrect assumptions, maladaptive attitudes, and other problems that users need help with. For example, 2C+ refers to a cognitive level 2 behavior that is positive because it is a problem-solving skill (e.g., thinking of an alternative expression for a query in a search window); 1A − refers to an affective level 1 behavior that is negative because it interferes with the progress of the search process (e.g., unwillingness to press a key in response to screen instructions). There is no limit to the number of behaviors that could be classified in any one of the nine zones. So, the taxonomic inventory can continue to grow in completeness and new behaviors can be readily discovered at any time by any researcher.

While such an inventory has many uses, both instructional and scientific, its potential value lies in helping us meet the new user-centered challenges in reference work and instruction. While merely reading classified self-witnessing reports can be enlightening, the 3×3 matrix of the classification scheme can serve as an intellectual map for information counseling activities by reference librarians and instructors. In one instance, it was used to successfully improve point-of-use instructions for CD-ROM based searching by novices.[12] This was achieved by consulting the inventory, and noting which items might apply to this instructional situation, then consulting Table 2 for guidance with solutions.

Typically, the cognitive aspect is well defined in point-of-use-instructions that describe the minimum set of required operations for a system. However, instructions tend to make fewer statements that are aimed at addressing the affective information needs of novices that are present in the inventory, and represented in Table 2. Several new types of sentences specifically directed to a novice searcher's affective concerns were inserted in an existing set of instructions for how to search a particular database. For example, level 1 affective sentences gave orientation (e.g., where to look for an option on a screen or how frequently committed errors [FCEs] can be avoided and corrected); level 2 sentences gave advice (e.g., when to consult an online thesaurus or select advanced search options); and level 3 sentences gave reassurance (e.g., reminders that it's not their fault if the system freezes or if a Web site is "not found").

Novice users found the longer, but gentler and more user-centered instructions more helpful. It seemed to strengthen their self-efficacy beliefs as searchers. They felt they could do better, just because the instructions were perceived as more benign. They behaved differently too.

For example, they were more efficient, made fewer search moves with better results, thus avoiding more errors. Apparently, knowing users' affective stumbling blocks, and providing for them, can influence their information behavior in an instructionally positive direction.

Information management in the new user-centered paradigm can use information counseling techniques to meet users' affective information needs. The generic ACS taxonomy in Table 1 can be applied to a variety of problems relating to the user's information environment. Table 2 describes some information counseling solutions for particular affective symptoms at all three levels. Each level of internalization serves a particular affective function (e.g., orienting or adjusting to the information environment [level 1] involves overcoming resistance to information seeking). Some affective symptoms of this include procrastination, dread, impatience, feeling lost, complaining, being disappointed, and feeling neglected. Specific information counseling solutions can be developed for these symptoms in written, online, and oral instruction. For example, instructions can include statements that help users to feel guided, such as warning novices about frequently committed errors (FCEs) and providing instructions that help them access FAQ files.

Advising or coaching solutions (level 2) are intended to strengthen "information intentionality," an expression that refers to users' motive to actively cooperate with and participate in the learning environment. Some affective symptoms to look for include the feeling "it is taking too long," feeling anxious, and feeling confused or lost. Information counseling solutions that strengthen users' intentionality include giving them convenient tips that save time and prepare them for what to expect of particular operations or commands. For example, to help novices gain in self-confidence as searchers, give feedback about what will happen if they enter a search statement in an Internet search engine with and without boolean operators.

At level 3, users experience powerful symptoms of displeasure and rejection or avoidance, to which we can to respond by reassuring and consoling them. These little acts of kindness encourage users' acceptance of the requirements of information environments. To help users feel enthusiastic and optimistic about the eventual outcome of their search efforts, we can assure them that, armed with their new knowledge about searching, they will be successful.

Table 2 provides only sample illustrations of affective symptoms and information counseling solutions. Librarians and researchers who obtain user-based data in a variety of information use contexts may add to these examples as needed. An information counseling orientation symbolizes a new behavioral avenue for reference work and information literacy instruction and management. No longer is the user treated as a black box, system-like. The ubiquity and complexity of systems requires the profession to address the user's need to acquire useful affective information skills, in order to manage ever-new cognitive skills. For every cognitive skill there is a complimentary affective skill, without which cognitive behavior devolves into helplessness. If affective behavior is negative or avoidant, cognitive behavior receives little or no support because internal motivation remains too low. The practice of beneficial information counseling hinges on our ability to match cognitive target skills with their affective facilitation skills. The Inventory is intended to help us in this task.

BEHAVIORAL INVENTORY OF INTERNET LEARNING

Each of the nine zones of the Internet information behaviors matrix contains illustrations from student self-reports while learning Internet. Each entry is clearly some variation of that taxonomic class or genre of information behavior. For instance, zone 2A+ includes self-confidence and a sense of being in control of the system, and their opposites (i.e., learned helplessness and low self-confidence). Each classification item can help someone with that particular affective information need. Each of us can experience almost any of these needs depending on the situation.

Another aspect of the inventory that needs further development is multiple classification. Since the illustrative entries represent the spontaneous productions of individual witnesses, they rarely describe a single domain. The longer the segment in an entry, the more difficult this problem becomes. These illustrations include enough context in each entry to enable readers to reconstruct the information episode or situation. Therefore, each entry could be classified in one or more zones to highlight various kinds of affective information needs present in that entry. Choosing titles for each entry is another developmental step in building the inventory. Eventually, the titles chosen for each entry will collectively represent a theory of information behavior. The illustrative inventory that follows is organized into the following zones:

	AFFECTIVE BEHAVIOR	*COGNITIVE BEHAVIOR*
Level 3	Accepting vs. Rejecting	Contextualizing and Personalizing vs. Not Creating a Personal Context

Level 2	Self-confidence vs.	Predicting and Making Inferences
	Learned Helplessness	vs. Not Figuring Things Out
Level 1	Persisting and Caring About	Identifying and Observing vs.
	Accuracy vs. Giving Up	Misidentifying and Not Observing

The Inventory begins with illustrations in the affective domain for the three levels of internalization, followed by the cognitive domain examples. Discussion of the entries follows each zone.

ACCEPTING (3A+) VS. REJECTING (3A −)

- "In conclusion, life on the Internet seems to be settling down a bit. Because I've identified some of the problems as minor inconveniences, they no longer bother me. I've decided not to label them as problems, but hurdles that can be overcome."(3A+)
- "I am becoming more at ease with the Internet system, and I'm able to recognize some of the computer's mannerisms. For example, noise on the telephone line causes my screen to become garbled. When the screen does become garbled I quit what I'm doing and try to move to various other areas."(3A+)
- "Throughout this navigation of women's studies, my feeling was basically one of enthusiasm or excitement. For some strange reason, my searches were coming forth accurately. I was amazed that I could find the information that I needed so quickly."(3A+)
- "As I sat to do my work I felt like a million bucks, as the saying goes. I started my lab session feeling fine. I did not have the previous feelings of frustration, backaches or headaches. I overcame my feeling of failure and braved trying to work through Netscape. I was in pure ecstasy as I maneuvered my way around Netscape. I was floating on cloud nine. I felt such a rush of adrenaline that I could not stop, I wanted to go on, but I had to get to class. After class I excitedly went to Keller and logged on to Netscape."(3A+)
- "I guess I'll never overcome this feeling of dread when I have to go online to get on the Net. I really don't think I'll ever love computers, but I guess I have no choice about using them."(3A −)
- "Why does society have to be so in love with technology? It never works anyway, and it's too expensive. I don't have time to waste learning something that's junk."(3A −)
- "I learned a lot, but I don't think I'll retain it because I don't have a computer and I don't plan to get one. I work with plants, so I don't need computers."(3A −)

In each case, these novices express their degree of acceptance of the information technology environment. Note that these responses are quite strong in both positive and negative directions. The positive comments reveal their coping skills, and their ability to overcome barriers to arrive at a sense of progress and ultimate success, even developing a genuine desire to continue to learn more Internet skills. If we expose new learners to these positive comments at the outset, it may facilitate their internalization of Internet skills.

SELF-CONFIDENCE (2A+) VS. LEARNED HELPLESSNESS (2A −)

- "My feelings in the past two weeks of Internet have been those of excitement and optimism. Once we were given the assignments for this report, I felt very excited to tackle a new challenge. After I completed the assignment I felt that maybe it was too easy, but then retrieving information shouldn't be too difficult or strenuous."(2A+)
- "My navigation process through Netscape was a success. I was able to use Netscape and I was even able to use Gopher through Netscape. This once seeming unconquerable giant has now become just another computer program that I will learn more about and hopefully get to master."(2A+)
- "What an accomplishment!!! I no longer feel controlled by or inferior to the computer. I am the one in control. After all, the computer is just a machine, right? It is only as good as its user and at this point, I feel that I can accomplish anything. What a power rush."(2A+)
- "With such confidence, I noticed I did not get so frustrated if I made any wrong choices or if I needed to back track to try another route. I just tried the next option without another negative thought. If I am pressed for time though, I can feel the frustration trying to creep in but, I try to catch it at first notice and change my attitude to a positive one and, IT WORKS!!!"(2A+)
- "What an increase in time saving from my first several sessions. I have learned that I am a person that is very time efficient. I like time management so, this really gave me an adrenaline rush. I seemed to have no problem in choosing which menu to get into in order to find subject topic that I need. What an improvement! My self-esteem when dealing with computers has grown tremendously. I did not realize how much a negative attitude hindered you from completing a task proficiently."(2A+)
- "I am able to accomplish much more without feeling negative or start to have headaches as I had previously. My eyes also do not get

as tired of looking at the screen. The beautiful graphics on Mosaic through the Mac also gives the eyes a break. The graphics are wonderful and just brighten up my day as well as my computer lab session. Overall, I have improved by leaps and bounds."(2A+)

- "Enter Lynx. I knew I didn't know too much about navigating this program but I had been so successful at evading frustration and anger so that I felt I could manage without any unwanted blow-ups. This just isn't very fun way to navigate, although, I like being able to flip back to the previous menu or even back to the main menu with just an arrow key. It took me a while to figure out the bookmark business, but with the help of the 'help,' I was able to get the hang of it. This just boosted my confidence some more."(2A+)

- "There was always a dark cloud floating around while I was using the computer, just waiting for some unsuspecting moment to provide the ideal atmosphere in which to work its work. I'm afraid the bell tolls for me. I'm not cut out for it, I guess."(2A −)

- "I was angry and frustrated at my failed attempts. I just couldn't believe it! I mean I would get so fired up and pissed that I just wanted to destroy the entire system. I don't know what it is. I'm just getting very used to not being able to accomplish a task on the computer. I don't feel in control and don't have a desire to continue trying. Sorry."(2A −)

The theme of these comments is elation at new found self-confidence as a searcher, in contrast to complaints about a variety of failures, no sense of control of the system, and intense negative emotions. Students who experienced a gain in self-confidence as Internet users demonstrated their affective coping skills while in the process of acquiring complex search strategy skills. Their positive statements represent adaptive affective approaches to managing the stress of learning to search a new system, e.g., appreciating something about the system; depending on Help functions; recognizing the value of maintaining positive attitudes; and expecting to attain mastery.

PERSISTING AND CARING ABOUT ACCURACY (1A+)
VS. GIVING UP AND NOT CARING (1A −)

- "My keystrokes slowed down when I was unsure about what to do. They also quickened after I had devised a plan and was following through on it. I smiled when I finally found what I was looking for."(1A+)

- "At the beginning of the search, I kept saying, 'You can do this.' I had adopted the same strategy I had before and knew I could access the information that way. Once I got the information I had set out for involving Women, I said, 'See I told you.' "(1A+)
- "After I selected Mosaic and got the same problem I had to reflect on why I felt so compelled to try again. It seems as though my mind wants desperately to clear up the confusion. It almost feels painful to continue without first answering the question in my mind. I then reflect back on my commitment to move ahead to avoid wasting a lot of time."(1A+)
- "I plan to spend more time on the computer trying to learn more about Mosaic as well as how to operate it. There are so many avenues of looking up information through Mosaic that I believe I may spend countless hours just navigating my way through Mosaic without anything specific in mind."(1A+)
- "This class is teaching me how to problem solve on the computer. Even though I don't want to experience the anxiety and frustration, I still continue to navigate through an assignment and I'm learning."(1A+)
- "It surprises me how I will try to set myself up for tasks I believe I'll have some degree of success with. I've actually noticed a pattern: In the beginning I would return to Windows if Pine got too hard. Then I would return to Pine if Gopher got too hard. I realize now the strategy behind that. I don't want to proceed too fast and accumulate too many failures so I set myself up for definite successes."(1A+)
- "I looked under environment in Lynx. I had to go deep into the directories but eventually turned up topics about ethics and social issues."(1A+)
- "Also, because my outlook has been a positive one, I type a lot quicker, but a lot gentler on the keyboard and with much less mistakes. Having mistakes takes up time because you need to go back and correct everything you did wrong."(1A+)
- "After trying WAIS unsuccessfully under Health, I really began feeling down. This was the first time the computer 'beat me.' This was also one of the few times I realized I was letting my negative self affect my confidence and performance."(1A −)
- "Initially I attempted to find the homework assignment of searching for Immanuel Kant's book, *The Science of Right*, through the Lynx program. I was very frustrated with this program. The UNIX system is very slow and I did not have the patience to work through this

slow process. It also seemed very confusing to me. I exited Lynx and decided to check my e-mail."(1A −)

- "Somehow on about my third search this day my mouse failed me [froze up?]. I was stunned! Here I was at LOGIN!! What could've happened I kept asking myself. Finally I decided it was my attitude that was affecting the mouse. Is this superstitious?"(1A −)
- "When I came across an obstacle, I would give up without searching the screen for some of the options that may be related to the problem, and I could have found a way around it. But I didn't."(1A −)

Students at level 1 have a variety of difficulties to overcome. This process requires persistence and attention to detail and order. These comments represent how Internet learners dealt with the resistance they felt when confronted with various types of Internet complexities. The positive comments reveal the strategies students used to cope with complexity, e.g., returning to a more familiar task if the current one isn't working out; adopting a consciously positive attitude toward learning the Internet; rewarding the self with smiles and appreciative self-talk when successful; and not giving up until satisfied that all efforts that could be made are made.

CONTEXTUALIZING AND PERSONALIZING (3C+) VS. NOT CREATING A PERSONAL CONTEXT (3C−)

- "I showed my friend that we could access the surf report and the movie listing with no problem, he was amazed. I'm kind of sorry about showing him this, because he calls me all the time to get the surf forecast. I don't really mind though because I usually access that everyday so I can plan my work for school accordingly. So finding the surf forecast on the Internet has been a great tool for me and many of my friends."(3C+)
- "I finally got to the subjects portion of WWW and searched Social Science subject for the word Wellness. This search turned up nothing. This didn't bother me because I could search for other things. I searched the same subject for the word Lifestyles and found many things dealing with this topic."(3C+)
- "Once I was in human rights, I went nuts. I spent about one hour clicking on everything and looking at everything. Finally, I felt I had brain overload and bookmarked what I liked and got out. I thought, "You can do this. My keystrokes slowed down as I was careful to absorb all of the information I could about the topic. A grin or two appeared across my face when I found something interesting or amazing."(3C+)

- "I bookmarked and read some of the "Women's Handbook (1992) Barnard College/Columbia University," which discusses many gender and female issues from academics to recreation to self-defense. I'll probably save this to my account too. After going through the entire list, I also bookmarked health care issues and will come back to it for the next project. I will definitely go back to my bookmark in Lynx because it also links to other relevant documents. By putting in Bookmark, I've automatically increased my search and the information that I can yield."(3C+)

- "Some things still bug me about Lynx though. Sometimes I don't like sitting there reading through those paragraphs trying to find the link that I'm looking for. That's only when I'm pressed for time though. So even though I get frustrated and don't find what I'm looking for in a timely fashion, I have actually accomplished something good for myself. This makes me feel better about the whole session in general."(3C+)

- "I put it down on my bookmark to read at a later date when I have more time. I also looked up religion to find any religion groups that I might join. I have not found one yet. The ones that I did look into seemed a bit too liberal or different for me."(3C+)

- "I found an electronic Psychology journal called Psycoloquy which offered a subscription, and a list of files (need to be requested). This is going to be a very useful later on, since it promises to be a primary means to access scholarly and scientific information in the future."(3C+)

- "I chose to look up Women's Health first because I felt it was an issue I was interested in. I'm trying to navigate through the Internet with specific personal goals incorporated into what is requested in class. I bookmarked the information on domestic Violence because after I graduate this semester I may try to work as a low level counselor at a domestic abuse shelter."(3C+)

- "My main activity these past two weeks has been reading information that I have found on-line. The cyberscope section in Newsweek magazine has been fun to read. They always have something useful or fun to share. I also just discovered PC Currents: The Computer Newsmagazine for Hawaii."(3C+)

- "I've had many problems besides school these last two weeks. These problems have definitely affected my motivation. If I did succeed in motivating myself, my attention span for the work was very short lived. Part of my problem is that I don't find much that interests me. All that stuff on Lynx . . . I don't know who it's for really."(3C −)

These comments reflect the degree to which these novices made Internet use a part of their personal lives as a result of the course, e.g., searching for a topic they have a genuine interest in; keeping current with new developments in that topic on the Internet; saving interesting sites in bookmark files for future reference; and acquiring masses of information that can be personally controlled. These cognitive skills emerged in response to learning the procedures for accessing the Internet.

PREDICTING AND INFERENCE MAKING (2C+) VS. NOT FIGURING THINGS OUT (2C−)

- "My last session I had such a terrible time with Lynx. Last time I tried using all the Help commands in the highlighted bar at the bottom of the screen. I pressed the arrow keys like it instructed me to do, but there was no change on the screen. The computer did beep at me to let me know I couldn't use that command. I had to think now. After a long reflective pause I tried the cursor keys on the calculator section of the keyboard but, I got the same beep response. Not surprised. I next tried the shift key. Nothing changed. Then I tried the Tab key and to my delight a new set of words was highlighted. This was a very exciting breakthrough for me. Next I took immense pleasure in just tabbing around to different highlighted words for awhile. At this point my mood had certainly changed. I was actually laughing out loud and screaming with pleasure."(2C+)
- "When I got into Lynx again I accessed Health Issues and realized that it was the same information I had previously accessed in Gopher. I became frustrated and challenged. I realized I was in a Hypertext type of searching so I decided to open up some documents and try to get access through links that way. I was successful in finding tips on Healthy Lifestyles and Prevention in terms of cancer and heart and lung disease."(2C+)
- "Since I had found Immanuel Kant's *The Science of Right* in Gopher last week, I wanted to see if I could find it in Lynx. After searching for Kant and finding his name in the Gopher of the American Philosophical Association, I was denied access to the document containing *The Science of Right*. Hoping to find a copy of it some other place, I worked my way through the WWW catalog and WWW Worm without finding it. Since I had found it through Gopher, I realized that the document was there, but that I did not know how to find it through Lynx. In frustration, I terminated this session."(2C+)
- "It seems that every time I set out to find something I found it the most direct and less problematic way. Whenever I came across an

obstacle I took a step back and headed off in a different direction and once I got there it felt like it was no problem at all."(2C+)

- In the beginning of the search I thought, "Where would the computer put this information." It kind of became a little game for me to figure out where the information can be stored. I tried to be clever. I thought of the remote subject matter before the obvious. As I browsed up and down the subject list, I kept saying, "Could it be there?" At last I decided on Human rights. I knew gender related topics would be there, yet in an abstract sort of way. I felt the material would be more centered on specific groups rather than if I had looked it up under Women's Studies."(2C+)

- "I thought that since this searches databases for information I would have a good chance. When I came up empty under Health, Wellness, Health Lifestyle, Health Food, etc., I decided to try good old Gopher Jewels. This server had gotten me out of a couple of ruts so far. When I found an abundance of information on Health, Medicine, and Disability, but none on Wellness, I decided the WWW was the best place for this. If I could find one link to Wellness I would be home free."(2C+)

- "I discovered Lynx for the very first time. I really felt a sense of enthusiasm upon discovering Lynx. Perhaps I felt less stress in using Lynx because it was easy to access and furthermore it was interesting. Initially I was puzzled by the title on the introduction page called Welcome to Honolulu Community College. I thought, What does Honolulu Community College have to do with Lynx? Surprisingly I figured out that the introduction page was a type of menu, whereby one can highlight the different topics and reach an entirely new gateway. I was amazed at the different topics on the menu and the numerous gateways, especially World Wide Web."(2C+)

- "I could not access my first bookmark, which was "readme.jokes." I sat there and thought, "I absolutely cannot give up because I have to figure out how this thing works." I continued to press Enter on the readme.jokes file but the computer kept on repeating its response to me, which was "Cannot open requested file." After many, many, many attempts I decided that maybe something was wrong with the computer system."(2C −)

- "While navigating the past two weeks I have caught myself time and time again just staring at the monitor, no movement, no thinking. Since there was no cognition evident and I was accomplishing absolutely nothing during these phase-outs, I decided that the instant I was aware of the onset of a phase out I would turn my vision elsewhere. It's kind of creepy the way computers can do this to you."(2C −)

These comments reveal the problem-solving strategies students used to learn things that were not taught directly in the course. They were given a conceptual orientation to menu structures and search engines, with some procedural instruction. So, they had to figure out many things for themselves by applying conceptual frameworks. The positive comments show how students successfully develop a reasonable inferencing strategy for learning a system, e.g., switching to a different Internet system when one system did not retrieve anything useful; recognizing menu structures and their functions; thinking in terms of system organization when approaching a search task; and exploring links to learn about the system.

IDENTIFYING AND OBSERVING (1C+)
VS. MISIDENTIFYING AND NOT OBSERVING (1C−)

- "I decided to see if I could make a directory in my account that I could transfer documents to from WWW. At the UHUNIX prompt I typed 'mkdir internet.' It gave me another UHUNIX prompt. I wondered if anything happened? At the new prompt I typed 'cd Internet.' It returned: /home/29/jodyr/internet. I wondered again what that meant. At the new prompt I typed 'dir.' It just gave me another prompt. So I typed 'cd' then pressed return. It read: /home/29/jodyr. I knew now that I was controlling the computer but, I wasn't clear on exactly what I was commanding the computer to do. I have never set up a directory before so their purpose and function are still a mystery to me. I recognize the need to master and understand directories. It's exciting to know that I'm increasing my understanding but, I also feel impatient and embarrassed and this prevents one from asking for help."(1C+)
- "The other day I was in Lynx and probably because I was more relaxed than at the beginning of the semester, I began experimenting with the printing options, which gave me good results. Afterwards I switched to Gopher and tried the same technique with the same positive results."(1C+)
- "My first setback was that I had not given my bookmark a proper name or string. What the heck did it mean by a 'string.' Well, I remembered that the name in the bookmark setting, in 'options,' had three separate names divided by a period. Then I remembered the string that the instructor gave in class, lynx bookmark.html, is what I had written in my notes. So, I typed in lynx.bookmark.html in the bookmark field. This obviously had done the trick because instead of getting an Error-unable to access bookmark message, I got the mes-

sage box for the bookmark command. I then pushed 'L' to link to bookmark, and it flashed a quick 'done' message. I was warm and fuzzy, let me tell ya."(1C+)

- "When I take position at the computer terminal I have set in my mind an idea of what I am interested in locating through my search. I chose to focus much more time these two weeks in Lynx rather than Gopher. My idea was to discover and understand what Lynx has to offer."(1C+)

- "I was not happy when the computer said, Cannot access directory. In my mind I was thinking, I really hate it when the computer cannot access the directory. All of a sudden a message appeared and read, Congratulations, you have found a bug in Lynx Ver 2.3 Beta. You cannot imagine my enthusiasm, finally the computer was congratulating me for something. However, I still am not certain whether this is a good thing or perhaps I destroyed something in the program or the program itself."(1C−)

- "I got really frustrated at myself because I thought I had saved a variety of files to my e-mail address, but I didn't. I realized this when I returned to Pine awaiting all those files and nothing was there. You can believe I took a few deep breaths. Here I thought I was navigating and getting a better grip on accessing the multitude of pathways that I was indeed saving to screen and sending the files to my mail."(1C−)

- "One of my searches began by double clicking on the NCSA Telnet 2.6 icon to access UHUNIX. For at least 5 mins. I waited while watching the sign at the upper left corner constantly flash opposite errors. This is the best description I can give of it."(1C−)

- "Once I figure how to print the information I would certainly like to print the information that my friend wants. I ran into retrieval problems and I discovered that printing from this area was not a simple procedure. I spent over 1 hour figuring why I could not get the information to print. I tried all options with no success. No doubt it was my fault. I didn't feel like asking anyone."(1C−)

- "I experienced tremendous anger and frustration at first when I initially got to Lynx. For one thing, I didn't totally understand the concept and as a result, kept performing string searches which led nowhere because it would only be looking through that particular document (the introduction page)."(1C−)

The comments at level 1 show how students struggled to acquire relevant distinctions in the Internet environment. Students dealt with the problems of learning new syntax for entering commands, using directories, and getting to addresses. Often, students would experience a sequence of repetitive errors, then would suddenly observe the critical piece of information that was overlooked before, and then they were able to perform the operation correctly.

CONCLUSION

Information counseling involves identifying users' skills and errors in a particular operation and using this information to make user-centered changes in instruction and other information services. Students as learners go through similar steps as they attempt to adapt to an information system. What one student experiences, another may also experience, either at the same level or in a different form. Identifying these common skills and errors in relation to specific systems or particular operations, empowers librarians to design services that respond directly to students' needs. The Inventory gives direction to instructors and system designers as to what the content could be for giving orientation (level 1), advice (level 2), and reassurance (level 3) to novice learners that facilitates their internalization of Internet learning.

The positive self-witnessing statements in the inventory can be used with new learners to help them acquire attitudes that will facilitate their learning new systems. In this way, students learn from each other what to expect, how successful they might be, that it's a challenge they can meet, and which attitudes are helpful and which are detrimental to learning the Internet. One student who reviewed some student comments on the first day of class wrote in response, "I'm very confused. I'm still not getting the big picture yet. But I know that I will because everyone must start somewhere, and the previous generations made it, so I should be able to do it too."

Testimonials that are written for the next generation of Internet learners, raise these comments to the level of peer-instruction. Thus, students are empowered by seeing themselves as information counselors to the next generation.

NOTES

1. Diane Nahl, "The User-Centered Revolution: 1970-1995." in *Encyclopedia of Microcomputers,* eds. Allen Kent and James G. Williams, *in press.* (New York: Marcel Dekker, Inc., 1995) [URL: http://www2.hawaii.edu/slis/nahl/ articles/user/ user67to90.html#RTFToC17.html#novices].

2. Carol C. Kuhlthau, *Seeking Meaning: A Process Approach to Library and Information Services* (Norwood, New Jersey: Ablex, 1993).

3. Ibid, p. 187.

4. Leon A. Jakobovits and Diane Nahl-Jakobovits, "Learning the Library: Taxonomy of Skills and Errors," *College & Research Libraries* 48:3 (1987):203-214; Leon. A. Jakobovits and Diane Nahl-Jakobovits, "Measuring Information Searching Competence," *College & Research Libraries* 51:5 (1990):448-462; Diane Nahl-Jakobovits and Leon A. Jakobovits, "A Content Analysis Method for Developing User-Based Objectives," *Research Strategies* 10:1 (Winter):4-16; Diane Nahl-Jakobovits and Leon A. Jakobovits, "Bibliographic Instructional Design for Information Literacy: Integrating Affective and Cognitive Objectives," *Research Strategies* 11:2 (Spring):73-88; Diane Nahl, "Affective Elaborations in Boolean Search Instructions for Novices: Effects on Comprehension, Self-Confidence, and Error Type, *Proceedings of the 58th ASIS Annual Meeting,* 32 (October, 1995):69-76; Diane Nahl and Violet Harada, '' Composing Boolean Search Statements: Self-Confidence, Concept Analysis, and Errors, *School Library Media Quarterly* (Summer 1996, *in press*); Diane Nahl and Carol Tenopir, "Affective and Cognitive Searching Behavior of Novice End-Users of a Full-Text Database," *Journal of the American Society for Information Science* 47:4 (1996):276-286; Diane Nahl and Leon James, "Achieving Focus, Engagement, and Acceptance: Three Phases of Adapting to Internet Use," *Electronic Journal of Virtual Culture* 4:1 (February 26, 1996) [URL: http://rdz.stjohns.edu/ejvc/ejvc4n1.james].

5. Jakobovits and Nahl-Jakobovits, "Learning the Library"; "Measuring Information Searching Competence."

6. Diane Nahl, "CD-ROM Point-of-Use Instructions for Novice Searchers: A Comparison of User-Centered Affectively Elaborated and System-Centered Unelaborated Text" (Ph.D. Dissertation, University of Hawaii, 1993).

7. Nahl, "User-Centered Revolution."

8. Ibid.

9. Herbert C. Kelman, "Compliance, Identification, and Internalization: Three Processes of Attitude Change," *Journal of Conflict Resolution* 2 (1958):51-60.

10. K. Anders Ericsson and Herbert A. Simon, *Protocol Analysis: Verbal Reports as Data* (Cambridge, MA: MIT Press, 1993).

11. Nahl and Tenopir, "Affective and Cognitive Searching Behavior."

12. Nahl, "Affective Elaborations in Boolean Search Instructions."

THE CHALLENGE OF THE INTERNET ORDER-CHAOS CONVERGENCE

It's WWWar!
A Rollicking New Comedy Series

Katharine A. Waugh

The illustrator, Katharine A. Waugh (kawaugh@vaxsar.vassar.edu), is Reference Librarian, Vassar College Library, Poughkeepsie, NY 12601.

[Haworth co-indexing entry note]: "It's WWWar! A Rollicking New Comedy Series." Waugh, Katharine A. Co-published simultaneously in *Internet Reference Services Quarterly* (The Haworth Press, Inc.) Vol. 2, No. 2/3, 1997, p. 35; and: *The Challenge of Internet Literacy: The Instruction-Web Convergence* (ed: Lyn Elizabeth M. Martin) The Haworth Press, Inc., 1997, p. 35. Single or multiple copies of this article are available for a fee from The Haworth Document Delivery Service [1-800-342-9678, 9:00 a.m. - 5:00 p.m. (EST). E-mail address: getinfo@haworth.com].

Finding Order in a Chaotic World: A Model for Organized Research Using the World Wide Web

May Y. Chau

SUMMARY. The World Wide Web (WWW) has a decentralized information environment and a non-linear (hypertext) information structure. This non-linear structure allows users to retrieve information at many different levels but also increases the difficulty of information retrieval. Unlike a well-developed CD-ROM database, the WWW does not have a controlled searching environment and information can be indexed in many different ways. It takes a well planned search strategy to perform an effective search in the labyrinth of the WWW. The SIRO (Systematic Information Retrieval/Organization) model offers a research planning process designed specifically for information seekers in the agricultural disciplines. The intention is to enhance search results and organize retrieved information. This process starts with the identification of the information structure on the WWW, then proceeds by organizing and analyzing information in a visual diagram or a "thinking map." This process leads searchers to logical sources on the WWW and a systematic analysis of the result. *[Article copies available for a fee from The Haworth Document Delivery Service: 1-800-342-9678. E-mail address: getinfo@ haworth.com]*

May Y. Chau (chaum@ccmail.orst.edu) is Agricultural Librarian/Assistant Professor, 121, The Valley Library, Oregon State University, Corvallis, OR 97331-4501.

[Haworth co-indexing entry note]: "Finding Order in a Chaotic World: A Model for Organized Research Using the World Wide Web." Chau, May Y. Co-published simultaneously in *Internet Reference Services Quarterly* (The Haworth Press, Inc.) Vol. 2, No. 2/3, 1997, pp. 37-53; and: *The Challenge of Internet Literacy: The Instruction-Web Convergence* (ed: Lyn Elizabeth M. Martin) The Haworth Press, Inc., 1997, pp. 37-53. Single or multiple copies of this article are available for a fee from The Haworth Document Delivery Service [1-800-342-9678, 9:00 a.m. - 5:00 p.m. (EST). E-mail address: getinfo@haworth.com].

37

KEYWORDS. Agricultural information, information organization, research planning process, SIRO, thinking map, World Wide Web, information flow

Technology has a significant impact on learning and curricula are predicted to be "more oriented to facilitate students' ability to master many types of intelligence."[1] The World Wide Web (WWW) is one of the many types of intelligence that requires human mastery due to its decentralized information arrays and the immense variety of materials available. Although search engines are powerful retrieval tools for the WWW, they have many limitations due to the lack of controlled vocabulary or an easily discerned overall logical structure.[2] It takes human intelligence to compensate for the search engines' limitations and turn the technology into a functional research tool. The SIRO model is a search process designed to build a bridge[3] between the query and the WWW system.

This model starts with an "understanding of the information structure"[4] of the agricultural discipline on the WWW. At present, this model targets the agricultural disciplines but may be modified to serve other disciplines as well. Based on this understanding, the searchers will be able to identify logical information sources to match their specific search needs. After the search, information retrieved is summarized and mapped on a visual diagram, or thinking map. This map facilitates the organizing and selecting of information and consequently gives some guidelines for further research. The SIRO model also emphasizes the importance of integrating the WWW as one of many research tools available rather than as the beginning and end of a serious search.

METHODOLOGY

The SIRO model is a search process that facilitates preplanning before and organization after the query on the WWW. All steps in this process are directly related to each other and should be executed in the suggested order. (See Figure 1.)

Step I: Identifying Categories of Information Providers in a Specific Discipline

This step applies Rubens's concept of characterizing institutional sources (government, courts, etc.) by their scope of activities and jurisdiction.[5] The purpose is to help the searcher establish general categories of logical information providers and understand the agricultural information struc-

FIGURE 1. Steps of the SIRO (Systematic Information Retrieval/Organization) Model

1.	Identify categories of information providers in a specific discipline
2.	Diagram the information flow between these categories
3.	Examine the organizational information providers
4.	Apply to a specific topic
5	Organize the retrieved results in a visual diagram

ture on the WWW. The identified institutional sources or categories for agriculture are government agencies, higher education, professional societies, and agribusiness corporations. Government regulates agricultural production and operation while higher education trains specialists in the field and faculty conduct an enormous amount of agricultural research. Professional societies publish refereed journals which provide scholarly information. Many large agribusiness corporations have their own research and development departments and provide useful information about the markets. Most importantly, many information providers under the selected categories have Web-sites with retrievable information. (See Figure 2.)

Searchers can use various resources to establish individual information providers under each selected category. These resources include reference librarians, reference tools (handbooks, encyclopedias, etc.), searchers' personal knowledge of the subject and WWW subject trees. Reference tools are available in both electronic and printed format, and they can be found in libraries and on the WWW. The subject trees provided by the search engines on the WWW index information in a hierarchical structure for various subjects. (See Figure 3.)

The process of selecting individual information providers under each category is explained below.

Category I: Government

By consulting the available reference sources (e.g., *US Government Manual*), the author selects the United States Department of Agriculture as the major information provider under the category of government. This agency is responsible for creating, applying and transferring agricultural

FIGURE 2. Reasons for Choosing Agricultural Information Providers

Categories of Information Providers	Reasons for Selection
Government	Imposes regulations on agricultural productions and marketing, conduct research, etc.
Higher Education	Train Specialists in the field and conduct research.
Professional Societies	Publish refereed journals and organize conferences.
Agribusiness	Have own Research & Development departments.

knowledge and technology [6] and has many branches. For example, the USDA's Cooperative State Research, Education and Extension Service (CSREES) links USDA activities with the research and education resources.[7] CSREES is also a state partner of land-grant universities. Another provider identified is the Commodity Future Trading Commission (CFTC). This agency regulates commodity exchanges and provides useful statistics.

Category II: Higher Education

Land-grant universities are recognized for their agricultural research and are state education partners of the USDA. These universities have excellent agricultural schools and house extension services. Faculty from these schools are agriculture subject experts; most of them actively engage in scientific research and publish in professional journals. Recently, these universities have begun posting information on the WWW, making contact between faculty much easier. Web sites of land-grant universities nationwide can be located under the subject of education in a web subject tree or from the CSREES homepage.

Category III: Professional Societies

Names and brief descriptions of agriculture-related societies and research centers can be obtained from reference sources such as the *Encyclopedia of Association and Research Centers Directory*. Traditionally, these pro-

FIGURE 3. Identifying Information Providers

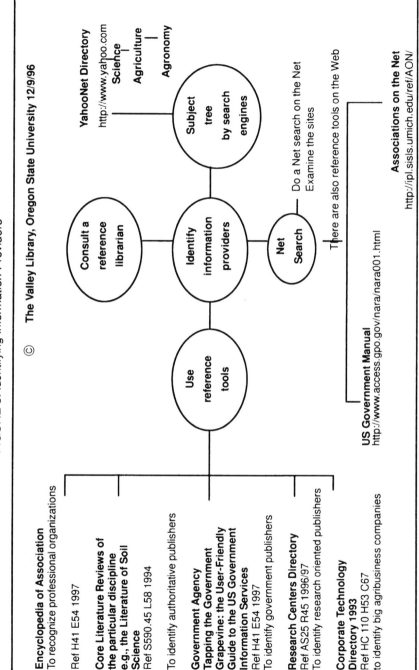

© The Valley Library, Oregon State University 12/9/96

YahooNet Directory
http://www.yahoo.com
Science
|
Agriculture
|
Agronomy

Subject tree by search engines

Consult a reference librarian

Identify information providers

Net Search

Do a Net search on the Net
Examine the sites

There are also reference tools on the Web

Associations on the Net
http://ipl.sisls.umich.edu/ref/AON/

Use reference tools

US Government Manual
http://www.access.gpo.gov/nara/nara001.html

Encyclopedia of Association
To recognize professional organizations

Ref H41 E54 1997

Core Literature Reviews of the particular discipline e.g., the Literature of Soil Science
Ref S590.45 L58 1994

To identify authoritative publishers

Government Agency Tapping the Government Grapevine: the User-Friendly Guide to the US Government Information Services
Ref H41 E54 1997
To identify government publishers

Research Centers Directory
Ref AS25 R45 1996/97
To identify research oriented publishers

Corporate Technology Directory 1993
Ref HC 110 H53 C67
to identify big agribusiness companies

fessional societies facilitate communications between agricultural scientists by organizing conferences and publishing refereed journals. Many of them have Web sites and include calendars of events.

Category IV: Agribusiness

Many large agriculture companies have excellent Research and Development departments (R&D) and can be accessed on the Web. By using the subject tree (e.g., Yahoo) on the WWW under the subject of science, a hierarchical path will lead to a listing of many commercial sites. The path derived from the Yahoo subject tree is shown below:

> Science
>> Agriculture
>>> Agribusiness
>>>> Ag Education
>>>> Agri-Business Assistance
>>>> Agribiz
>>>> Farm and Research Business Center
>>>> GIC Group
>>>> PSA-Assist

For example, the links provided by the site Agribiz include: Objective Agricultural Market Analysis; Provincial and Canadian Crop Condition; Market Commentary and Weather Reports; Daily Agricultural Options Analysis; Daily Price Charts; Monitoring Commodity Exchange Delivery Markets; Export Oriented Gopher Links from USDA AMS; USDA NASS Graphic Grain and Livestock Fundamentals; USDA F.A.S. Weekly Export Sales; USDA ERS-NASS-WAOB Reports and Historical Databases; Weekly State Crop Condition and Weather Reports; and Barge Freight Rate Table.

Step II: Diagram the Information Flow (Relationships) Between Categories of Information Providers

Diagramming the relationships between categories of information providers creates an information path and uncovers additional access points for similar information. For example, Agribiz furnishes information created by the USDA (e.g., *USDA F.A.S. Weekly Export Sales*) in addition to links to various commercial sites.

The diagram in Figure 4 illustrates collaboration/partnership between information providers. For example, CSREES of USDA is a state education

FIGURE 4. Information Flow Between Information Providers

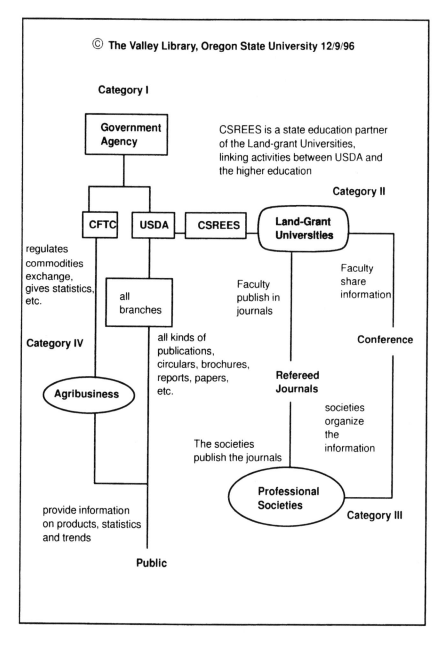

partner of the land-grant universities. Knowledge of information flow helps end users understand the WWW's information environment better. Such understanding also helps in planning the search path.

Step III: Examine a Major Information Provider's Organization

After linking the relationships between the selected categories, the searcher should advance to the level of understanding the internal information flow within individual information providers. Knowledge about the institution that creates the recorded information in terms of its subject scope and information flow[8] is important for an effective search. Due to the WWW's massive volume of information materials, knowledge of information-providing institutions will lead to finding a logical search pathway. For example, the USDA has jurisdiction over U.S. agriculture and has many different branches. Each branch publishes specific types of information. By studying the internal structure of such an information provider, the searcher will understand what branch in this agency is most likely to publish a required type of information. By examining the "Government Manual," the searcher will learn that the USDA's Animals and Plant Health Inspection Service (APHIS) is responsible for enforcing regulations governing the import and export of agricultural products in the USA. Therefore, APHIS is the most likely publisher of requirements for importing and exporting agricultural products. The extent of examination of an information-providing institution's organization varies with the searcher's research interest. It is beneficial to construct a simplified organizational chart for the USDA, including only those branches that are related to a specific research interest. (See Figure 5.)

Step IV: Apply to a Topic Under the Selected Discipline

After the searcher has an understanding of the information structures and how they relate to each other, he or she is ready to perform the search on the WWW. A sample search is conducted here to illustrate how to apply the SIRO model to specific topics.

A Sample Search

Topic: Corn rootworm (an agriculture related topic)
Search interest: General information posted on the WWW on this topic.
Background: corn rootworm is caused by corn rootworm beetles and is very damaging for corn production.

FIGURE 5. A Simplified Diagram for USDA's Organizational Structure

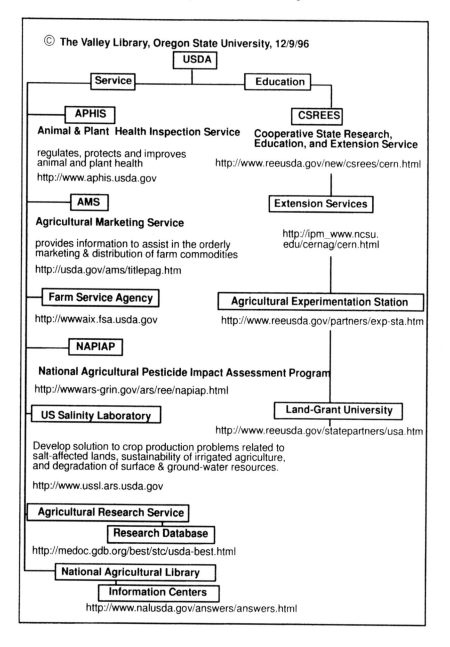

Planning Before Searching

1. Ask Key Questions

Questions:

   A. Corn rootworm disease destroys corn crops. Will it have a large economic impact on the infected areas?
   B. Which are the major corn production states?
   C. Corn rootworm disease is related to the corn rootworm beetle. What institutions are most likely to deal with this problem?

Responses:

   A. It will probably have a very huge economic impact on the infected area if corn production is the major crop in the state.
   B. It is known that the major corn production area is the corn belt which includes Illinois, Indiana, Iowa, Michigan, Minnesota, Missouri, Nebraska, Ohio, South Dakota and Wisconsin.
   C. Corn rootworm disease is caused by corn rootworm beetle and will therefore require pest management. There are many land-grant universities in the corn belt. They have entomology departments and extension services.

2. Utilize Knowledge Obtained from Step I Through Step III

The USDA is identified as one of the major information providers for agricultural information on the WWW. From the organizational chart of the USDA in Step III, the identified branches include CSREES (Cooperative State Research Education Extension Service), ARS (Agricultural Research Service), and NAL (National Agricultural Library). These branches in turn provide links to useful Web-sites. For example: CSREES links to the sites of the Integrated Pest Management Program, agricultural experimental stations, extension services, and land-grant universities nationwide. The ARS links to the CRIS research database; the NAL links to ten information centers. Agribusiness sites are also identified by a subject tree (e.g., Yahoo) on the WWW.

3. What Types of Information Are Needed

The searcher needs to find out what information related to corn rootworm is posted on the WWW and then will use this knowledge to determine a more specific research direction.

4. Decision

Based on the previous planning steps, the searcher decides to use all the categories of information providers suggested by the model and to compare the outcome to a search performed by a search engine. (See Figure 6.)

Search engines: EXCITE, chosen for its "sort by sites" feature. This feature groups documents under individual servers (e.g., www.iastate.edu. for Iowa State University).

Keywords: corn and rootworm (since the search interest is general).

Search results: over 6000 hits (sorted by confidence), dramatically reduced when sorted by sites.

5. Result Analysis

The result of this search is tabulated in Figure 7 and servers (individual information providers) retrieved by the search engine are compared to those selected by the SIRO model.

The EXCITE search confirms that the corn belt land-grant universities are indeed conducting active research on corn rootworm as predicted by the model. Their extension services and entomology departments publish circulars, newsletters, and research papers. The professional society retrieved is the Illinois Natural History Survey. The search results also provide a list of individual corn rootworm researchers.

The EXCITE search missed some information providers suggested by the model. These missing information providers include branches under the USDA (e.g., CSREES and ARS). By using the USDA's research database (CRIS) as suggested by the SIRO model, seven research projects (5 from ARS and 2 from land-grants) are retrieved. Four news items on corn rootworm are also retrieved from the USDA's Integrated Pest Management site. When examining the search results from EXCITE, only one item is shown under the server provided by Purdue University. When the searcher uses Purdue's Entomology Department Web site directly, as suggested by the model, forty-seven more items are retrieved. The EXCITE search retrieved no agribusiness site and very little statistical data. In this case, the agribusiness sites suggested by the SIRO model are most useful. For example, agribusinesses retrieved by the Yahoo subject tree include the Agribiz Web-site. The Agribiz Web-site links to many sites that provide agricultural statistics. These links are: the Daily Price Charts, Monitoring Commodity Exchange Delivery markets, USDA NASS Graphic and Livestock Fundamentals, and Weekly State Crop Condition and Weather Reports.

In the case of corn rootworm, the SIRO model correctly predicted the major information providers on the WWW such as the corn belt land-grants and

FIGURE 6. Planning for the Corn Rootworm Search

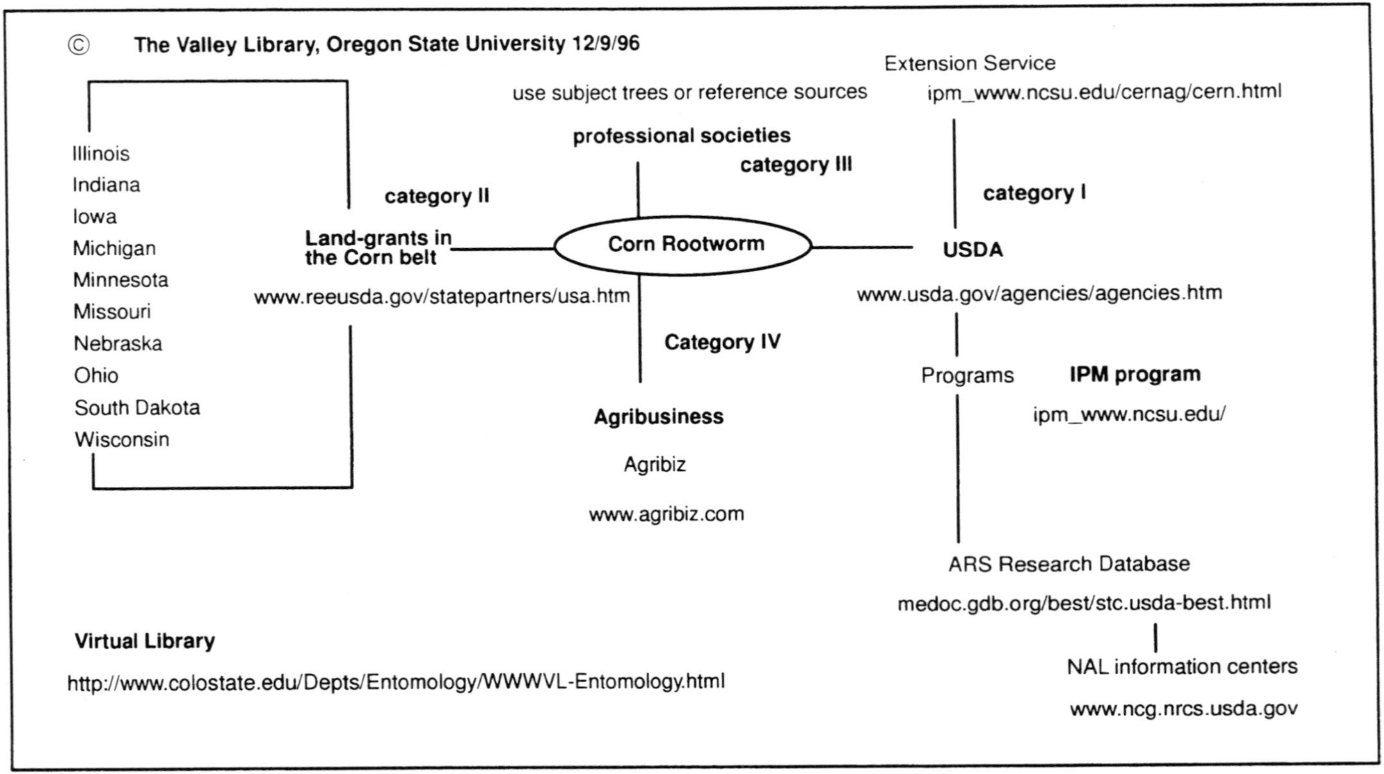

© **The Valley Library, Oregon State University 12/9/96**

use subject trees or reference sources

professional societies
category III

Extension Service
ipm_www.ncsu.edu/cernag/cern.html

category I

USDA

www.usda.gov/agencies/agencies.htm

Corn Rootworm

Programs   **IPM program**
           ipm_www.ncsu.edu/

ARS Research Database
medoc.gdb.org/best/stc.usda-best.html

NAL information centers
www.ncg.nrcs.usda.gov

category II

Land-grants in the Corn belt
www.reeusda.gov/statepartners/usa.htm

Category IV

Agribusiness

Agribiz

www.agribiz.com

Illinois
Indiana
Iowa
Michigan
Minnesota
Missouri
Nebraska
Ohio
South Dakota
Wisconsin

Virtual Library
http://www.colostate.edu/Depts/Entomology/WWWVL-Entomology.html

48

FIGURE 7. Comparing Search Results

Categories	Excite	SIRO Model
1. Government Agency	Missed ADA research projects	Retrieved 7 research projects Newsletter from the USDA IPM program
2. Land-grant universities	Information includes entomology dept. and extension service from these universities	Same, but closer search yields more results
3. Professional Societies	Illinois National History Survey	Missed
4. Agribusiness	None	Statistical information found

extension services. It also provides supplemental links missed by the search engines such as the research database (CRIS) and the Integrated Pest Management program under the USDA and the statistical data from the Agribiz website. The SIRO model is best used as a reference to check if any information sources are missing from the search results performed by search engines.

Step V: Organizing the Results

Organizing search results helps manage information, making it more meaningful to the searcher. By grouping the information into different research aspects, searchers can decide which areas need further research or what type of information is most relevant to their work. The SIRO model suggests the use of visual aids to organize the information so that searchers can investigate the result of a particular search in a single diagram. Thinking maps are used as "graphic organizers for structuring information" in schools because they help students think better.[9] The searcher can organize the search results of corn rootworm into a thinking map for inventory purposes. Search results are grouped into reports on injury, current issues, forecast on egg hatching, pest control, etc. (See Figure 8.)

This map groups and simplifies information in a very simple way for demonstration purpose. This thinking map can also be modified to exclude any unrelated information and focus on the searcher's immediate informa-

FIGURE 8. Using a Thinking Map to Organize the Results

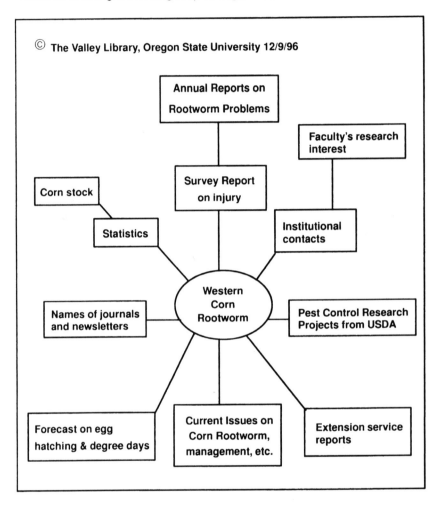

© The Valley Library, Oregon State University 12/9/96

tion need, or to help the searcher decide what is missing from the retrieval. Documents should be downloaded and organized according to the searcher's own organizing scheme for a specific search. Since the WWW is not responsible for archiving, downloading documents is a practical solution. As mentioned earlier, the WWW is not the only research tool and findings on the WWW are normally not comprehensive enough for serious research. For example, information about corn rootworm from several of the selected land-grant universities is not posted on the WWW, but this does not mean that they are not doing research on the topic. It may only mean that further follow-up is necessary. After searching and organizing the information, the next question is how to continue the search. Searchers should first decide in what direction they wish to go, and what other search tools (e.g., CD-ROM databases, monographs, journals, books, etc.) can help them to take advantage of the resources at their own institution. For example, the Valley Library at Oregon State University offers access to several agricultural CD-ROM databases and a current table of contents service provided by UnCover for journals in many disciplines. In this case, the search on the WWW serves as a starting point to obtain current information, but the search will not stop at the WWW level.

DISCUSSION

The SIRO model (summarized in Figure 9) benefits from the theory of existing sophisticated models on searching[10] and question formulation[11] as well as from literature (since 1995)[12] on locating agricultural information. However, the unique characteristics of the SIRO model are the systematic planning process and its visual presentation. This model is not purely theoretical, but rather concentrates on the actual planning process on a specific discipline. This style of presentation is directly related to the developmental history of the model. This model began as a series of flow charts intended to track the agricultural information flow on the WWW. It later developed into a bibliographic workshop and has been tested in classrooms at Oregon State University since the winter of 1995. All workshop participants were asked to give input on the model and their responses were taken into serious consideration. As a result, the model evolved to the present stage with the benefit of active participation. It was generally well-accepted by the workshop participants, but the biggest challenge is still how to sell it to the participants in customers' terms. Users need to be convinced that time spent on planning is a worthy investment.

This model needs further testing of its suitability for research in other disciplines. The first test will be conducted in the winter of 1997 in the field of Social Science. Adaptations and modifications are anticipated for identifying information providers due to the different information structure different disciplines require. In fact, one of the strengths of this model is its adaptability to different research needs. Most importantly, this model provides a means to mediate human and machine interaction and encourage searchers to apply their subject knowledge to better the machine performance.

FIGURE 9. A Visual Summary of the SIRO Model

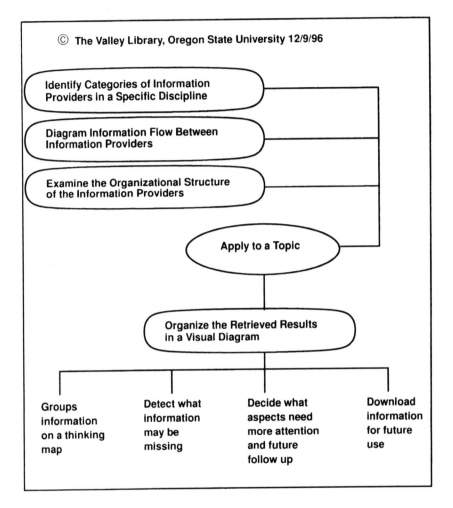

NOTES

1. C. W. Kaha, "Mastering Technology: Studies in Cognitive Styles," *College Teaching* 43:1 (Winter 1995): 25-27.

2. Blaise Cronin and Carol A. Hert, "Scholarly Foraging and Network Discovery Tools," *Journal of Documentation* 51:4 (December 1995): 388-403.

3. James Benson, and Ruth Kay Maloney, "Principles of Searching," *RQ* 14:4 (Summer 1975): 316-320.

4. Diane K. Kovacs, Barbara F. Schloman and Julie A. DcDaniel, "A Model for Planning and Providing Reference Services Using Internet Resources," *Library Trends* 42:4 (Spring 1994): 638-647.

5. Donna Rubens, "Formulation Rules for Posing Good Subject Questions: Empowerment of the End-User," *Library Trends* 39:3 (Winter 1991): 271-298.

6. Office of the Federal Register National Archives and Records Administration. *The United States Government Manual.* (Washington, DC: GPO, 1995): 137.

7. Ibid., 123.

8. Donna Rubens, and Mary M. Huston, "Thinking Like a Searcher" *Building on the First Century (Proceedings of the Fifth National Conference of the Association of College and Research Libraries)* ed. J.C. Fennell. (Chicago: ALA, 1989): 337-342.

9. David Hyerle, "Thinking Maps: Seeing is Understanding," *Educational Leadership* 53:4 (December-January 1996): 85-89.

10. Benson and Maloney, "Principles of Searching," 316-320.

11. Rubens, "Formulation Rules for Posing Good Subject Questions: Empowerment of the End-User," 271-298.

12. Hugo Besemer, and Irene Verman, "Agricultural Information on the Internet: What is Out There and How to Find It," *Quarterly Bulletin of the International Association of Agricultural Information.* 40:2/3 (1995): 61-67.

Library Instruction on the Web: Inventing Options and Opportunities

Corinne Y. C. Laverty

SUMMARY. With the establishment of the World Wide Web as a standard information tool in academic libraries, there is greater demand for research assistance than ever before. Reference questions involve more teaching time given the number of interfaces clients confront as they navigate the book catalog, electronic databases, and the Web. Librarians require expert knowledge of multiple search strategies at their fingertips as well as the ability to teach others how to apply them effectively. How can instruction librarians use this new medium to serve as a dynamic learning aid to students in the classroom, at the reference desk, in distance education courses, and as a self-directed learning tool? This paper outlines how the Web can function as our latest desktop publishing system, revitalize subject pathfinders and "how-to" guides, and promote the invention of interactive library tutorials. A Web site presenting design ideas accompanies this article at: http://stauffer.queensu.ca/inforef/tutorials/cla/clahome.htm. *[Article copies available for a fee from The Haworth Document Delivery Service: 1-800-342-9678. E-mail address: getinfo@haworth.com]*

KEYWORDS. Library instruction, bibliographic instruction, World Wide Web, Internet research, search strategies

---

Corinne Y. C. Laverty (lavertyc@stauffer.queensu.ca) is Instructional Services Librarian at Stauffer Library, Queen's University, Kingston, Ontario, Canada K7L 5C4.

[Haworth co-indexing entry note]: "Library Instruction on the Web: Inventing Options and Opportunities." Laverty, Corinne Y. C. Co-published simultaneously in *Internet Reference Services Quarterly* (The Haworth Press, Inc.) Vol. 2, No. 2/3, 1997, pp. 55-66; and: *The Challenge of Internet Literacy: The Instruction-Web Convergence* (ed: Lyn Elizabeth M. Martin) The Haworth Press, Inc., 1997, pp. 55-66. Single or multiple copies of this article are available for a fee from The Haworth Document Delivery Service [1-800-342-9678, 9:00 a.m. - 5:00 p.m. (EST). E-mail address: getinfo@haworth.com].

55

Librarians are charged with learning to perform expert searches on the Web and teaching others how this system extends the traditional information-tion continuum and research strategy. Library users are both fascinated and frustrated with this new medium as they encounter the pleasures and pitfalls of the Web. Given the serendipitous mystique of surfing, the medium offers an educational opportunity which holds appeal for a captivated audience. Not only is it popular, as a learning tool it is visually engaging, point-and-click friendly, and can enable quasi-interactive manoeuvres that make information-gathering appear to be seamless and transparent.

Around the world, library home pages reveal efforts to deploy the Web as an instructional tool with varying degrees of success. A discussion follows outlining how the Web can be used to serve a library instruction program from facilitating access to basic guides and pathfinders at workstations throughout the library, to the creation of complex library tutorials.

INSTRUCTION PROGRAM

The instruction program I coordinate has a home page at http://130.15.161.74/inforef/instruct/index.html. This page is the jumping off point for advertising sessional workshops, describing successful library research strategy assignments, and linking patrons to subject pathfinders, how-to guides, and library tutorials. Types of instruction are outlined so faculty get a sense of the range of workshops available. One type of library assignment that has proved very successful with large classes called "Research Strategy," is advertised using the results of student evaluations of the exercise. Calendars are provided for Internet workshop times and will include direct sign-up capability in the future. Apart from generic sessions on "Searching the World Wide Web," library instruction is formally integrated into the curriculum or occurs informally at the reference desk. Consequently, a call for instructors to reserve a time slot for library instruction and consultation with the librarian is also included here.

This site is continually revised because of the evolutionary phase our library system is undergoing in terms of changing interfaces and available research tools. Examples of Web instruction presented throughout this paper are taken from the Stauffer Library instruction page at Queen's University, Kingston, Ontario, Canada.

OVERHEADS

Where there is Web access with a browser and projection system in a lab or classroom, the simplest use of the Web is as a tool for creating overheads. HTML files serve as readily transportable overheads that are just as easy to create and use as slides made using graphics software such as PowerPoint or Freelance Graphics. Hundreds of HTML files can fit onto a single 1.44 MB diskette. Since most library instruction in a wired classroom will have Internet access, using the Web to display key points eliminates the need to maintain a graphics package at the presenter's workstation. Overheads for display through a browser are best sized so they fit into the visible window without need for scrolling. When displaying HTML files in Netscape, maximize the display area by removing the toolbar and directory buttons via the "Options" menu. Apart from showing overheads from the instructor's station, files can also be loaded onto classroom computers so students can follow a series of HTML files linked with a forward arrow or icon from their own screens.

Application of this overhead technique allows librarians to concentrate on mastering HTML rather than having to manipulate a separate graphics program for overheads and HTML for Web pages. Overheads designed using HTML can also become permanent Web pages that students refer back to and that link directly to live examples of library databases or Web sites that illustrate aspects of a given presentation or provide exercises for a particular class. Demonstration of the medium as a desktop publisher also enhances instruction about the uses of the Web and how it works. An introduction to searching the Internet should include discussion and demonstration of the lack of standardization and evaluation of Web information and homemade overheads can be used to reveal the construction of simple text files.

BACKUP SYSTEM

Teaching in an electronic classroom invites hands-on, active learning exercises, as long as your network connections are secure. Experienced instructors take "glitch" management seriously and prepare more than one backup system knowing that technological problems will arise on a regular basis. While regular overhead transparencies and blackboards may serve as a last resort, captured screens readily simulate a live demonstration. Sophisticated video tools such as Lotus Screen Cam or Camera Man actually create movies of entire research strategies including the action of the cursor, individual menus and databases, and the sound of the keyboard and typist. The resulting files are realistic but they are huge and not as transportable between machines as a series of individual screen captures which can run on any machine with basic Web access. Paint Shop Pro (PSP) is an inexpensive program that captures individual screens which can be saved as GIF or JPG files and displayed through a browser such as Netscape. The basic steps for this process follow.

1. Open PSP and the database screen you wish to capture.
2. Use [Alt] [Tab] to switch from the PSP screen in front of you to the preceding Windows screen. Use [Alt] [Esc] to clear unwanted screens (such as menus) until every time you use [Alt] [Tab] you move between PSP and the desired screen for capture.
3. Under the "Capture" menu in PSP, select "Area" or "Full Screen." Area allows you to size the space to be captured. Once you select an option, PSP automatically jumps to the preceding screen to make the capture. This is the reason you must first align it.
4. Save the file as a GIF image, format version 89a, in a designated backup folder.

While this process is necessary to capture database screens and menus, Web files can be saved directly to disk as complete entities. To create the impression of a live demonstration, captured screens can be retrieved as single files from Netscape under the "File" menu. A smoother presentation is achieved when files are sequenced in HTML with the addition of a single forward arrow or preferred icon below each screen which is linked to the next screen capture. In this way the instructor moves quickly and systematically through a series of screens rather than opening individual files one at a time. In the case of Web pages, links should be changed so that the browser is directed to the drive where the backup file folder is stored. Where graphics are an important part of the file, these can be captured separately and linked into the backup folder. If they are not essential, they can be deleted from the backup file so they do not clutter the screen.

COMPREHENSIVE PATHFINDERS

Many libraries are making their subject guides available on the Web. Take a tour of library sites across Canada at http://stauffer.queensu.ca/inforef/tutorials/cla/clahome.htm to see an array of pathfinder formats and content. Given the versatility of the Web in terms of its graphic capabilities and hypertext connectivity, traditional pathfinders can be significantly enhanced and extended when disseminated via this interface. A number of features that I have adopted can be viewed at http://stauffer.queensu.ca/inforef/english/ and include:

1. Use of a menu system within a table format (Figure 1) so all choices are visible from the initial screen.
2. Addition of a complete research strategy within a subject area rather than limitation to the traditional list of reference tools. For example, an overview of how to undertake research within a discipline is included in the example above, along with a list of key Internet resources, search techniques for pertinent databases, how to critically evaluate information, prepare a bibliography, and write an essay.
3. Wherever possible, build in active links to databases and tutorials or guide sheets for how to use them. For example, the file describing strategies for searching the catalog can provide a link directly to the application and an option to work through the accompanying tutorial.
4. Information should be separated into individual files for quick loading and ease of printing. A comprehensive file combining all smaller files can also be made available as a printing option with a warning of loading time so users can print a single continuous copy if they wish to do so.

Expansion of the traditional pathfinder on the Web becomes a useful teaching tool in the classroom, at the reference desk, and for self-help at any time. The table of contents allows patrons to select their area of interest or concern rather than read through a long file of various types of resources. Providing this option of selection in the form of a simple visual

FIGURE 1. Sample Table of Contents for a Subject Pathfinder

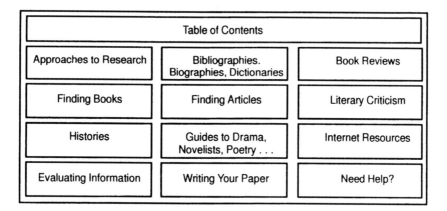

display is often missing from library guides. Requiring users to read through long lists of reference tools is both frustrating for them and unwarranted given the nature of questions these tools are created to address. Researchers do not wish to peruse entire lists and more often have a particular need in one area. Menu systems are a critical part of engaging a user and successfully steering them to purposeful information.

In the wired classroom, this form of pathfinder can become the central teaching resource which presents an overview of the research process as a starting concept. It provides students with a map of inter-connected research choices from which they can explore different avenues according to their need. The instructor can begin a workshop by asking students what types of resources they would use for the assignment at hand, then move to the file "Approaches to Research" and "Research Strategy" to focus responses. From here, a class can move directly to the online catalog to observe a demonstration and undertake exercises for finding books. The instructor can then guide them to the summary at "Finding Books" within the pathfinder to reinforce the principles of searching and the place of books as information sources within the confines of the assignment or discipline. In the future, I intend to build in individual class exercises and evaluation forms as part of the pathfinder.

"HOW-TO" GUIDES

With the ability to display captured screens at workstations throughout the library via a graphical Web interface, technical instructions are easier to illustrate. Desktop publishing programs such as PageMaker offer precise design controls but cannot be mounted on workstations across the library system or accessed remotely from offices or home. With the commonality of a single Web interface by provision of a browser such as Netscape, available free to our campus community, we finally have a shared medium through which to commune.

The use of HTML tables is a good way to present command summaries. An example of such a summary for an online catalog appears at http://stauffer. queensu.ca/inforef/guides/qcat.htm. This guide was designed so that it could be printed and distributed as a double-sided handout if necessary. Tables force the concept of teaching by direct example through the physical limitation of input fields. They cater to quick scanning of succinct examples rather than prose descriptions of how a command operates.

Pictures and diagrams not only speak a thousand words, they can also be interpreted by the user at a glance. Instruction librarians can use the capture process to quickly illustrate technical procedures that almost defy explanation through verbal description. An example of downloading records from an online catalog is illustrated at http://stauffer.queensu.ca/inforef/tutorials/ qcat/down.htm. A screen from this guide is illustrated in Figure 2. This example shows the capture of an open menu which requires a different technique from the copying method described previously for a single image.

In this case, the capture process is as follows:

1. Open the database and the pull-down menu you wish to display.
2. On a PC, use <Alt> <Print Scrn>, or <Print Scrn>, to capture the screen with the open menu. Paint Shop Pro cannot be used to capture open menus. The image is stored as a bitmap (BMP) on the machine's clipboard.
3. Paste the image into a versatile desktop program such as Claris Works that allows easy manipulation of graphics. Word Perfect is not suitable for this. After opening a new graphics file in Claris Works, open the "Edit" menu and select "Paste."
4. Edit the image by adding arrows and captions to draw attention to particular features.
5. Capture an area of this edited file using Paint Shop Pro and save it as a GIF image.

Obviously, these descriptions of technical procedures should be illustrated on Web pages!

FIGURE 2. Capturing and Editing an Open Menu

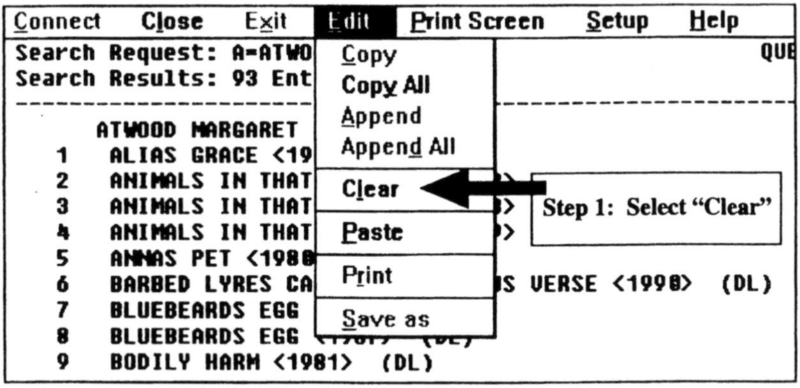

User-Centered Instructions

User-centered instructions are of prime importance in the construction of guides attempting to convey technical information. How frequently we have despaired of our software manuals in trying to learn a new program! Instructors who are technical experts may find it challenging to write guides that are accessible to novices. A common problem that I have encountered is the use of too much written description in place of an example of the action or command required to make something actually happen.

Whatever medium is used to disseminate library instruction guides, there are several tips regarding language usage that remain constant:

1. Avoid unnecessary technical terms and jargon.
2. Use point form action language when illustrating commands.
3. Do not give overviews or introductions other than a simple line of explanation. Unfortunately, people tend not to read these and they take up valuable space.
4. Consider what the user wants to know about the product (which is not usually the technical details of what enables it to work).
5. Avoid descriptive language in sentence format to explain how to use software. Instead, prefer charts and boxes to illustrate the use of various commands.
6. Replicate commands exactly as seen on the screen rather than substituting a description of them.
7. Give commands in context on the screens where they can be applied.
8. Use precise examples that you know will work rather than hypothetical ones.
9. Explain acronyms and abbreviations.
10. Maintain consistency of terms. Once you use a term do not use other words to describe it.

For example, choose one of: command line, command prompt, next command, prompt.

11. Incorporate frequently asked questions into publications.
12. Keep documents short and directed at selected users. Prefer a separate advanced document on a product to a long document with both introductory and advanced techniques.
13. Use instructions to teach basic principles that can be built on in successive publications such as the relationship between support-

ing communications software and a product and the general use of read-me files for installation assistance.

14. Provide last revised date and e-mail contact.

Graphics and *Layout*

1. Use a standard layout for similar types of databases or software. For example, common sections for an application could include: what is xxx? (simple coverage; key functions); how to install; how to search; special tips; how to print or download; how to exit.
2. Use captured screens for clarity. Alternatively, design miniature screen replicas which remove confusing and extraneous information from the screen and identify only what a user must be aware of to execute a step.
3. Show consistency in the use of graphics, their size, and organization.
4. Use graphics for a purpose and limit content accompanying them so that a single page loads quickly, preferably within about 12 seconds.
5. Accompany graphics with a short point form explanation and required action for the user.
6. Use white space and boxes (tables on the Web) to draw attention to frequently used commands that a user would be expected to refer back to.
7. Highlight search strategy whenever possible by grouping steps to form a process that would be used repeatedly.
8. Colour-code related handouts (printouts of the most frequently used Web guides) and use a clearly recognizable logo which identifies their origin.
9. Provide an option to download or print the entire guide with a warning of loading time.

"INTERACTIVE" TUTORIALS

An example of a quasi-interactive tutorial for the online catalog can be viewed at http://stauffer.queensu.ca/inforef/guides/qcat.htm. The sections for title, periodical title, author, subject, keyword, and call number provide exercises for students to test themselves by attempting questions with links to correct and incorrect responses. Incorrect answers reiterate basic search principles and offer the user a chance to select another answer. The tutorial does not offer bonafide interaction in the sense of live participation by the user in the catalog.

terms and concepts that the instructor targeted in a tutorial demonstrating use of an online catalog.

INTO THE FUTURE

Web guides and tutorials are only useful if they are well-designed, well-advertised, and readily accessible from workstations across the library system, the campus, and the community. All student residences at Queen's University are now wired enabling thousands of students access to the library system at any hour of the day or night. Many other students and faculty dial into the system remotely from offices and home. With increasing numbers of part-time and distance education students, there is a greater need for library instruction of the self-help variety. While electronic tutorials are no replacement for personal interactions at the reference desk or in the classroom, they are definitely in demand.

The creation of teaching aids on the Web is labor intensive at the outset, mostly as a result of initial design considerations. Achieving mastery of HTML and supporting software is, however, no more difficult than learning any desktop publishing application. The challenge for instruction librarians is to take advantage of the versatility and accessibility of the Web in a way that enhances the library learning process. If your teaching materials are not used by librarians at the reference desk and in library instruction classrooms, perhaps both the design of the tools and the reference interview interaction should be examined. Our way of thinking about how we assist people to build on their information-finding prowess may need to evolve as we attempt to field increasing numbers of questions with fewer human resources. Now that we have tools with which to conjure interactive learning aids that can potentially reach all our clients, the need for technologically capable and inventive librarians has never been greater.

The Two Instructional Faces of the Web: Information Resource and Publishing Tool

Aniko L. Halverson

SUMMARY. The World Wide Web represents the final step in the evolution of the Internet as a tool worthy for practical applications in instruction. Two particular applications for the Web are discussed in light of projects which have been undertaken in the Helen Topping Architecture and Fine Arts Library at the University of Southern California. First, the World Wide Web may be used as a resource in the library. The Web is a source of content which, like all library resources, must be taught. It should be presented to users along with the same information literacy skills which must accompany any resource. Second, the Web may be used as a publishing tool where the content is created according to the particular instructional need or situation. This usage involves the technology of the Web rather than the content of the Web; this technology is the interface and access capabilities, either local or on a server, provided by the Web browser. *[Article copies available for a fee from The Haworth Document Delivery Service: 1-800-342-9678. E-mail address: getinfo@haworth.com]*

KEYWORDS. World Wide Web, humanities, digital images, HTML, bibliographic instruction

---

Aniko L. Halverson (halverso@calvin.usc.edu) is Reference and Instruction Librarian, Helen Topping Architecture and Fine Arts Library, University of Southern California, University Park, Los Angeles, CA 90089-0812.

[Haworth co-indexing entry note]: "The Two Instructional Faces of the Web: Information Resource and Publishing Tool." Halverson, Aniko L. Co-published simultaneously in *Internet Reference Services Quarterly* (The Haworth Press, Inc.) Vol. 2, No. 2/3, 1997, pp. 67-76; and: *The Challenge of Internet Literacy: The Instruction-Web Convergence* (ed: Lyn Elizabeth M. Martin) The Haworth Press, Inc., 1997, pp. 67-76. Single or multiple copies of this article are available for a fee from The Haworth Document Delivery Service [1-800-342-9678, 9:00 a.m. - 5:00 p.m. (EST). E-mail address: getinfo@haworth.com].

The Internet is a constantly evolving global network of networks. It is comprised of many different information resources, and numerous applications are available for the purpose of Internet access. Prior to the introduction of the World Wide Web, the library community found the use of Internet resources to be a challenge to learn as well as to teach to users. The first generation of Internet applications were largely character-based, and often cumbersome to navigate. The World Wide Web now offers a more flexible means of presenting Internet information resources. Graphical and user-friendly, the hypertext-based interface is intuitive and easily maneuverable; in fact, the Web is itself referred to more and more as "the Internet." Conversely, we hear the term "the Web" used to refer to the Internet overall, a misnomer which indicates the widespread acceptance of the Web as a medium, a mode of communication, a resource. The Web is rapidly overshadowing such unappealing, character-based Internet applications as Gopher and ftp. The advent of the Web marks the arrival of a mechanism with which to explore creativity in a variety of media in a networked environment. The rich content of global information networks has at last been granted a visually oriented, multimedia vehicle for its expression.

Because of the emergence of the Web, the Internet may at last be considered a tool worthy of exploration for numerous practical applications in instruction. The literature concerning library user education refers widely to the common problems and challenges associated with the evolving information universe. The increasingly complex stratosphere of resources raises many questions as to how best to welcome and motivate students to potentially alien new technologies. The inherent challenges in providing students and scholars in the Humanities with information are also well documented. Resistance to new technologies and rigid information-seeking habits create a challenge for librarians in introducing this user population to new information resources, including the task of convincing them of the often tremendous benefits of these sources, which include digital formats and multimedia applications. Humanities scholars are characterized in particular by their need for visual information. The enhanced capabilities for access to visual information in this digital era, as well as the democratization of multimedia publishing available with HTML, the mark-up language used in the creation of Web documents, will dramatically change the sphere of visual resources, and certainly the role of the librarian and curator.

The World Wide Web has the potential to solve the twofold problem of educating library users and introducing users to new realms of visual information. This is especially true for the community of art and architecture historians, who will benefit greatly from new ways to access the information upon which they rely. Given this context of the information needs of a visually-oriented user population, including art and architecture historians, artists, and architects, the World Wide Web will have an impact on instruction in two ways.

First, the World Wide Web may be used as a resource in the library. The Web is a source of content which, like all library resources, must be taught in order to maximize its effective use. It should be presented to users along with the same information literacy skills which must accompany any resource. Users must be introduced to the Web in conjunction with a set of skills with which to use it responsibly and productively. This instruction must be approached in terms of where it fits into the bigger picture of library resources. It is easy to construe the Web as a be-all, end-all resource because of its vastness, with estimates of scores of millions of Web sites available; rather it is a resource which provides certain kinds of information. Information on the Web is unwieldy as it is created and shared by individuals and institutions with varying purposes and intended audiences. The inherent value of the information should be subject to the same evaluation and critical thought processes as should published print sources. Libraries which promote the use of and access to the World Wide Web must adopt policies for instructing patrons to effectively use it.

Second, the Web may be used as an publishing tool where the content is created according to the particular instructional need or situation. This usage involves the technology of the Web rather than the content of the Web; this technology is the interface and access capabilities, either local or on a server, provided by the Web browser. Local use can be either on a single workstation or on a campus network. Files are not necessarily situated on the Web where external, anonymous users may have access. It is this use of the Web, as an instructional medium, which will be explored in light of the numerous projects in place and in progress in the Architecture and Fine Arts Library Slide Collection at USC.

THE WORLD WIDE WEB AS AN INFORMATION RESOURCE

Instruction for use of the Web should be much like instruction for traditional library resources; however, the Web does possess its own unique traits which should drive instructional methods. The World Wide Web, under the control and governance of no single entity or body, is a fascinating mix of often unique information, of both the useful and the useless. It is vital that instruction includes responsible use and critical thinking components. Pask and Snow, in their 1995 article "Instruction and the Internet" assert that "to be successful Internet users, students must have a clear understanding of the broad context of the Internet . . . students still need to be able to use the same basic information literacy skills librarians have stressed in the last decade."[1]

The teaching methodology I have adopted for Web instruction is in the form of a Web page, created for a "Basic Introduction to the World Wide Web" class, which is mounted on a local server. The page serves as both an outline for the class and a way for students to perform hands-on exercises as a group. Objectives for the hour-and-a-half long session are followed by basic Web terminology, a brief history of the evolution of the Web, and an explanation of what appears in the browser window. Hypertext is introduced, and concepts are presented on the Web page, with emphasis placed on the advantages, as well as the pitfalls, of multimedia Web devices. The capability for images and sound is presented as part of the intrinsic advantage of the Web; I explain the potential problems associated with these features, which include the often slow loading as well as cumbersome large image files. Newcomers to the Web should be aware of these elements so as not to hinder their enthusiasm.

The class is taught in one of two state-of-the-art networked Learning Rooms in Leavey Library, the undergraduate teaching library at USC which opened in August 1994. The room is equipped with 25 workstations, a teaching station which is projected onto a large screen with a Barko projector, and whiteboards. For classes of ten or more students, it is desirable for the instructor to be accompanied by a Web-savvy assistant, or "floater," who can roam about the room, ensuring that students are able to follow along, and also to help answer questions.

Rather than following the much-used "a list of links is provided" approach to the introduction to the Web, I focus on the use of indexes and search engines in order to provide students with the skills to find information independently. This is followed by an exercise in critical thinking—a vital concept in the practical use of the sometimes content-questionable arena of the Internet. A search is conducted; the results are used to illustrate the difference between sites with reliable content and sites which have relatively low content merit. Students may suggest search topics; I also bring search ideas to the class which are tailored to produce results which will generate discussion and illustrate critical thinking concepts.

The URL for the Web page used in the class is provided to students on a handout. Students must have it to access the page as it is not linked to any other page and is thus not available for use by outsiders. It may be accessed at a later date, as links are provided as an incentive for further exploration. In this regard, the Web page becomes a reference tool for students who may wish to have a familiar point of departure when surfing the Web independently. The page also includes information for more advanced users, such as sending email from a Web page, and links to sites which provide Web authoring tools and instructions for mounting a personal page on the USC servers.

The relative merits of the Web for reference fall into two areas. There are well-known general reference tools which are appearing more and more as Web sites. These sites, as they are produced by well-known, reputable publishers, free the user from the necessary critical thinking processes when analyzing the relative merits of Web sites. USC has licensed the Encyclopedia Britannica Online Web site and has it linked to the University Libraries Web site. Some commercial sites may require licensing of products before access can be obtained.

Secondly, the Web is an invaluable tool for research involving "Internet-rich" topics. These are topics which by their nature are likely to be well-represented on the Internet. Two examples of such topics are contemporary art and electronic journals. The latter example refers to journals published electronically that are not necessarily electronic counterparts of the printed journal (which do exist in large number), but are journals published solely in an electronic format. Electronic journals are heralded as an illustration of the Web's potential as a publishing medium. "Internet-rich" topics dictate a necessity for the Internet, or the Web, to be consulted for research.

Issues of access and staff training must be considered when addressing the use of the Web for reference. On the USC campus, the University Libraries are grappling with a number of issues in terms of providing networked resources for reference use: not all reference desks are equipped with networked workstations, patron access to the Web varies from library to library, and not all reference personnel are equally trained on the use of the Web.

WEB TECHNOLOGY AS A PUBLISHING TOOL

I will focus on course-related Web sites as an example of the Web as a medium for instruction. In this sense, "the Web" does not refer to the Internet, nor to the physical networks that carry information globally. An important semantic question should be posed: does the term "the Web" refer to the content which exists on the Web, or is it the interface, access and multimedia capabilities provided by Web technology? I use the term "the Web" for instruction to refer to the latter. Katherine Whitley, at the Untangling the Web conference at the University of California, Santa

Barbara, in April 1996, refers to what I call Instructional Web Sites as "HTML tutorials." Whitley asserts that "HTML provides an almost ideal vehicle for teaching methods that require visual impact, that take advantage of the hypertext nature of the Web, and that can be used remotely."[2] While she discusses the use of HTML and Web documents as a means for educating users specifically for computer-based information systems, her methodology is the same. Whether termed "Web-based instruction" or "HTML tutorials" the idea is to use the Web as a medium for creating instructional materials as it is a way to publish information quickly and easily. It is equally a way to provide access locally and remotely to a variety of course-related information, including images in a digital format.

The first use of digital images in the USC Architecture and Fine Arts Library Slide Collection was in the form of Kodak Photo CDs. Instructors selected groups of images from the collection to be digitized and stored on Photo CD. The CDs were placed on reserve where four Kodak Photo CD players were available for viewing. While this seemed to solve the problem of providing access to students to images outside of class, it proved to be a very limited method. Not enough workstations or CDs were available to meet the demands of users, particularly during the period prior to exams, when many students needed to review these images for study. CDs provided high quality resolution images which were otherwise unavailable to students, but limitations were discovered. Lists of images were maintained as separate, printed documentation. The lack of textual accompaniment to the images rendered the Photo CD format a fairly limited tool for study. It was, however, an indication of the potential for digitization of images for improved access. In addition, the Photo CD format is an excellent medium for the storage of images.

The next stage of the development of the use of digital images was with the commercial database ImageAXS. This application provided an interface in which text could be included along with the digital images. Text included descriptions of images as well as notes or instructions written by the instructor. It was discovered that networked access to the information would be advantageous. The application provided a good public interface and the capability of providing access to many images. The ImageAXS database is not very structured, but provides limited capabilities for providing textual accompaniment to the images. Fields provided are of relatively short length, with a maximum of six fields. The new problem which arose was the lack of multiple user access. The application required installation and routine maintenance on each workstation, which proved to be ineffective on a large campus. It was discovered that students would benefit from access from different libraries, particularly from Leavey Library, which provides 24-hour access. Thus the idea for access to the images and text required for courses on a multi-user platform was born.

The discoveries generated by the ImageAXS experiment, that is, limited descriptors as well as the issue of access, came about at a time when the World Wide Web appeared on the USC campus. Libraries and computer labs were beginning to promote Web access. In the summer of 1995 a number of ideas converged which led to the development of a prototype instructional Web site. Dialog took place concerning the issue of access to images and other course-related information, as a form of electronic reserve materials, as well as the concept of a digital classroom. The "digital classroom" refers to a physical room with digital equipment used for teaching. A group of individuals from the University Library system, which included Librarians, the Slide Curator, and Systems personnel, collaborated with the instructor of the Fine Arts 121 Survey of Western Art summer course to launch a Web site for the class. After a brief seven-week development time, the experimental site was used as a teaching tool and as a course manual. The class was small enough, with about 20 students, to take place in a digital classroom equipped with a projector.

The course was a grand success. In addition to its use for teaching the class, the Web page was used as a communication medium, providing students with the ability to post messages in an electronic discussion forum, as well as a means to send email to the instructor. The major feature of the site was to provide access to the images used to teach the class. The instructor, Andrea Pappas, has said that the use of the site in teaching the class has wholly changed her teaching pedagogy, with a move away from the lecture format. The projection of digital images in the classroom in a hypertext format allows for nonlinear access to images in a way which textbooks and traditional slide lectures cannot provide. Classroom time may be used for more dynamic interaction between teacher and student, creating a collaborative learning environment.[3] This atmosphere goes hand in hand with the collaborative teaching inherent in the team effort involved in creating the Web site.

Issues of copyright must be responsibly treated in the provision of networked digital images. Images were taken directly from the Slide Library and scanned for use on the Web page. These images are generally photographed from books and used in classroom teaching only; in terms of copyright, this use has generally been treated as acceptable under the realm of Fair Use. For use on class Web site however, in order to protect the copyright, which is not owned by USC, subsequent sites have been password encrypted, with only students and faculty given the login and password information necessary to access the site.

While Web-based instruction solved many problems, new ones were created. Among these problems are demands on staff time. Basic Web authoring is not labor intensive, given a knowledge of HTML; it is the scanning of images which places the most demands on staff time for generating these Web sites. It was initially uncertain as to how these tasks would be incorporated into established, day-to-day process in the Slide Library as no additional staff hours were added as a result of taking on Web projects. So far there has been no significant impact on the functioning of the Slide Library. With the increased demand for instructional Web pages (three sites are currently being created for Spring 1997) it remains to be seen how the existing staff availability, as well as the current hardware and equipment situation, will serve.

The biggest shift in focus for Slide Library operations has been from the physical use of slides to a digital arena with the need for computer equipment and networks. We continue to create slides, with the photography done in-house, and to scan them as part of the everyday procedures of providing images for use in teaching. The idea of a Core Image Database is being explored, where new acquisitions to the collection will be added and indexed in a database. Faculty will eventually be able to select and group slides for lectures using workstations, rather than the light-table. Commercial image database software is currently being reviewed for selection to facilitate such a database.

Another potential problem involves issues of access. As more students are required to use the Web in order to fulfill course requirements, issues of access to networked workstations must also be carefully considered. In the Architecture and Fine Arts Library, two networked computers are currently available, with no printing capabilities. Across campus in Leavey Library, the networked Learning Rooms as well as another, larger area with networked machines known as the "Information Commons" provide 24-hour access to the Web in a variety of platforms during the school year. Students are dependent on this facility for access to the course Web sites. In the Spring 1996 semester, two additional courses were taught which involved the use of class Web sites. One of these courses was a survey of Western architecture which had 200 students. The challenge of ensuring that each student was given the tools to effectively use the site, as well as gain access easily, was a learning experience for the instructor as well as the librarian charged with Web instruction.

Instruction is another vital element to requiring student use of instructional Web sites. Ideally, faculty must be willing to devote class time to Web instruction in order for the sites to be most effective. Through trial and error we have discovered that classes held on a drop-in basis had little turnout. For the Fall 1996 semester, classes were mandatory, which proved to be more effective. Faculty involvement is also an important element. Faculty should encourage attendance and should be present at Web instruction sessions, whether held in or outside of regular class time, in order to answer content-based questions and also to reinforce the role of the Web site in the class. The aforementioned "Basic Introduction to the World Wide Web" classes serve the purpose of getting students to be comfortable with their class Web site as well as to generate interest about the Web at large.

The key to the success of the class Web site concept is the involvement of the faculty member throughout the process. Participation on the part of the instructor is necessary—they may contribute to the design and creation of the site, even to do some of the HTML mark-up. With the increased demand for instructional Web sites, a "template"-like site has been created to facilitate the work.

The success of the instructional Web sites has led to faculty web sites showcasing their work, has created a forum for communication in and around the two Schools, and has furthered the climate of collaboration and sharing between academic departments and the library. Further ideas for applications of the Web have been generated, including the creation of a virtual gallery of student work. The positive results of the use of the Web in this context have changed the role of the Slide Library from production line to that of a technological leader and a vital link in providing the Schools of Architecture and Fine Arts with a much-needed boost in their effective use of technology. This has been and continues to be critical for the overall visions of the Architecture and Fine Arts Library, which seeks to play an active role not only in providing information but also to the teaching, study, and communication in the two Schools.

NOTES

1. Judith M. Pask and Carl E. Snow, "Undergraduate Instruction and the Internet," *Library Trends* 44:2, (Fall 1995): p. 311.

2. Katherine Whitley, "Instruction on the Web: Authoring Tutorials in HTML," available http://www.library.ucsb.edu/untangle/whitley.html

3. Andrea Pappas, "Wolfflin Meets Nintendo: New Instructor-driven Challenges for Visual Resource Libraries," Art Libraries Society/North America Annual Conference, Miami Beach, Florida, April 1996.

APPENDIX

URLs

Helen Topping Architecture and Fine Arts Library
http://www.usc.edu/Library/AFA/

Standish K. Penton Family Slide Library
Http://www-lib.usc.edu/Info/AFA/#slide

Basic Introduction to the Web
http://www.usc.edu/dept/finearts/hs/webclass.html

THE CHALLENGE OF SPECIFIC CONVERGENCES: INTERNET INSTRUCTION SITE APPLICATIONS

For the Purpose of This Assignment

Katharine A. Waugh

The illustrator, Katharine A. Waugh (kawaugh@vaxsar.vassar.edu), is Reference Librarian, Vassar College Library, Poughkeepsie, NY 12601.

[Haworth co-indexing entry note]: "For the Purpose of This Assignment." Waugh, Katharine A. Co-published simultaneously in *Internet Reference Services Quarterly* (The Haworth Press, Inc.) Vol. 2, No. 2/3, 1997, p. 77; and: *The Challenge of Internet Literacy: The Instruction-Web Convergence* (ed: Lyn Elizabeth M. Martin) The Haworth Press, Inc., 1997, p. 77. Single or multiple copies of this article are available for a fee from The Haworth Document Delivery Service [1-800-342-9678, 9:00 a.m. - 5:00 p.m. (EST). E-mail address: getinfo@haworth.com].

Electronic Instruction at Carlson Library: Emerging Challenges

John C. Phillips
Marcia King-Blandford

SUMMARY. In this age of increasing electronic instruction in academic libraries, the University of Toledo's Carlson Library, like many other academic libraries, is trying to come of age. The library's instruction program has traditionally used a paper-based instructional format. However, with the introduction of the library's OPAC, CD-ROMs, the Internet, and OhioLINK in recent years, we are faced with a number of challenges which this paper will discuss. The main challenge is that we are trying to teach electronic resources without a mediated classroom in the library. We need to bridge the gap between the paper-based instruction program and electronic resources because our current teaching methods do not always allow for patron interaction with the technology. Increasingly, instruction is having to take place at the Information Desk, where there are time constraints and library users are unclear about the kinds of information they want or which electronic resources they need. Adapting to these new and growing resources and developing the skills needed to teach them are among the important challenges librarians at Carlson Library face. *[Article copies available for a fee from The Haworth Document Delivery Service: 1-800-342-9678. E-mail address: getinfo@haworth.com]*

John C. Phillips (jphilli@utnet.utoledo.edu) is Map Librarian and Marcia King-Blandford (mkingbl@utnet.utoledo.edu) is Reference Librarian, William S. Carlson Library, The University of Toledo, 2801 W. Bancroft Street, Toledo, OH 43606.

[Haworth co-indexing entry note]: "Electronic Instruction at Carlson Library: Emerging Challenges." Phillips, John C., and Marcia King-Blandford. Co-published simultaneously in *Internet Reference Services Quarterly* (The Haworth Press, Inc.) Vol. 2, No. 2/3, 1997, pp. 79-92; and: *The Challenge of Internet Literacy: The Instruction-Web Convergence* (ed: Lyn Elizabeth M. Martin) The Haworth Press, Inc., 1997, pp. 79-92. Single or multiple copies of this article are available for a fee from The Haworth Document Delivery Service [1-800-342-9678, 9:00 a.m. - 5:00 p.m. (EST). E-mail address: getinfo@haworth.com].

KEYWORDS. OhioLINK, library instruction, electronic classrooms, individual instruction appointments, information and reference desk, World Wide Web, bibliographic instruction

Rowe's statement concerning teaching patrons how to use electronic research tools is truly indicative of one of the most important challenges facing academic librarians nationwide, and we at Carlson Library are trying to meet that challenge. She states that during the past ten years, automation has appropriated increasing resources in the academic library environment. Teaching patrons how to use sophisticated electronic research tools is one of the major challenges confronting most college and university librarians. Librarians have responded to this challenge by dramatically revising their bibliographic instruction programs to accommodate technologically advanced tools.[1] Electronic instruction at Carlson Library is a relatively recent phenomenon. It has only been since 1989 that our card catalog went online as a NOTIS site. The library's serials holdings were already online as Innovative Interfaces in anticipation of our OhioLINK membership. In 1990, the library was awarded a local area network grant to acquire several CD-ROM networks with different search engines for the reference area which were used for database searching of the periodical literature and government publications. The library's online catalog, the various CD-ROM databases, and the automation of the serials check-in process marked the beginning of what was to become a rapidly growing network of electronic resources available to the users of Carlson Library. This first round of electronic resources was our introduction to the additional responsibility for teaching library patrons how to use the variety of technologies.

Just five years later, in the fall of 1994, Carlson Library migrated to Innovative Interfaces for both its books and serials holdings as its membership in OhioLINK began. OhioLINK is comprised of public and private universities, some private colleges, community colleges in Ohio, as well as the State Library of Ohio. Its main purpose was to provide a statewide library and information network to access the state's collective wealth of research materials for faculty, students, and other library users. As part of a five-year plan, OhioLINK would provide a single electronic library catalog and a statewide document delivery system.[2] During this time, the OhioLINK central catalog contained 5.7 million records from over 40 libraries including library materials in law, medical, and special collections.[3] In addition to the central catalog, OhioLINK was to provide a core of bibliographic databases across a wide range of subjects. This membership created new opportunities for electronic access and also made demands on the searching skills of our library users and reference librarians. Page and Kesselman observed that there are two basic challenges facing all librarians. They will need "to develop expertise in this rapidly changing environment and teach patrons about the network and its wealth of resources."[4] Their remarks would indeed define the two biggest challenges facing reference librarians at Carlson Library.

The authors became interested in writing about these challenges faced by the library because we participate in the library instruction program and are teaching electronic resources. The main challenge we face at Carlson Library is the lack of a mediated classroom for group instruction. We need this classroom to introduce and teach library patrons to use the various levels and kinds of electronic resources our OhioLINK membership provides. With no immediate plans for mediated classrooms in the library, we face the difficult task of trying to teach electronic resources classes using an instructional approach essentially based on a paper format and overhead transparencies. Transparencies have been very useful in the classroom over the years to illustrate components of a bibliographic entry from printed indexes or in more recent years, to replicate some of the screens from the OPAC and the research databases. They have also been used as backup for electronic resources in the event that the technology malfunctioned. However, Rowe asserts that "though they serve as an acceptable means of conveying aspects of printed resources, transparencies prove ill-suited to the fluidity of computerized systems."[5]

HISTORICAL DEVELOPMENTS

Some form of bibliographic instruction at the University of Toledo's Carlson Library has existed for many years. In the earlier days of bibliographic instruction at the library, a small group of library faculty members was involved in bibliographic instruction. However, in 1975 the library set out to establish a separate bibliographic instruction program as part of the Library Programs Division, which would include Reference, Bibliographic Instruction, and Collection Development Departments.[6] Several years later, Carlson Library was awarded an educational grant (NEH/CLR funded) which made possible an experimental three-year program of bibliographic instruction for the College of Education. This program marked the beginning of an ongoing and comprehensive bibliographic instruction program for that college in particular and the bibliographic instruction program in general. Four librarians, each with an expertise in the humanities, education, sociology and international students, were the first members of the department.[7] Eventually, two additional subject specialists with expertise in the physical sciences and business were added to the B.I. department. During the years immediately following the formation of the new department, efforts were made to "regularize" instruction in order to reach the largest possible number of students by teaching them in the required courses of several departments. In those days there was limited end-user access to searching electronic resources.

In 1989 the division's name was changed from Library Programs Division to the Bibliographic Instruction and Reference Division, which denoted the new separate B.I. department. However, in 1994 the division underwent yet another name change as a result of another reorganization. No longer would there be a separate Bibliographic Instruction Department and all reference librarians were expected to participate in the library instruction program. The division's new name became the Information and Instruction Services Division. No one in the new division is referred to as a subject specialist. All reference librarians are generalists and are expected to provide instruction in all disciplines.

TECHNOLOGICAL CHALLENGES

At the beginning of our active OhioLINK membership in 1994, our online public access catalog, named UTMOST, provided three menu options for library users. A user could choose either UTMOST, for library materials from the three campus libraries (Carlson, Scott Park Learning Resource Center, and Law), or the OhioLINK Central Catalog, representing 15 OhioLINK members, or choose from among the five research databases initially offered (ABI/Inform, Dissertation Abstracts International, Periodical Abstracts, Newspaper Abstracts, and WorldCat).[8] This level of access, each with its unique features, would be available from all public access terminals in the library. As August of 1994 got under way with the newly-formed Information and Instruction Services Division, Carlson Library began the final stages of implementing the new technology associated with its OhioLINK membership.

Just five months later, by January 1995, the fifteen OhioLINK libraries had grown to twenty-seven institutions contributing records to the Ohio-LINK central catalog.[9] In addition, plans to add additional databases on a regular basis had begun. Twenty research databases were then available directly through OhioLINK, with an additional six more available through gateways on the network.[10] The OhioLINK research databases are represented by at least four different search engines, which are III, OCLC/First Search, OVID, and RLG-EUREKA. By the end of 1995, 41 OhioLINK schools provided OhioLINK service to their users.[11] The five year plan to tie Ohio's academic institutions and the state library together into a net-worked system was fully operational and the number of participating institutions continued to grow. The number of OhioLINK libraries is now 43 and there are currently 48 research databases.[12]

To say this is a tremendous growth in technological access to information within Ohio is an understatement. The above timeline does not include the different revisions to the software (currently at release 10), and the unique features within the networked system. One of the most important developments for Ohio's students and faculty is the availability of online borrowing. When the Central Catalog shows an item at another OhioLINK institution, all the user has to do is to make a few keystrokes to tell OhioLINK's Central Catalog to deliver the book and the user will have it within three to five working days.[13] In addition to online borrowing, a "Do-It-Yourself Article Requesting" capability is available for many articles indexed by Periodical Abstracts (a multidisciplinary database) and ABI Inform (a business database), two of the many research databases offered. This feature allows library users to request some articles from their computer terminals and have them printed a few minutes later at a cost of 10 cents per page.

During this same time, OhioLINK announced plans to deliver the body of OhioLINK services through a graphical interface on the World Wide Web.[14] Local libraries completed BETA testing in mid-1996 and have implemented Web interfaces for OhioLINK services to allow network users another access point. Web interfaces for the central site and research databases are available. At the beginning of fall quarter 1996, eight public access terminals in Carlson Library offered Web access while twenty-five public terminals had telnet access.

This is the OhioLINK technology that is available to the users of Carlson Library. As a reference tool, Internet resources have been available at Carlson Library for a number of years and, initially, there were some librarians in the library who used it occasionally to answer reference questions. As the Internet has taken on greater importance as a source of information, and the World Wide Web has drawn unparalleled interest, both domestically and internationally, all reference librarians at Carlson Library are expected to develop some expertise in using the Internet to answer reference queries. Reference librarians are also expected to teach Internet access in the classroom as requested and at the Information Desk when it is appropriate.

The rapid pace at which technological change is occurring in the library has caused legitimate concerns for reference librarians. As an example, in only eighteen months the number of research databases at Carlson Library increased from five to 30. For many librarians this rapid change makes them feel inadequate. Mellendorf contends that learning to use the technology efficiently will allay many of those concerns librarians have.[15] He also states that "perhaps no resource has ever provided such a wealth of information while simultaneously producing such unique frustrations."[16] One technique we use to allay some of those concerns at our library is to provide in-house training sessions for librarians on the use of the various technologies. OhioLINK has recently begun regional training sessions taught by individual vendors. These sessions provide librarians with the basic searching skills they need to use and teach electronic resources. Reference librarians at Carlson Library attend these OhioLINK training sessions on a rotating basis and return to the library to train their colleagues.

INSTRUCTION CHALLENGES

The Information Desk at Carlson Library can be a very busy service point. Reference librarians are faced with the task of answering a myriad of reference questions requiring the use of the library's online services. It is oftentimes necessary to provide one-on-one assistance at the Information Desk in the use of OhioLINK and Internet technologies. There are several computer laboratories on campus where hands-on electronic instruction for groups could take place but the library has to compete with other units on campus to use these facilities. Scheduling the labs in advance would be a problem since we are given relatively short notice by professors who want to bring their classes to the library for instruction. One of the difficulties inherent in providing such assistance at the Information Desk is that it requires librarians to spend a great deal of time assisting patrons in using the online services while other patrons in need of other kinds of assistance are left waiting. Page and Kesselman stress the importance of using an electronic classroom when teaching users how to search electronic resources. They state that "hands-on sessions in an electronic classroom provide users with contextual reinforcement. Being able to try out tools and resources in the classroom is likely to lead to more successful experiences when users try searching on their own."[17] In addition, Rowe noted that most libraries in recent years have installed electronic classrooms to meet the challenges of electronic instruction. "The classroom environment most conducive to learning modern library skills is one with a computer lab that allows students to have hands-on practice," according to Rowe.[18] As in most academic libraries, reference librarians go to great lengths in trying to meet the informational needs of library users, but the Information Desk is not the place where a considerable amount of time can be spent with patrons on a one-on-one basis. We believe that teaching them how to use the various online services is most effectively done in an electronic classroom. However, until such time when a mediated classroom for library instruction becomes available at Carlson Library, the Information Desk will be one of the most important service points for teaching the Internet and other OhioLINK electronic resources.

An alternative to one-on-one, in-depth instruction at the Information Desk is a service provided to students and faculty called the "Individual Instruction Appointment" (IIA). This service is, as the name indicates, an individual instruction session in which a reference librarian meets with a patron for one hour to assist the user in meeting their research needs. Arrangements for an appointment are made in advance. The librarian and the patron schedule an appointment based upon a mutually agreed upon time. Part of that session involves hands-on instruction using the various networks of OhioLINK resources. This is uninterrupted assistance and the librarian is not under pressure to get back to the Information Desk and assist other patrons. This service is very popular with students and requests for it continue to increase. A written explanation of the service, including procedures for making an appointment, is available in a library guide. The appointment allows the librarian some preparation time to try various search strategies and perhaps test some ideas based on the user's information needs before meeting with the library user. This preparation time can be very useful for the librarian and the user.

An additional recent challenge to library instruction has been the students' ability to access OhioLINK and the Internet from their dormitories, networked campus computer clusters, and their homes. OhioLINK users have one-stop shopping to all of the OhioLINK resources wherever they have online access. Attempting to instruct users who are not physically present in the library presents a specific problem. It requires that library instruction take on a marketing approach. Although help screens are available and are continually updated, it is still necessary to "get the word" out to students and faculty that remote access is one of their options. We feel that it is necessary to promote the library's remote electronic access service through all the various "marketing" tools available. Since every student at the University of Toledo does not participate in library instruction classes and many faculty do not use the library regularly, it is necessary to reach out to both students and faculty. This outreach includes using various techniques designed to get the word out through departmental newsletters, library displays in the Student Union, bookmarks, and library guides. Another challenge is created by the faculty's lack of exposure and access to the library's technology-based services. Since much of the technology is new and some of the faculty's offices are not wired for electronic capabilities, many faculty are unaware of the electronic services available and are unable to access them remotely.

In the fall of 1994 when OhioLINK was being introduced to the campus, two reference librarians initiated meetings with some of the various academic departments to introduce OhioLINK and to identify subject-specific Web resources that would be of interest to faculty members in those departments. These instructional sessions were taught in the various academic departments. During these sessions, the librarians discovered that many individual faculty offices were not wired for electronic access. Remote electronic access to library resources is one of the more challenging teaching tasks we face at Carlson Library.

When library instruction is held in one of the four library classrooms, another challenge becomes apparent. Library instruction for the lower level courses, such as English writing classes and classes for students whose native language is not English, includes the use of a course-specific, subject-related worksheet. The worksheets, with assigned topics, take the students step by step through the research process and require them to locate books and journals using UTMOST and OhioLINK. Since the worksheets have been pre-designed for students to succeed, they also have the advantage of exposing students to the complex process of selecting the most appropriate electronic resources to use, for example, UTMOST, OhioLINK, the Internet, etc. These worksheets assist students in selecting the correct access point for the type of information they are seeking (books vs. journals) and in determining the appropriate search method (keyword vs. subject). They also introduce the students to the location of both books and periodicals within Carlson Library. As the students complete the worksheets, they encounter retrieval options that may not have been discussed during the classroom presentation. This opens the door to introducing special features in the systems, such as limiting searches and requesting full-text journal articles. Students will also discover that they can borrow books online from other libraries when a title is not available at Carlson Library. While the students are completing the worksheets in the reference area, the librarian who taught the class is available to assist them and librarians staffing the Information Desk are also available to assist as time permits.

Using worksheets in our non-mediated environment allows for a controlled hands-on experience for lower division students. They also reinforce the instruction which took place in the classroom. A challenge in using the worksheets is the continuing need to revise and reprint them. Although we have graduate teaching assistants assigned to revise and update the worksheets, this is an ongoing, expensive, and laborious task. Initially, the worksheets were tied to paper indexes but two factors have forced the movement away from instructing with paper indexes. The first and foremost factor is due to library budget cuts. The availability of these indexes on OhioLINK has resulted in the cancellation of many of the paper indexes. We no longer have the luxury of maintaining indexes in print if they are available in electronic form. And secondly, most students simply prefer to use computers rather than print indexes to find information they need.

Moreover, another challenge associated with using worksheets to bridge the gap between technology and a paper based instruction program is that worksheets are not as suitable for use in upper-level, subject-specific courses. Oftentimes, as is appropriate, library instruction is tied to an already defined research topic assigned within the parameters of course syllabi. The uniqueness of the individual research process is not conducive to a worksheet. For upper-level undergraduate and graduate instruction, one of our library's four classrooms is equipped with an LCD (liquid crystal display) projection unit attached to a computer in order to demonstrate the capabilities of online systems. It allows for a combined lecture and live presentation, but this classroom is not equipped with individual workstations for the critical hands-on, self-paced computer learning experiences. This capability is better than having to use transparencies but, again, students are unable to experience their own searching. This classroom is scheduled on a first-come, first-served basis. If graduate or upper-level undergraduate division classes need to be taught at the same time, one class must then be assigned to use a regular library classroom with an overhead projector.

Unforeseen Events/Challenges

Much of the one-on-one instruction in using the various electronic resources continues to be carried out at the Information Desk. Although this type of instruction has its limitations, librarians are feeling more confident about providing it at the desk because of OhioLINK training sessions in using the electronic resources. These sessions are occurring more frequently and there has been an improvement in the training documentation. Each time a new database is introduced OhioLINK provides regional training sessions around the state. They are usually conducted during mornings and afternoons to allow more librarians to be trained. Opportunities for librarians to practice using the various new databases through a staff mode prior to the introduction of those databases to the public are also available. Moreover, the newly-created OhioLINK listserv affords members the opportunity to communicate and discuss, informally, any problems with the system or any new features or discoveries. There are several watchdog persons at the various libraries who volunteer their services to oversee and evaluate the systems. They report any problems or unusual occurrences with OhioLINK. This exchange of information regarding the various technologies and those opportunities to practice using the various systems in staff mode increase the confidence level of librarians who teach OhioLINK.

Interest in the Individual Instruction Appointment is growing rapidly. For example, in fall 1995 there were two requests for IIAs but during fall quarter 1996 there have been 48 such requests thus far. However, we are beginning to discover that some students are not prepared for in-depth instruction, for which the instructional appointment was intended. They have not identified a research topic and are unclear about their assignments as well as their information needs. Since reference librarians at the Information Desk usually recommend the individual instruction appointment, we are discovering that it has become necessary to do more initial screening of patrons at the Information Desk to make sure that the appointment is what they really need. As word of the service spreads by students, some misunderstandings about it are beginning to surface. Students are beginning to ask for a general orientation to the library and its resources and some graduate research assistants working for their professors are hoping that the librarian will be doing their work for them when they meet. It seems that many library users are learning about the service from friends and by word-of-mouth and perhaps misinformation is being disseminated in the process. We announce this service in graduate classes because research at that level is individualized, although the service is available to undergraduate students and faculty as well. The primary purpose of the individual instruction appointment is to offer in-depth, hands-on individual instruction. Perhaps we need to do a better job of defining this service and thus minimize the possibility of unreasonable expectations. In our opinion, those persons whose research needs are best met by the individual instruction appointment are graduate students with clearly defined research needs.

As fall quarter 1996 geared up, and requests for library instruction began, focus once again shifted to the need to use worksheets for instructional purposes. Some further revisions had to be made in the worksheets. For example, changes made on the computer workstation screens, either by our automation staff or OhioLINK, have to be reflected in the worksheets. Oftentimes, screen changes are discovered while students are completing the worksheets. In addition, there is the problem of not having enough public access terminals for both the public to use and for a class to use at the same time. During peak public use, people are waiting to use terminals. If a librarian brings their class to the public terminals, there simply are not enough terminals available for individual use. Because of time constraints and a limited number of workstations, students are forced to work in groups. This limits their opportunities for individualized, hands-on computer experiences.

In an attempt to avoid using worksheets and tying up the public terminals in the reference area, the library began to offer classroom hands-on computer experiences for classes at locations outside the library. During summer quarter 1996, a reference librarian and a teaching faculty member team taught an English Organizational writing class which focused on Internet resources and business information. To provide hands-on searching capabilities, a computer classroom was used for one-half of the class sessions. The Tuesday class met in a standard university classroom while Thursday's class meeting was held in a university computer lab classroom. Each student had access to a computer workstation for hands-on searching. Instructions on utilizing the Internet to retrieve business information resources that supported the technical writing component of the class were provided. Searching the library's homepage was also a component of the course. The actual hands-on experiences were received very favorably by the students. This was the first opportunity Carlson Library had to provide an in-depth, hands-on electronic searching opportunity for students in a computer lab classroom.

To continue this effort during fall quarter 1996, the English instructors have been given the option to call Computer Services to schedule their English Organizational writing classes in a computer lab classroom. A librarian then meets the class at the computer lab to provide remote access searching of OhioLINK resources and to introduce Internet access to the students. Out of fourteen sections, six instructors have taken advantage of this option. To do this requires advanced planning by the course instructor because s/he must reserve the mediated classroom. To schedule an instructional session in a library classroom, the course instructor only needs to notify the library one week in advance. But in order to use the computer lab, classrooms must be reserved early in each quarter. In addition, some course instructors are unsure of how to incorporate remote electronic access into their courses. The library continues to work with the teaching faculty to advise them in this area.

The problem of the library's not having a mediated classroom for instruction was a concern to the College of Engineering. The engineering faculty felt that the traditional paper-based library instruction program was not meeting their students' needs. Since that college had recently moved into a new building with multiple mediated classrooms, the engineering faculty were approached by the library about the possibilities of conducting library instruction at their facilities for their students. The engineering faculty were enthusiastic about those possibilities and agreed. We are eager to meet the College of Engineering students' needs but there are two challenges for librarians associated with this approach. One is scheduling and the other is logistical. Reference librarians staff the Information Desk and teach library instruction classes. Teaching library instruction in the College of Engineering's mediated classrooms requires librarians to resolve scheduling conflicts between having to be in the library and providing instruction outside the library. Unlike some libraries where a team of librarians is responsible for just outreach services, Carlson Library must rely on the same group of librarians to staff the Information Desk, teach classes in the library and also do outreach instruction in other departments. The College of Engineering is located on the opposite side of campus from the library, and the librarian must allow for not only travel time but site preparation time as well. Contrary to what the literature recommends regarding the need for an assistant in the lab, there is not another librarian or graduate assistant available to be a "floater" in the mediated classroom. The librarian must teach the class alone when the faculty member is not present. Teaching alone is definitely a challenge when there are at least thirty students at individual workstations. We welcome this opportunity to provide library instruction to the College of Engineering but this opportunity is a challenge as well. The librarian is given a fifty-minute time slot to teach information retrieval using the library's homepage and introducing the variety of science databases available through OhioLINK. The student population is a mix of traditional, non-traditional, and international students. Working alone with at least thirty students at individual workstations, with varying levels of computer skills, diverse language and cultural backgrounds, and time constraints challenges even the most dedicated librarians. But the feeling among the librarians is that every opportunity to provide hands-on teaching experiences is a good one. Students must be given this opportunity to develop information retrieval skills if they are to succeed as students and later as professionals.

The library instruction program at Carlson Library is undergoing change to reflect the growing infusion and use of electronic resources in academic libraries and departments on campus. The transition from a paper-based instructional program to electronic instruction has resulted in a number of challenges. Our teaching methods must bridge the gap between traditional library instruction and the growing need for electronic instruction with the ultimate goal of replacing our paper base instruction with electronic instruction. On the one hand, there are the technology challenges. We welcome OhioLINK and the Internet because they allow for the rapid retrieval of information and they are relatively easy to use. On the other hand, however, the technology has been coming in unrelenting waves. Librarians are beginning to deal with the continuing flow of technology by attending systematic training sessions for use in the electronic resources. As we face the challenges of electronic instruction without a mediated classroom in the library, we realize that we must use alternative methods for teaching these resources. We are convinced that when we teach electronic resources while staffing the Information Desk, provide hands-on experiences through both the Individual Instruction Appointment and the various worksheets, and seize opportunities to teach in departmental mediated classrooms, we are meeting our challenges and bridging this gap.

NOTES

1. Caroline Rowe, "Modern Library Instruction: Levels, Media, Trends, and Problems," *Research Strategies* 12, no. 1 (Spring 1994): 4.

2. Public Information, "What is OhioLINK?" (OhioLINK, Columbus, Ohio, photocopy), 107 1/94.

3. "The Ohio Library and Information Network," Update April 1996 (http://www.ohiolink.edu).

4. Mary Page and Martin Kesselman, "Teaching the InternetChallenges and Opportunities," *Research Strategies* 12 (Summer 1994): 157-67.

5. Rowe, "Modern Library Instruction: Levels, Media, Trends, and Problems," 9.

6. Bibliographic Instruction Department, "Bibliographic Instruction Report for Library Annual Report, 1980-81" (Carlson Library, The University of Toledo, Toledo, Ohio, 1981, photocopy): 1.

7. John Grothouse, "UT Library Program Most Extensive in U.S.," *The Collegian* (Student Publication of the University of Toledo), 3 February 1983, 3.

8. Karen Sendi, conversation with authors, Carlson Library, Toledo, Ohio, 6 May 1996.

9. "Snapshot of OhioLINK: Libraries, Services, Faculty, Students," OhioLINK Update, 1, no. 1 (January 1995): [1].

10. "OhioLINK begins a New Database Expansion," *OhioLINK Update*, 2:1 (March 1996): [1].

11. "Snapshot of OhioLINK: Libraries, Services, Faculty, Students" [1].

12. "The Ohio Library and Information Network," Update November 1996 (http://www.ohiolink.edu).

13. "Snapshot of OhioLINK: Libraries, Services, Faculty, Students" [1].

14. "What's coming," *OhioLINK Update*, 1:2 (August 1995) :3.

15. Scott A. Mellendorf, "Pounding the Pavement With Purpose: Utilizing the Information Superhighway for Daily Work Tasks," *RQ*, 35:2 (Winter 1995):231-35.

16. Ibid., 231

17. Page and Kesselman, "Teaching the Internet: Challenges and Opportunities," 163.

18. Rowe, "Modern Library Instruction: Levels, Media, Trends, and Problems," 9.

WORKS CONSULTED

Arp, Lori. "Reflecting on Reflecting: Views on Teaching and the Internet," *RQ* 34 (September 1995): 453-455.

Blumenthal, Caroline, Howard, Mary Jo, and William R. Kinyon. "The Impact of CD-ROM Technology on a Bibliographic Instruction Program," *College and Research Libraries* 54 (January 1993): 11-16.

Glogoff, Stuart. "Library Instruction in the Electronic Library: The University of Arizona's Electronic Library Education Centers," *Reference Services Review* 23: 2 (Summer 1995): 7-12.

Gratch, Bonnie B. "Rethinking Instructional Assumptions in an Age of Computerized Information Access," *Research Strategies* 6:1 (Winter 1988): 4-7.

Nickerson, Gord. "Networked Resources," *Computers in Libraries* (September 1991): 25-29.

Pask, Judith M. and Carl E. Snow. "Undergraduate Instruction and the Internet," *Library Trends* 44:2 (Fall 1995): 306-17.

Swan, John. "Books and Screens, Readers and Reference: Bridging the Video Gap," *Reference Library* 37 (1992): 65-74.

"Technology is Dramatically Changing the Way Librarians Work," *Library Journal* 119 (November 1994): 49.

The Information Literacy Challenge: Addressing the Changing Needs of Our Students Through Our Programs

Elizabeth A. Dupuis

SUMMARY. Technological changes are occurring rapidly. As one result, students entering college are bringing very disparate computer skills and attitudes. Some students are reluctant to embrace new technologies; others demand electronic resources for all assignments. By considering the computer access and Internet resources available to elementary school students today, we can only imagine what our users of tomorrow will expect from libraries. Although college students may arrive at our libraries with increased computer skills, their knowledge of electronic information may be lacking. Definitions of information literacy and an overview of information literacy skills are outlined. The Digital Information Literacy program at The University of Texas at Austin, as well as the technological environment and facilities at the institution, serve as a case study for integrating information literacy skills into traditional services and partnerships. *[Article copies available for a fee from The Haworth Document Delivery Service: 1-800-342-9678. E-mail address: getinfo@haworth.com]*

Elizabeth A. Dupuis (beth@mail.utexas.edu) is Head of the Digital Information Literacy Office at The University of Texas at Austin, Undergraduate Library Services Division, The General Libraries, Flawn Academic Center (FAC) 101, S5443, Austin, TX 78713.

[Haworth co-indexing entry note]: "The Information Literacy Challenge: Addressing the Changing Needs of Our Students Through Our Programs." Dupuis, Elizabeth A. Co-published simultaneously in *Internet Reference Services Quarterly* (The Haworth Press, Inc.) Vol. 2, No. 2/3, 1997, pp. 93-111; and: *The Challenge of Internet Literacy: The Instruction-Web Convergence* (ed: Lyn Elizabeth M. Martin) The Haworth Press, Inc., 1997, pp. 93-111. Single or multiple copies of this article are available for a fee from The Haworth Document Delivery Service [1-800-342-9678, 9:00 a.m. - 5:00 p.m. (EST). E-mail address: getinfo@haworth.com].

KEYWORDS. Information literacy, bibliographic instruction, college students, The University of Texas at Austin, computer and library skills, student expectations, library programs

As librarians and instructors, we face great challenges. Past decades have proven that change is occurring at a remarkably quickening pace with each day. In "The Age of Social Transformation," Peter Drucker declared, "No century in recorded history has experienced so many social transformations and such radical ones as the twentieth century . . . Learning will become the tool of the individual–available to him or her at any age–if only because so much skill and knowledge can be acquired by means of the new learning technologies."[1] With these predictions, it is not surprising that our patrons, their personal experiences with information resources, and their expectations for us are also evolving.

CURRENT STUDENTS

With each new class of freshmen at The University of Texas at Austin, the growing diversity of computer backgrounds and information skills is striking. Freshman Orientation sessions are a wonderful opportunity to talk to incoming students about their experiences with and attitudes towards computers. Some students have used computers to write term papers or pass a computer-oriented high school class; others do not use computers and may feel uncomfortable with high-technology environments. On the other hand, some freshmen are far more sophisticated users. These students have already explored the Internet either at school or at home. They have experience using electronic databases and CD-ROMs as information resources. Some of them have learned when to use each tool and how to distinguish between the types of information retrieved from different systems.

Growing numbers of students are already coming to colleges and universities with higher expectations for our libraries. Our entering students at UT-Austin look to use new technologies for each assignment. Many students especially seek out electronic resources that provide full-text. Generally, these students are reluctant to search traditional sources or use conventional methods for research. One reason for this reluctance may be that they do not understand how or when to best use those sources. Without realizing it, they may also have a false sense of confidence in regards to some information attained via the computer and the Internet.

Presumably most librarians can relate to this type of diversity in the backgrounds of their students.

> While 75 percent of public schools have access to some kind of computer network, and 35 percent of public schools have access to the Internet, only 3 percent of instructional rooms (classrooms, labs, and media centers) are connected to the Internet . . . Despite past investments in technology, many schools still lack the basic technology infrastructure to support the most promising applications of educational technology. About half the computers in U.S. schools are older, 8-bit machines that cannot support CD-ROM-sized databases or network integrated systems or run complex software.[2]

Although this study finds that the majority of schools do not have Internet access, many students–either in school or at home–are advancing their skills at a remarkable pace. The schism between students with computer knowledge and students without may be widening. One hope is that the upsurge of K-12 initiatives across the country, such as Goal 2000, will soon offer all students access to remarkable resources.

FUTURE STUDENTS

Consider these resources available on the Internet and their applications for elementary and secondary students.

- *The Exploratorium Digital Library Exhibits*
  (http://www.exploratorium.edu/exhibits/exhibits.html)
  " . . . the Exploratorium is a collage of 650 interactive exhibits in the areas of science, art, and human perception. The Exploratorium stands in the vanguard of the movement of the 'museum as educational center.' "[3]
- *Teaching and Learning on the Web*
  (http://www.mcli.dist.maricopa.edu/tl/)
  "This searchable collection includes sites that are using the World Wide Web for more than just surfing . . . places that are using the technology for learning."[4]
- *Welcome to CU-SeeMe Schools*
  (http://www.gsn.org/gsn/cu/)
  "This list will put you in touch with other K-12 schools around the world who have the capability to do CU-SeeMe videoconferencing over the Internet. The list will be used to announce upcoming special events and opportunities for schools to participate in live videoconferences with schools, scientists, authors, government, business, and community leaders."[5]
- *Global SchoolNet's Internet Projects Registry*
  (http://www.gsn.org/gsn/proj/)

"This Registry is the one central place on the Internet where you can find projects from the Global SchoolNet Foundation (GSN) and other organizations such as I*EARN, IECC, NASA, GLOBE, Academy One, TIES, Tenet, TERC, as well as countless outstanding projects conducted by classroom teachers all over the world. We glean projects from across the Internet to include in this registry. . . . "[6]

- *Quest: NASA's K-12 Internet Initiative*
  (http://quest.arc.nasa.gov:80/)
  "Our mission: To provide support and services for schools, teachers and students to fully utilize the Internet, and its underlying information technologies, as a basic tool for learning. We are supported by the NASA Information Infrastructure Technology Applications (IITA) project and the High Performance Computing and Communication (HPCC) program."[7]

- *Reinventing Schools: The Technology is Now!*
  (http://www.nap.edu/nap/online/techgap/welcome.html)
  "The document is based on a meeting at which hundreds of leaders from government, education, and the entertainment and information technology industries, developed strategies for reinvigorating the K-12 educational process by integrating the school experience with the information technology that has captured children's imaginations. Funding for the project was provided by the National Science Foundation, National Aeronautics and Space Administration, Academy Industry Program of the National Research Council, Coca-Cola Endowment Fund of the National Research Council, and Kellogg Endowment Fund of the National Academy of Sciences and Institute of Medicine."[8]

- *Homework Helper*[(tm)]
  (http://www.infonautics.com/products.htm#homework)
  "Homework Helper[(tm)] is the world's most extensive online library for kids. Using Homework Helper, students can pose a question in plain English and launch a comprehensive search through millions of pages of content, including more than 100 full-text newspapers, nearly 800 full-text magazines, two newswires, multiple reference books, hundreds of maps, thousands of photographs as well as major works of literature and art."[9] (A fee-based service)

These seven sites are only a small sample of the types of collaborative and innovative uses of the Internet for educating primary and secondary students. As the K-12 initiatives increase, the number of projects and the sophistication of those projects will likely increase as well; hence, the number of students acquainted with the Internet will also probably rise.

The Department of Education offers the following statistics for student use of computers at school and at home. The chart below (Figure 1) compares data collected in October 1989 and October 1993 for Grades 1-8, 9-12, and the first through fourth years of college. From 1989 to 1993, the percentage of students who used computers in school had risen in every category. In grades 1-8 the percentage of students had increased from 52.3% to 68.9%; in grades 9-12 the percentage of students had increased from 39.2% to 58.2%; for college students the percentage had increased from 39.2% to 55.2%.[10]

Consider that the elementary school students of today will have even more familiarity with electronic sources, including Internet resources, when they reach college age. Their expectations for libraries may be beyond what we can imagine considering the limitations of our resources today.

INFORMATION LITERACY SKILLS

As more people gain computer skills at an early age, they will be more familiar with the computer as a tool. However, familiarity with the keyboard

FIGURE 1. Comparison of Student Computer Use at Home and at School

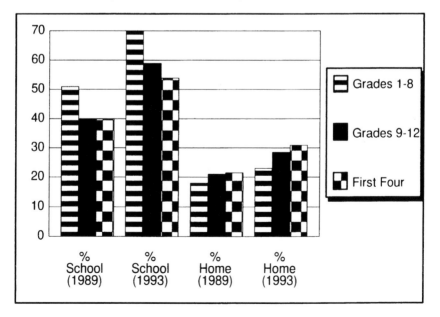

and general use of computers leads some people to falsely believe that they also know how to effectively use all the electronic resources accessible through that medium. Although their enthusiasm for computers is often high, their awareness of electronic resources is often low. Many freshmen do not have an appreciation for the sheer number of sources offered at higher education institutions. "Most library users are unaware of the quantity and variety of information available. They are often satisfied with materials that an experienced librarian would find wholly inadequate and/or inappropriate. Unless librarians educate users about finding information, users will continue to underutilize and misuse information."[11]

To address this problem in terms of user education, libraries first created bibliographic instruction programs. Many of those programs are now working with or evolving into information literacy programs. Definitions of information literacy vary slightly from source to source, though the focus is helping students gain a broad understanding of information sources–including those outside of the library–and honing their ability to deal with that information. The American Library Association gives this definition:

> To be information literate an individual must recognise when information is needed and have the ability to locate, evaluate and use effectively the information needed . . . Ultimately information literate people are those who have learned how to learn. They know how to learn because they know how information is organised, how to find information, and how to use information in such a way that others can learn from them.[12]

A search of library literature and World Wide Web provided a long list of skills suggested for creating and nurturing an information literate. The complete list of those skills is outlined in the Appendix. A summary of the basic awareness and skills an information literate should possess includes:

- understanding of the complexities of the information environment and technologies involved
- ability to articulate when and what information is needed
- ability to select appropriate tools or sources and search them effectively
- ability to evaluate materials across mediums and formats
- ability to manipulate and organize the information retrieved
- ability to communicate to others the location and content of the information found

Literacy, beyond embracing the basic abilities of reading and writing, now embodies the general ability to understand and perform functions successfully. The term is often paired with areas such as media, computers, culture, and information. The goal of information literacy is to ensure that people understand how to, and why they need to, learn about sources in the information society. Some of these sources will be in the library; others will be in the world at large.

We should attempt to teach a set of skills that are not specific to a source, tool, or place. Students should learn to search, select, evaluate, and manipulate content based upon general processes rather than memorize steps for attaining information from certain sources. Students, with guidance when necessary, should be encouraged independently or collaboratively to discover effective methods for dealing with information.

INFORMATION LITERACY PROGRAMS AND SERVICES

How can we integrate these skills into a successful program? Librarians have suggested various formats for instructional programs and styles for teaching. The most prevalent models for bibliographic instruction programs include course-integrated classes, library-based classes for credit, self-paced instruction via handouts, and computer-assisted instruction via a stand-alone workstation or the Internet. Alternately, in the works consulted most librarians agreed that broad information literacy skills are best taught within the academic curricula.

The American Library Association states, "What is called for is not a new information studies curriculum but, rather, a restructuring of the learning process. Textbooks, workbooks and lectures must give way to a learning process based on information resources available for learning and problem solving throughout people's lifetimes. . . . "[13] With the assistance of professors and other instructors, this method encourages students to build their skills through structured assignments incorporating print, electronic, and Internet resources. Although they will be repeatedly exposed to the information world, each time they will approach it from a new field and with a new goal.

Virginia Tiefel suggests "As to methods, instruction should employ short modules that allow self-directed study with more emphasis on instructional content and less on the media used. The system should be one that users are comfortable in using and gives them a sense of control over it. Users should receive guidance on which resources are best for their needs, and basic instruction on search technique. . . . "[14] Assisting students becomes even more complicated, though no less important, as many of our services are requested remotely. Libraries must integrate information skills into not only instruction, but also orientation, reference, and liaison responsibilities.

DIGITAL INFORMATION LITERACY AT UT-AUSTIN

To make an information literacy program most effective, a variety of resources are imperative. Those resources include: basic Internet instruction classes, a wide array of electronic library services, hands-on training rooms, and numerous Internet-based resources of high quality and diverse content. The General Libraries at UT-Austin offers each of these basic components for a successful implementation of such a program.

An ideal information literacy program includes information in all formats. On our campus the number of students and level of technological advancement has necessitated the creation of a special program whose goal is to enable students, faculty, and staff to find, evaluate, and make effective use of digital information. That program is managed within the Digital Information Literacy Office (DILO). This office works closely with librarians at all campus libraries; information-related campus departments and centers; faculty and instructors; and students. The Head of the DILO is responsible for emphasizing basic information skills related to digital formats by:

- developing, promoting, and publicizing a formal program for training members of the UT-Austin community
- collaborating with faculty and instructors to promote effective use of electronic information services within the curriculum
- planning and developing a library-wide training program related to the Internet, new databases, new technologies, and instructional techniques for staff
- collaborating with library staff and other information-related departments to create instructional programs and materials
- managing the Electronic Information Classes program, the Internet Consulting Office and mentoring program, and an instruction clearinghouse
- developing measures to evaluate the effectiveness of training programs and materials

Although the DILO emphasizes electronic resources, it is important to note that this office works with other librarians to ensure that students are educated about the complete range of information resources available. The

Digital Information Literacy program is dedicated to promoting electronic resources to the students and faculty, as well as to our own staff. With the number of services and resources competing for librarians' time, the DILO offers support by coordinating the instructional programs related to this format of information.

"The General Libraries continues to follow its strategic plan of using computing and information technologies to enhance and extend library information services to the UT Austin community. The UT Library Online information system, a World Wide Web offering, forms the core of the electronic information services offered by the General Libraries."[15] It includes resources such as:

- *UTNetCAT:* UT-Austin library catalog offering a Web interface and integrating Internet resources
- *Indexes and Abstracts:* Collection of more than 40 general and subject-specific electronic databases and tools
- *Electronic Journals:* Current electronic journals and digitized archival titles
- *Universal Times Electronic Newspaper:* Synthesis of ClariNet newswire stories, USENET newsgroups, and Internet resources related to news
- *Perry-Castañeda Library Map Collection:* Approximately 1,500 maps digitized for the Web, relating all parts of the world.

The Undergraduate Library's (UGL) mission emphasizes teaching students to do research. We strongly promote core resources and services for lower-division undergraduates. An increasing portion of our collection development is devoted to digital content. Our student body is fairly computer and Internet-literate. Students and faculty routinely publish their own World Wide Web pages. Many professors have integrated listservs, newsgroups, Web pages, and Internet resources into their class curricula. Our instructional programs have changed in response to a changing environment. On a campus where there are approximately 50,000 students—including more than 30,000 undergraduates—it is possible for us to base most of our digital information literacy program on the Web. We are outnumbered by students, but thanks to a university-wide Information Technology student fee, there are Internet-connected computer labs and classrooms positioned around campus.

Student Microcomputer Facility and Hands-On Classroom

The largest general purpose computer lab is located on the second floor of the UGL and is open 24 hours a day, 5 days a week and regular business hours the other 2 days each week. That lab, called the Student Microcomputer Facility (SMF), includes 144 Macintosh computers and 49 486 Intel computers. Included on each of these workstations is software for Internet access, word processing, spreadsheets, presentations, database creation, desktop publishing, mathematical applications, statistics, and graphics. Laser printers and scanners are also available. Although each of the workstations is handicapped accessible, a separate room offers hardware and software for students with visual disabilities including a voice output device and a braille printer. To date, over 1,730,200 logins have been counted since the lab opened in 1994. More information about the hardware, software, and statistics in the SMF can be found at: http://www.utexas.edu/smf.

Within the SMF is a hands-on networked training room equipped with projection equipment and 15 Macintosh Quadras directly connected to the Internet. These machines have the same software and configurations as the stations in the main facility. Classroom use is shared equally between the General Libraries and the Computation Center. The room has a capacity of 30 seats and is occasionally reserved for course-integrated instruction. More information about the types of library classes taught in that training room can be found in the LOEX paper entitled: *The World Wide Web as an Instructional Medium.*

Students in my library instruction classes seem most attentive and engaged in hands-on sessions. Within the format of a hands-on session, students can pursue answers to questions through their own exploration. The Internet provides an expanded communication medium and a non-linear format which broadens the scope of the class and increases the potential for reaching students at all levels of skill, interest, and learning styles.

Electronic Information Center and Internet Consulting Office

"Electronic Information Centers (EIC) serve as learning laboratories where students can receive assistance with research using electronic information resources. Library staff are available to answer questions, help refine research strategies, identify additional information resources appropriate to the topic, and work intensively with students, when appropriate."[16] The two centers are located in the Perry-Castañeda Library (the main library) and the UGL. The UGL EIC offers 18 Power Macintosh computers and 10 Pentium-class PCs for members of the UT-Austin community to access the Internet, the library's CD-ROM network, and the databases purchased by the General Libraries and provided via the Internet. The primary distinction between this computer center and the SMF is our emphasis on research and assistance.

To respond to students' need for help with electronic information, we created the Internet Consulting Office (ICO) in 1994. During the first few semesters this office was based in the SMF to complement Computation Center consulting with a research-oriented Internet reference desk. Now the ICO has been integrated into the UGL EIC and service is available from late morning until early evening. The Internet Consulting Team consists of librarians, library assistants, and library school volunteers knowledgeable about Internet software, databases, and electronic resources. Initially, consulting is offered on a first-come, first-served basis, though expansion of services may later include appointment consultations. Students ask questions on a wide range of topics and skill levels. Some need assistance with developing search strategies and choosing resources; others need assistance manipulating more obscure formats and developing Web pages.

With the integration of the ICO into the EIC, the library is now providing a laboratory where students can learn about information resources, ask for assistance, and complete the research for their assignments. The EIC is physically adjoined to the Information Desk and close to our print materials as well. This symbiosis of service desks and resources allows students to explore and learn about the entire range of information sources from one point.

Integration of Skills Within the Curriculum

Class assignments are the main reason students seek our guidance. Some of the courses with which the UGL works closely are the English 306, English 309, the Student Success Program, and the Substantial Writing Component classes. Increasingly these courses are integrating electronic resources and the Internet into their curriculum. It is refreshing to work with instructors who are convinced of the benefits of teaching these skills.

Listed below are two examples of class assignments suggested by instructors from these programs and taught in conjunction with librarians last year.

- *Evaluation of a Web Site*
  Students in a Rhetoric and Composition class participated in a hands-on session and discussion of the Internet, World Wide Web, and evaluation of electronic resources. When reviewing Web sites, discussion included: how sites organize information, how sites rate and evaluate other Web sites, what features are beneficial or detrimental on a Web page, and whether the information stated is biased or assumed. The instructor encouraged students to apply the rules of

argumentation and rhetoric to these pages and the librarian assisted with search and evaluation strategies.

- *Examination of Internet Resources on a Topic*
  Students studying black holes in an Astronomy class attended a hands-on session discussing the various formats of information which can be found on the Internet. The information viewed included text, images, sound, and movies. Information from a personal home page, magazine, scholarly report and journal were also analyzed. Students learned to search for, compare, retrieve, and cite electronic information.

By allowing students to engage in inquiry and exploration in groups, they build upon each other's discoveries and conclusions. In these classes our role becomes that of a facilitator.

Electronic Information Classes

Many students, faculty and staff also enjoy attending lecture and hands-on workshops about the Internet and electronic information resources that interest them. Since summer 1992 we have had a free, organized Internet training program called the Electronic Information Classes. Each semester the program evolves, though we maintain a variety of topics and levels offered. During fall and spring semesters we offer about 150 classes; each summer we offer roughly 75 classes. Many of these classes are open to the general public as well as the UT community. Through Spring 1996 semester, the Electronic Information Classes program has offered over 1,500 classes and reached nearly 13,000 users. For more information about the Electronic Information Classes offered this semester, visit: http://www.lib.utexas.edu/cgi-bin/calendar.

Approximately 50 librarians and library assistants volunteer to teach these sessions. Everyone participating in the program has the opportunity to suggest new classes and comment about changing the direction of current classes. It is a very participatory and open environment. We solicit suggestions from attendees on our print questionnaires which are handed out at the end of each class, through our electronic questionnaire on the Web, and via e-mail.

Electronic Services and Assistance

In an effort to reach a large number of students at many hours of the day, many of our services and resources are available via the Internet. We provide typical reference assistance through services and products such as Ask a Reference Question form and our General Libraries Publications site. Increasingly we are designing instructional materials that are Web-based and interactive. It is important to our mission to support our students' educational goals; the more widely we can distribute our assistance the easier it is for our students to find it when they need it.

Additionally, students indirectly benefit from the services we offer to faculty and instructors. The Digital Information Literacy Office publishes a series of Web pages which explain strategies for integrating information literacy skills into the classroom. Among other tips, we offer instructors common descriptions and comparisons of resources; special suggestions are made to faculty who create assignments for large numbers of students. Effective assignments are possible when faculty understand the limitations imposed by subject, accessibility, and location of the resources they suggest to their students. This method of assistance is efficient and non-intrusive; instructors can peruse the information at their leisure and refer to it at any time. Additionally, by offering this information in such an open medium, perhaps it will open the door to new partnerships with faculty.

Partnerships

Collaboration and partnership are the keys to the success of information literacy programs. Libraries and related information departments must work together to promote information literacy skills for our students. Alliances with computer centers, international offices, writing centers, English as a second language departments, Dean of Students offices and faculty in the colleges will be crucial for students' complete understanding of the information resources available to them.

The General Libraries has initiated or participated in a variety of joint projects to reach this goal on our campus. We joined efforts with the Computation Center and Data Processing to form "Team Web," a group supporting and promoting Web publishing and Web use at UT-Austin, and offer Weekly Internet Seminars. We collaborate with the Dean of Students Office and other student services on instruction to benefit incoming students, minority programs and international students. Members of the library staff have given special presentations to the Development Office and members of the administration about the technologies within and the challenges facing libraries today. This past Spring we participated, with the Undergraduate Writing Center and Center for Teaching Effectiveness, in a Faculty Fair for professors who teach Substantial Writing Component courses. The Graduate School of Library and Information Science at UT-Austin is another good resource. We work closely with library school students and offer volunteer opportunities at service points such as the Internet Consulting Office. The graduate students benefit from the public service experience and the undergraduate students benefit from the peer tutoring.

Without this interaction, our organization would become insular and unresponsive. By sharing our goals and ideas we create more dynamic, practical, and responsive programs.

CONCLUSIONS

Literacy implies confidence, competence and acceptance. The quantity, quality, and diversity of sources, access methods, delivery methods, and formats creates a potentially disorienting environment for new users. Students must learn to embrace future possibilities without disregarding traditional avenues for information. Sharpening students' information skills is a vital challenge. It will demand creativity and critical thinking skills from library professionals. It will require cooperation with departments and staff within our libraries, partnerships with related departments across campus, and promotion to our faculty and other instructors. It will require a reassessment of our current services and perhaps of our own skills. I, for one, welcome the challenge.

NOTES

1. Peter F. Drucker, "The Age of Social Transformation," 1994. [URL: http://www.theatlantic.com/atlantic/issues/95dec/Chilearn/drucker.htm].

2. Congressional Office of Technology Assessment, "Teachers and Technology: Making the Connection," April 3, 1995. [URL: http://www.gsn.org/web/reform/ota/home.htm].

3. The Exploratorium, "Exploratorium Digital Library Exhibits," 1996. [URL: http://www.exploratorium.edu/exhibits/exhibits.html].

4. Maricopa Center for Learning and Instruction, "Teaching and Learning on the Web." [URL: http://www.mcli.dist.maricopa.edu/tl/].

5. Global SchoolNet Foundation, "Welcome to CU-SeeMe Schools," 1996. [URL: http://www.gsn.org/gsn/cu/].

6. Global SchoolNet Foundation, "Global SchoolNet's Internet Projects Registry," 1996. [URL: http://www.gsn.org/gsn/proj/].

7. NASA, "Quest: NASA's K-12 Internet Initiative." [URL: http://quest.arc.nasa.gov:80/].

8. National Academy of Sciences, "Reinventing Schools: The Technology is Now!," 1995. [URL: http://www.nap.edu/nap/online/techgap/welcome.html].

9. Infonautics, "Homework Helper(tm)," 1996. [URL: http://www.infonautics.com/products.htm#homework].

10. United States Department of Education, "Chapter 7: Learning Resources and Technology," in *The Digest of Education Statistics, 1995.* [URL: http://www.ed.gov/NCES/pubs/D95/dintro7.html].

11. Virginia M. Tiefel, "Library User Education: Examining Its Past, Projecting Its Future," *Library Trends* 44:2 (September 22, 1995):318.

12. American Library Association Presidential Committee on Information Literacy. *Final Report.* (Chicago, IL: American Library Association, 1989), 1.

13. Ibid.

14. Tiefel, "Library User Education: Examining Its Past, Projecting Its Future," 320.

15. The University of Texas at Austin, The General Libraries, *Libraries and Information Skills for Students: Support Through Computing and Information Technology.* (Austin, TX: The General Libraries, 1996-97), 1.

16. The University of Texas at Austin, The General Libraries, *Libraries and Information Skills for Students: Support Through Computing and Information Technology,* 1995-2000. (Austin, TX: The General Libraries, 1995-96), 3.

WORKS CONSULTED

Alberico, Ralph, "Serving College Students in an Era of Recombinant Information," *Wilson Library Bulletin* 7:119 (March 1995):29-32.

Alberico, Ralph and Elizabeth A. Dupuis, "The World Wide Web as an Instructional Medium," 1995. [URL: http://sawfish.lib.utexas.edu/~beth/LOEX/].

American Library Association Presidential Committee on Information Literacy. *Final Report.* (Chicago, IL: American Library Association, 1989).

Arp, Lori, "Information Literacy or Bibliographic Instruction: Semantics or Philosophy?" *RQ* 30:1 (Fall 1990):46-9.

Atton, Chris, "Using Critical Thinking as a Basis for Library User Education," *Journal of Academic Librarianship* 20:5-6 (November 1994):310-13.

Behrens, Shirley J., "A Conceptual Analysis and Historical Overview of Information Literacy," *College & Research Libraries* 55:4 (July 1994):309-22.

Blake, Virgil L. P. and Renee Tjoumas, *Information Literacies for the Twenty-First Century.* (Boston, MA: G. K. Hall, 1990).

Breivik, Patricia Senn and Gee, E. Gordon, *Information Literacy: Revolution in the Library.* (New York: Macmillan, 1989).

Bruce, Christine Susan, "Information Literacy Blueprint," 1994. [URL: http://www.gu.edu.au/gwis/ins/infolit/blueprnt.htm].

California Media and Library Educators Association, *From Library Skills to Information Literacy: A Handbook for the 21st Century.* (Castle Rock, CO: Hi Willow Research and Pub., 1994).

Carlson, David and Ruth H. Miller, "Librarians and Teaching Faculty: Partners in Bibliographic Instruction," *College & Research Libraries* 45:6 (November 1984):483-91.

Congressional Office of Technology Assessment, "Teachers and Technology:

Making the Connection," April 3, 1995. [URL: http://www.gsn.org/web/reform/ota/home.htm].

Cooper, Tasha and Jane Burchfield, "Information Literacy for College and University Staff," *Research Strategies* 13 (Spring 1995):94-105.

Dillon, Dennis, "An Internet Experience: Electronic Information Training Program at the University of Texas," *Library Issues: Briefings for Faculty and Administrators* 14:5 (May 1994):1-2.

Drucker, Peter F., "The Age of Social Transformation," 1994. [URL: http://www.theatlantic.com/atlantic/issues/95dec/Chilearn/drucker.htm].

Foster, Stephen, "Information Literacy: Some misgivings," *American Libraries* 24:4 (April 1993):344-6.

Grassian, Esther, "Thinking Critically About World Wide Web Resources," May 9, 1996. [URL: http://www.ucla.edu/campus/computing/bruinonline/trainers/critical.html].

Huston, M. M. (Ed.), "Toward Information Literacy–Innovative Perspectives for the 1990s," *Library Trends* 39:1 (1991):186-366.

Kaufman, Paula T., "Information Incompetence," *Library Journal* 117:19 (November 15, 1992):37-40.

Keefer, Jane, "The Hungry Rats Syndrome: Library Anxiety, Information Literacy, and the Academic Reference Process," *RQ* 32:3 (Spring 1993):333-9.

Kohl, David F. and Wilson, Lizabeth A, "Effectiveness of Course-Integrated Bibliographic Instruction in Improving Coursework," *RQ* 26:2 (1986):206-11.

Kuhlthau, Carol Collier, "The Process of Learning from Information," *School Libraries Worldwide* 1:1 (January 1995):1-12.

MacAdam, Barbara, "Information Literacy: Models for the Curriculum," *College & Research Libraries News* 51 (1990):948-51.

McCrank, Lawrence J., "Academic Programs for Information Literacy: Theory and Structure." *RQ* 31:4 (Summer 1992):485-97.

McCrank, Lawrence J., "Information Literacy: A Bogus Bandwagon?" *Library Journal* 116:8 (May 1, 1991):38-42.

Mellon, Constance A., "Process Not Product in Course-Integrated Instruction: A Generic Model of Library Research," *College & Research Libraries* 45:6 (November 1984):471-8.

Mensching, Glenn. E. and Teresa B. Mensching (Eds.), *Coping with Information Illiteracy: Bibliographic Instruction for the Information Age.* (Ann Arbor, MI: Published for Learning Resources and Technologies, Eastern Michigan University by Pierian Press, 1989).

Miller, Marian I. and Barry D. Bratton, "Instructional Design: Increasing the Effectiveness of Bibliographic Instruction," *College & Research Libraries* 49:6 (November 1988):545-49.

Murdock, Jeanne, "Re-engineering Bibliographic Instruction: The Real Task of Information Literacy," *Bulletin of the American Society for Information Science* 21:3 (February 1995):26-7. [URL: http://www.asis.org/Bulletin/Feb-95/opinion.html].

Naito, M., "An Information Literacy Curriculum: A Proposal," *College & Research Libraries News* 52:5 (1991):293-6.

National Commission on Excellence in Education. *A Nation at Risk: The Imperative for Educational Reform.* (Washington, DC: U.S. Government Printing Office, 1983).

Page, Mary and Martin Kesselman, "Teaching the Internet: Challenges and Opportunities," *Research Strategies* 12:3 (Summer 1994):157-67.

Rader, Hannelore B., "Bibliographic Instruction or Information Literacy," *College & Research Libraries News,* 51:1 (1990):18-20.

Rader, Hannelore B., "Information Literacy: A Revolution in the Library," *RQ* 31:1 (1991):25-9.

Rader, Hannelore B., "Information Literacy and the Undergraduate Curriculum. The Library and Undergraduate Education," *Library Trends* 44:2 (September 22, 1995):270-9.

Rockman, Ilene F., "Challenges in Teaching End Users Access to Internet Resources," in *13th National Online Meeting Proceedings* (New York: Learned Information, May 5-7, 1992):321-4.

Ruess, Diane E., "Library and Information Literacy: A Core Curriculum Component," *Research Strategies* 12:4 (Winter 1994):18-23.

Shirato, Linda (Ed.), *Judging the Validity of Information Sources: Teaching Critical Analysis in Bibliographic Instruction*: Papers and Session Materials Presented at the 18th National LOEX Library Instruction Conference, May 11-12, 1990. (Ann Arbor, MI: Published for Learning Resources and Technologies, Eastern Michigan University by Pierian Press, 1991).

Tiefel, Virginia M., "Library User Education: Examining Its Past, Projecting Its Future," *Library Trends* 44:2 (September 22, 1995):318-24.

United States Department of Education, "Chapter 7: Learning Resources and Technology," in *The Digest of Education Statistics,* 1995. [URL: http://www.ed.gov/NCES/pubs/D95/dintro7.html].

The University of Texas at Austin, The General Libraries, *Libraries and Information Skills for Students: Support Through Computing and Information Technology.* (Austin, TX: The General Libraries, 1996-97).

The University of Texas at Austin, The General Libraries, *Libraries and Information Skills for Students: Support Through Computing and Information Technology, 1995-2000.* (Austin, TX: The General Libraries, 1995-96).

University of Washington Libraries, Core Curriculum Team, Subgroup on the Future of Library Instruction. *Integrating Information Literacy into the Curriculum at the University of Washington.* (Seattle, WA: University of Washington, 1995).

White, Herbert. S., "Bibliographic Instruction, Information Literacy, and Information Empowerment," *Library Journal* 117:1 (1992):76-8.

APPENDIX

INFORMATION LITERACY SKILLS

Understanding Information World and Needs

- Familiarity with the variety of information sources, including libraries
- Understand the diversity of technologies involved
- Learn when and how to use computers and other machines for information needs
- Understand all information can not be found via the computer
- Understand how information is gathered, organized, packaged, and stored
- Understand the publication cycle and system of scholarly communication
- Recognize the need for information to make educated and intelligent decisions
- Learn how to articulate their information needs
- Learn to transfer skills between platforms and systems
- Accept that information searching can be time-consuming
- Understand phenomenon of information explosion
- Learn ways to keep current and deal with information overload
- Understand concepts of intellectual property and other political, social, and economic agendas associated with information creation and provision

Assessing and Selecting Resources

- Assess sources of information, including computer-based and other technologies
- Know when to use print, CD-ROM, online and full-text sources
- Evaluate the effectiveness of channels for different needs
- Understand the difference between primary and secondary sources

Searching and Locating Information

- Understand database structure and content
- Know how to build successful search strategies using boolean logic, field searching and limiters

- Understand when to use controlled vocabulary
- Understand difference between precise and comprehensive searches
- Understand how to interpret citations and use call numbers to locate print items
- Recognize how to alter the search if the first attempt does not find information or finds too much information

Evaluating and Interpreting Information

- Employ critical thinking skills
- Distinguish relevant from irrelevant information
- Determine the strength of the argument
- Determine the factual accuracy of a statement
- Consider currency, authority, bias, viewpoints, and assumptions

Manipulating and Organizing Information

- Understand the process for saving, downloading, e-mailing, or printing search results
- Understand how and when to use document delivery to retrieve documents
- Organize information for practical applications, including within documents such as World Wide Web pages

Citing and Communicating Information

- Know relevant terms and acronyms
- Understand how to cite sources, including electronic resources
- Know how to communicate results to others
- Understand how to integrate new information into an existing body of knowledge

THE CHALLENGE OF SPECIFIC CONVERGENCES: SUBJECT-ORIENTED INTERNET SOURCES

Ours Is a Highly Interactive Web Page

Katharine A. Waugh

The illustrator, Katharine A. Waugh (kawaugh@vaxsar.vassar.edu), is Reference Librarian, Vassar College Library, Poughkeepsie, NY 12601.

[Haworth co-indexing entry note]: "Ours Is a Highly Interactive Web Page." Waugh, Katharine A. Co-published simultaneously in *Internet Reference Services Quarterly* (The Haworth Press, Inc.) Vol. 2, No. 2/3, 1997, p. 113; and: *The Challenge of Internet Literacy: The Instruction-Web Convergence* (ed: Lyn Elizabeth M. Martin) The Haworth Press, Inc., 1997, p. 113. Single or multiple copies of this article are available for a fee from The Haworth Document Delivery Service [1-800-342-9678, 9:00 a.m. - 5:00 p.m. (EST). E-mail address: getinfo@haworth.com].

Untangling the Web
of Legislative Histories:
A Web Page for Bibliographic Instruction
on the Legislative Process

Elaine Hoffman

SUMMARY. The Government Documents department at Stony Brook was traditionally allotted only one classroom session to introduce undergraduate students to the intricacies of researching federal legislative histories. This paper describes a first attempt to create a Web page that guides students through the essential steps of a legislative history search and provides explanations of unfamiliar terms, the library location of needed items and direct links to important legislative sites (such as THOMAS and GPO Access). The article also surveys other, similar and related Web pages that have recently been developed on the World Wide Web. *[Article copies available for a fee from The Haworth Document Delivery Service: 1-800-342-9678. E-mail address: getinfo@haworth.com]*

KEYWORDS. Legislative history/histories, legislative process, bibliographic instruction, legislative research

To many undergraduates enrolled in political science and legal research classes at the State University of New York (SUNY) at Stony Brook the

Elaine Hoffman (ehoffman@ccmail.sunysb.edu) is Senior Assistant Government Documents and Reference Librarian, Frank Melville Jr. Memorial Library, State University of New York at Stony Brook, Stony Brook, NY 11794-3331.

[Haworth co-indexing entry note]: "Untangling the Web of Legislative Histories: A Web Page for Bibliographic Instruction on the Legislative Process." Hoffman, Elaine. Co-published simultaneously in *Internet Reference Services Quarterly* (The Haworth Press, Inc.) Vol. 2, No. 2/3, 1997, pp. 115-132; and: *The Challenge of Internet Literacy: The Instruction-Web Convergence* (ed: Lyn Elizabeth M. Martin) The Haworth Press, Inc., 1997, pp. 115-132. Single or multiple copies of this article are available for a fee from The Haworth Document Delivery Service [1-800-342-9678, 9:00 a.m. - 5:00 p.m. (EST). E-mail address: getinfo@haworth.com].

115

writing of a United States federal legislative history must seem as challenging and intricate as the spinning of a spider's web. It is very easy to lose one's way and get caught in that web. Using HTML (Hypertext Markup Language), I have developed a Legislative History Web Page in an attempt to make it easier for students to find their way through this morass.

Stony Brook is one of the four major research universities in the SUNY public education system that also includes 60 other schools. The Government Documents section, which is a subdivision of the Reference Department, is a selective U.S. federal depository. As such we receive about 60 percent (previously 80 percent) of what the federal government publishes and we also have a backup Readex microfiche collection that provides us with even more government documents than those we select. Although Stony Brook does not have a law school, as part of the depository system our collection includes a basic law collection of such sources as federal laws, hearings, prints, documents, budget materials, presidential documents, supreme court cases, commercial and government indexes and regulatory sources.

Every year Political Science professors call upon the Documents section to do a few introductory classes, usually lasting about an hour and a half, to introduce undergraduates to the basics of conducting a federal legislative history search. When I first came to the Documents section four years ago, the sources used for these classes consisted almost entirely of paper indexes, microfiche sources and CD-ROM indexes. One of the documents librarians would outline the basic process of conducting the search, quickly showing each paper volume, and distribute handouts afterwards. Some students would attempt to take notes while others merely listened and tried to absorb all the information. Eventually, by the middle of the session, some of their eyes would glaze over from the information overload. A few years later we began to add Internet sources to the lecture, demonstrating them in the classroom using an LCD cube, a personal computer and an overhead projector. We distributed another handout, including Internet sources, along with the traditional handouts.

PURPOSE

The outcome of these classes was not completely satisfactory. Some students would show up in the Documents section later that semester having a rough idea of what to do. Others seemed to be completely lost in the "legislative web" and we had to guide them through each step from the beginning. Another problem was that due to staffing shortages and a job freeze in the State University system, we were rapidly losing librarians and Government Documents Reference assistance was only available from 8:30 a.m. to 5:00 p.m. weekdays, and 2:00 p.m. to 6:00 p.m. Saturdays. Even physically finding each source became a time-consuming process because they were scattered in various sections of the Documents collection on the second floor of the Reference Department. The locations included the Law collection (arranged by Library of Congress [LC] numbers), the Documents Reference, Reserve and Desk areas, separate rows of paper hearings (earlier ones arranged by Congress, year, House or Senate, committee name and alphabetical title order; later ones by Superintendent of Documents [Sudoc] number) prints, and the microfiche collections including GPO and Readex microfiche (earlier ones located by Monthly Catalog Numbers and later ones by Sudoc numbers). To say the least it was very confusing!

In discussions with both my supervisor and the head of the Reference department, the idea emerged of developing a Web page outlining the steps involved in doing a legislative history, so that students would be able to consult it at any time they liked, day or night, from their rooms if they had a personal computer, or from one of the instructional computer laboratories located in various buildings on campus including the library.

Congress, especially in the past year, had become particularly enamored of the idea of converting the majority of depository and public information into electronic format and making it available on the World Wide Web. Not only would such documents be much more current than was possible with paper texts but also much less costly to produce. Combining this trend with the desire to explore more innovative ways to conduct bibliographic instruction sessions in legislative history and the awareness that students were going to have to learn to use the Internet soon in order to be able to access many documents at all, I decided to attempt such a Web page.

The major purpose of the page was to guide and simplify the process of doing a legislative history, allowing the students to "plug in" to whatever information they needed, to copy down or print out the location of the sources they required, to provide additional, explanatory information about each of the sources and tools discussed, and to provide instant, easy links to major sources of legislative information on the World Wide Web.

LITERATURE SEARCH

The work for the Web page actually began before I conceived the idea of writing a paper about it. Thus, I conducted the literature search simultaneously with the writing of the page. An initial search of Library Literature (using the EPIC system) produced several articles combining the terms "bibliographic instruction" and "Internet" or "World Wide Web," but very few including the words "legislative history" or "legislative process" as well.

Interestingly, the few articles that were applicable, had several relevant ideas and terms that seemed to predate the actual arrival of the World Wide Web.

Especially striking were two articles written by Professor I. T. Hardy. In his first article[1] Professor Hardy describes his development of Project CLEAR's (Computers in Legal Education) Paper Choice, a computer program that combines hypertext software techniques and "question-and-answer decision trees"[2] to teach law and other students about legal research. In his paper he discusses first developing an "experimental hypertext system called the Paper Choice/graphics edition"[3] which seems to be an actual precursor to today's World Wide Web browsers such as Mosaic,[4] Internet Explorer[5] and Netscape.[6] After describing how with hypertext one can "establish links among the various topics"[7] and store a "page or two of text or a single computer-screen-sized picture"[8] he concludes later in the article that "few law schools in the 1987-88 academic year had computers that were capable of running graphics programs. Continued development of an all-graphics system . . . became impractical"[9] and abandons that project in favor of "The Paper Choice/Text Edition."[10] Today the development of World Wide Web browsers seems to have solved this problem of combining hypertext searching and links with graphics capability.

In his second paper Professor Trotter[11] discusses his creation of Lexpert, a continuation of his previous Project Clear. Lexpert is "a software system running on IBM-compatible personal computers that gives advice about doing federal legislative history research . . . contains information about finding the basic documents of legislative history . . . suggests the use of . . . research aids . . . suggests which specific section of the aid would be best used . . . and offers narrative information describing each of the research aids."[12] Lexpert was designed as a "decision tree"[13] of many linked files that makes it a hypertext system according to Professor Hardy's definition. When reading the article I discovered that many of his goals were the same as those in my Web page:

- To give advice about how to do federal legislative history research.
- To suggest possible sources for conducting such research.
- To provide the library location of the selected resources.

- To provide narrative information and date coverage about many of the research aids.
- To provide links between the different sources.

The third article of particular interest in the literature search was by Patrick Ragains[14] in which he discusses how he used "an active learning technique known as the jigsaw method to review the federal legislative process"[15] as part of a bibliographic instruction session for a community nutrition course at Montana State University-Bozeman. Many of Mr. Ragains' stated objectives in using this method were similar to my own:

- "to review the federal legislative/regulatory process,
- [to] link available information sources with each point in the process,
- [to] outline the search strategies needed to track legislative and regulatory activities."[16]
- "to desensitize students to their . . . fear of government documents."[17]

His desire to achieve these goals grew out of some of the same frustrations as my own: the limited amounts of time librarians have to present the legislative history research methods and bibliographic sources, the feeling that we were not serving students as well as possible through traditional Bibliographic Instruction (BI) techniques and the distribution of handouts, the lack of currency of some of the materials and the students' confusion over both the roles of various government federal departments and their failure to distinguish between the different sources leading up to the passage of a law. Using the jigsaw method Mr. Ragains had his students "work together in small groups to . . . examine publications providing information about discrete points in the development, enactment, and implementation of federal law."[18] In session two of the class he showed "how to access and search the Federal Register on the Internet,"[19] just as in our classes we demonstrated the use of the Government Printing Office (GPO) Access and THOMAS using an LCD monitor and overhead projector.

CREATION OF THE WEB PAGE

World Wide Web pages are currently written using a computer language named HTML, Hypertext Markup Language. Although many introductory guides are available on the Internet, nothing substitutes for a personal teacher. Luckily for me the head of Bibliographic Instruction,

Richard Feinberg, was already involved in writing a Web page for the library and showed me the basics of writing HTML and using Netscape, a World Wide Web "browser" which enabled us to view the finished product. The editor that we used to produce the Web page was HTMLed,[20] a text editor that we had downloaded from the Internet.

The Web page was created using a few very basic HTML commands. It is not fancy or sophisticated compared with some of the sites that we will discuss later. Nevertheless, it was quick, relatively painless and served the purpose. Many excellent introductory materials exist for learning HTML on one's own. One I would like particularly to recommend is called "Computer Now: Crash Course on Writing Documents for the Web"[21] and as it states it was written "to help people . . . put a page on the web [who] could care less about most of the technical details and don't want to read a book."[22] The guide covers just a little bit more of the commands that I will be discussing below, the "absolute essentials"[23] for putting a bare bones Web page out on the World Wide Web.

The basic HTML "tags" or commands that I had to learn in order to create a rudimentary page were:

<HTML> . . . </HTML>	<P> . . . </P> (paragraph)
<HEAD> . . . </HEAD>	<U> . . . </U> (underline)
<TITLE> . . . </TITLE>	<B> . . . </B> (bold)
<BODY> . . . </BODY>	<I> . . . </I> (Italics
<CENTER> . . . </CENTER>	<H1> . . . </H1) through <H6> . . . </H6>

 (line break)	<HR> (horizontal rule, plain white line)
<DD> . . . </DD> (indent)	

The HTMLed editor provided me with the ability to enter the line break, paragraph, bold, italics, H1 through H6 formatting and a few other commands automatically by clicking a button with my mouse.

Additionally I had to create two different types of links. In the following Web page reproduction, Illustration 1, titles that are underlined and are in bold type show the first category of Web link. The underlining and bolding indicate the fact that they have been linked to separate pages that contain further explanatory and locational information about them. By clicking on a particular title they would automatically link the user to that separate page. By pressing the left arrow key the user could return to the main Web page. In the future I plan to add "RETURN" buttons to make this function even more apparent. If, for the purposes of this article, we could reproduce this page in color, the reader would be able to see that the bolded and underlined titles (links) change from blue to pink once they have been used. This feature deals with one of the problems that Professor

Ragains encountered, that of the user becoming confused or lost as to where they were in the database.

The basic command for linking the title or term being expounded upon to the linked page is <A HREF="NAME OF PAGE ITEM IS BEING LINKED TO">NAME IF ITEM BEING LINKED</A>.

The second type of link is for linking the name of a site to that actual site on the World Wide Web. For example, when I made a link to the THOMAS site the command I used was <A HREF="HTTP://THOMAS. LOC.GOV">HERE</A>. Please note that incorporated into the link is the actual URL (Universal Resource Locator) or "address" of THOMAS. Thus, the user does not actually have to know the URL in order to be linked to different sites. The word HERE appears instead of the word THOMAS because the sentence reads "If you wish to connect to THOMAS please click _HERE_".

My hope is to provide many more links on the page in the same manner that I have done so far. Most of these should be straightforward links. When I was doing my research, I found a very interesting page located at the THOMAS home page. It is called "Direct Links to THOMAS Documents"[24] and states "occasionally developers of Web pages may wish to make a link directly to a THOMAS document . . . Below are some examples of how a Web developer might build links directly to THOMAS documents."[25] Following this statement is a list of seven already prepared HTML format commands for linking one's page to different explanations in the THOMAS document, such as "Making a link to the full text of a bill" or "Making a link to a Congressional Record search."

In order not to have to reinvent the wheel I worked from the handouts that my supervisor, Jyoti Pandit, had developed over the past several years and organized the material into the following sections: Welcome, Background Information (including Primary and Secondary sources), and Steps in Conducting a Legislative History (which so far includes information on Bills, Hearings, Committee Prints, Committee Reports, Documents, Debates, Public Laws, and Rules and Regulations). Illustration 1 shows how one of the pages from the Legislative History Web Page looks. Please note that the URL for the page itself is found in the upper right-hand corner and is "http://www.sunysb.edu/govdocs/legproc.htm" without the quotation marks. Illustrations 2 and 3 show the same page written in actual HTML code.

At this point I would like to stress that the Legislative History Web Page is an ongoing, unfinished project. I hope to be adding to and developing much material for it over the next several semesters.

IMPLEMENTATION AND PROBLEMS

Of course there were several problems involved with the creation of the Legislative History Web Page. The first of these was the loading of software onto our office personal computer, including Windows 3.1, HTMLed, and Netscape Navigator 2.0. The next difficulty involved getting a World Wide Web subdirectory created on my e-mail account by the campus webmaster. In the middle of all these difficulties it was already time to teach the class so that although I could not show the students the actual, working Web page, I could display what it would look like and tell them what it hopefully would achieve. Once we received the correct address for the page I could distribute it to the class via the professors and graduate teaching assistants.

Another problem involved loading the material onto our campus VAX network. To do so was a rather tedious process, involving many manual steps. Then, because we did not yet have a proper SLIP or PPP connection in our office, I had to go to our library administration office to view the actual page on Netscape. After a few months this situation improved dramatically with the installation of a "temporary" SLIP connection so that by merely following a simple, twenty step process, we can connect to the World Wide Web using Netscape and then view the page! When I was in the middle of writing this paper I had to learn to use Windows '95, an updated version of HTMLed, and Netscape Navigator 3.0 because we had received new computers and equipment in our office. The advantage of switching to and learning all this new equipment is that when we receive our direct Ethernet connection, I will be able to load my material onto the network in a much quicker manner, using File Transfer Protocol (FTP) from my computer terminal instead of having to do it from the library administration office or using the long and tedious process already mentioned.

Since I was in a hurry to get the Web page going, I did not spend any time looking at other editors, of which there are a multitude on the market.

Perhaps the most vexing problem of all was finding time to continue writing the page, developing the ideas and creating the links. Writing HTML code is not very glamorous; spotting mistakes is hard on the eyes, difficult and time consuming. I would personally favor having a computer student do the actual formatting of the page once a librarian had outlined or typed it up in a text editor.

One problem that quickly became apparent when I started to write the page was the difficulty of going back and forth on the page itself to find or check some item of information that I had already written. To solve this problem I used "radio buttons," the section that you can see in Illustration 1

ILLUSTRATION 1. Netscape View of Legislative History Web Page

LEGISLATIVE PROCESS   http://www.sunysb.edu/govdocs/leggproc.htm

LEGISLATIVE HISTORY

WELCOME TO THE LEGISLATIVE HISTORY HOME PAGE

Dear Visitors: This page is still in the early stages of construction. Please be patient with any errors or "garbage" links. Corrections may be sent to: ehoffman@ccmail.sunysb.edu

This page was last updated 4/19/96.

This webpage is intended to help you through the lengthy and intricate process of doing a legislative history. We will attempt to take you through the procedure step by step so that you can review things which you learned in class or in the bibliographic instruction session which you attended for this course.

When you see *highlighted* items you may click your mouse on those items. Sometimes you will then see more information about that item and other times you will be directly connected to an Internet site or source such as a site for bills or the **Congressional Record**. The Internet site will often be able to give you more up to date or additional information to what we have here in the library.

If you wish to connect directly to a certain topic click on any of the items below:

Bills | Hearings | Prints | Reports | Documents | Debates |Public Laws |Rules and Regulations

BACKGROUND INFORMATION

Primary Sources

The first problem you have to deal with is how to select a topic for the legislative history. How do you pick a bill which may interest you and which may have become a law? There are several sources which you may consult. They are as follows:

PAIS Bulletin (Public Affairs Information Service Bulletin) Location: Ref Main H1.P82, Index Table PAIS is now also available on CD-ROM at the Government Documents Desk at the top of the second floor of the Reference Department. The CD-ROM provides coverage from 1972 to the present.

Congressional Quarterly Almanac, 1954- Location: Doc/Ref JK1.C66 is another excellent source which is accessible by subject search and has a non-partisan approach.

Congressional Quarterly Weekly Report 1964- Location: Doc/Ref JK1.C66) is similar to CQ Almanac but it is published every two weeks.

Congressional Information Service (CIS) Index , 1970- Location: Doc/Ref KF49.C623 is another excellent source to use as a subject approach. This commercial indexing services comes out monthly with annual cumulations.

CIS Index is also available on two separate CD-ROMS located at the Documents Reference Desk, both of which are called **Congressional Masterfile**, 1970-1986 and 1987-present.

The **Congressional Index**, Commerce Clearing House Inc. 1963- Location: Doc/Ref J69.C6 is a looseleaf

1 of 6   5/29/96 1.29 PM

that looks like the following:_ Bills_ _Prints_ _Reports_ _Documents_ _Debates_ _Public Laws_ _Rules and Regulations_ These buttons not only help Web page users tell right away what the page contains and go to the information that they require, but they help me find what I am searching for in the text much more easily. As one can see from Illustrations 2 and 3, these radio buttons were achieved by typing, for example, the command <A HREF="#Bills">Bills</A> at the word Bills that appears underlined as above and then typing in the command <A name=Bills>BILLS farther down in the text where the "Bills" section actually begins.

ILLUSTRATION 2. HTMLed Version of Previous Legislative History Page

```
Author:    Elaine Hoffman
Date: January 17, 1996
-->

<HEAD>
<TITLE>LEGISLATIVE PROCESS</TITLE>

</HEAD>
<BODY>


<CENTER><I><H4><B>LEGISLATIVE HISTORY</B></H4></I></CENTER>

<CENTER><B>WELCOME TO THE LEGISLATIVE HISTORY HOME
PAGE</B>.</CENTER><BR>

Dear Visitors:  This page is still in the early stages of construction.
Please be patient with any errors or "garbage" links.  Corrections may
be sent to:
ehoffman@ccmail.sunysb.edu<P>

This page was last updated 5/29/96.<P>

This webpage is intended to help you through the lengthy and intricate
process of doing a legislative history.  We will attempt to take you
through the procedure step by step so that you can review things which
you learned in class or in the bibliographic instruction session which
you attended for this course.<P>

When you see <B><I>highlighted</I></B> items you may click your mouse on
those items.  Sometimes you will then see more information about that
item and other times you will be directly connected to an Internet site
or source such as a site for <B>bills</B> or the <B><U>Congressional
Record</U></B>.  The Internet site will often be able to give you more
up to date or additional information to what we have here in the
library.<P><HR>

If you wish to connect directly to a certain topic click on any of the
items below:<P>

<A HREF="#Bills">Bills</A>        <A HREF="#Hearings">Hearings</A>
<A HREF="#Prints">Prints</A>    |   <A HREF="#Reports"> Reports</A>
|    <A HREF="#Documents">Documents</A>   |   <A HREF="#Debates">Debates
|<A HREF="#Public Laws">Public Laws</A>   |<A HREF="#Rules and
Regulations">Rules and Regulations </A>
<P><HR>
```

The more I work on the Web page the more techniques I am finding to improve it. I had created all the explanatory material in separate, new HTML files so that information on all the highlighted or underlined items such as bills, hearings, reports, documents, THOMAS, the Monthly Catalog, etc., have their own file to which the words are linked. Now that I realize how time consuming creating a separate file for each explanation is, I will probably be changing the format so that most of the terms are

ILLUSTRATION 3. HTMLed Version of Legislative History Page

```
<CENTER><B>BACKGROUND INFORMATION</B></CENTER><P>

<CENTER><B>Primary Sources</B></CENTER><P>

The first problem you have to deal with is how to select a topic for the
legislative history.  How do you pick a bill which may interest you and
which may have become a law?  There are several sources which you may
consult.  They are as follows:<P>

<B><U><A HREF="pais.htm">PAIS Bulletin</A></U> (Public Affairs
Information Service Bulletin</U>)</B>   <B>Location</B>: Ref Main
H1.P82, Index Table.  PAIS is now also available on CD-ROM at the
Government Documents Desk at the top of the second floor of the
Reference Department.  The CD-ROM provides coverage from 1972 to the
present.<P>

<U><B><A HREF="cqalmnc.htm">Congressional Quarterly Almanac</A></B></U>,
1954-   <B>Location</B>: Doc/Ref JK1.C66 is another excellent source
which is accessible by subject search and has a non-partisan
approach.<P>

<B><U><A HREF="cqwr.htm">Congressional Quarterly Weekly
Report</A></U></B> 1964- <B>Location</B>: Doc/Ref JK1.C66) is similar to
CQ Almanac but it is published every two weeks.<P>

<B><U><A HREF="cisindex.htm">Congressional Information Service (CIS)
Index </A> </U></B>, 1970-  Location: Doc/Ref KF49.C623 is another
excellent source to use as a subject approach. This commercial indexing
services comes out monthly with annual cumulations.<P>

<B><U>CIS Index</U></B> is also available on two separate CD-ROMS
located at the Documents Reference Desk, both of which are called
<B><U>Congressional
Masterfile</U></B>, 1970-1986 and 1987-present.<P>

The <U><B>Congressional Index</B><U>, Commerce Clearing House Inc. 1963-
Location: Doc/Ref J69.C6 is a looseleaf commercial service which is
updated constantly.  It is published in two volumes each year, one for
the House and one for the Senate. Both volumes provide subject access
and a brief description of each bill as it is introduced.<P><HR>
```

defined in a glossary that will come after the main body of the Legislative History Web Page. In that way I can connect each word or phrase to its explanation without having to create so many different files. The glossary would work in a similar manner to "buttons" in that when one clicked on an individual term, they would be taken to the proper explanation in the glossary.

EVALUATION

There is no question that in the future the World Wide Web will continue to be the most up to date way to access current information on such material as bills, new laws, Federal Register material and more; information for which we previously had to wait at least a month or two for its arrival in paper.

It seems to be too early to evaluate the success or usefulness of the Legislative History Web Page for a few different reasons. The Web page itself has had limited distribution because of the delay in obtaining its actual address to distribute to professors and students. I did have one e-mail inquiry from a student asking for help in finding it. At first it was only accessible if one knew its exact address, "http://www.sunysb.edu/govdocs/legproc.htm". After a few months of initial preparation and having it stand alone, it was added as a link to the Stony Brook Library Home Page. Since at that time we did not have any software for counting the number of hits on the page we really did not have any way of knowing how many people were using it. Also, because it still needs a lot more material, links and information added to it, I have not yet listed it with any of the indexing or announcement services available on the World Wide Web, such as "Net-Happenings"[26] or "Yahoo."[27]

Although supportive of the project itself, one of the Political Science professors expressed his doubt that it would be used very much this past semester because of the lack of expertise by many undergraduates in using the Web itself. His feeling was that in a few years students will be coming to college well versed in the use of the Web and that at that point they would use the page. One of the things that I would like to do at the end of the forthcoming academic year is to send out a questionnaire to both students and faculty to assess the usefulness of the Legislative History Web Page.

A helpful exercise was displaying the Web page as a poster session at the SUNYLA (State University of New York Librarians Association) annual conference in June 1996. A few people made helpful formatting and organizational suggestions that I hope to implement in the future.

OTHER LEGISLATIVE HISTORY SITES

It was only after I had substantially developed my Web page and was doing research for this paper that I began looking at what else existed out on the World Wide Web itself. Time constraints prevented an exhaustive search but I did use The Open Text Index,[28] Alta Vista,[29] Magellan,[30] and Lycos[31] to conduct various searches using the phrases "legislative process" and "legislative history." Limiting the search words to title or combining them with the Boolean term "ADJ" helped narrow down the results. What I discovered were many variations and innovative approaches for presenting guides to doing legislative histories using Web pages. Librarians, professors, students and commercial services are developing these types of Web pages. Please keep in mind, however, because of the rapidity of changes on the Web some of the following information could be updated or changed by the time this paper appears in print.

The sites mentioned in the following discussion exemplify the different types of legislative history Web pages that are to be found. The first type I would call traditional pathfinders and library research guides. The writers have essentially transferred them, via HTML, to the World Wide Web. A good example of this is the "Legislative History Research Guide"[32] at the Washington University Law Library. This straightforward guide of how to do legislative histories has been done in HTML but has no active links attached to it to lead anywhere else. Another example of this type is the page entitled "The Legislative History of a U.S. Law"[33] done at Wesleyan University. This traditional pathfinder does include simple back links such as "Up to Table of Contents" and "Return to Library Home Page" to help the user find their way back to where they started.

An example of a more sophisticated approach is that used at the U.S. House of Representatives site entitled "The Legislative Process–Tying it all Together."[34] Part of a complex, detailed site, this page, along with definitions included in the text, includes a special and helpful feature that we have not seen before, links to searchable databases that are using gopher or WAIS as search engines. Thus clicking on the term "Bill Text" connects one to a database of bills that can be searched by individual words or terms. Similarly clicking on "Committee Meetings" or "House Schedules" takes one to the appropriate information. There are also links to other sources such as "For more information on bills and resolutions see 'Consideration by Committee' in 'How Our Laws are Made.' "

The commercial group Vote-Smart has done a page similar to the previous one.[35] Part of a larger page entitled "An Introduction to Government," the section on "How a Bill Becomes a Law" is notable for its definitions of legislative terms that may not be familiar to the average citizen such as "discharge petition," "Calendar Wednesday" and "cloture." Clicking on any of these terms brings one automatically to a glossary of definitions at the end of the Web page. This page does not feature any links to other home pages.

A completely opposite approach, but still in the tradition of research guides, has been done at the UC Davis General Library. Entitled "Guide to Congressional Information in Electronic Form"[36] it only provides links to legislative information on the World Wide Web without giving a description of the legislative history process or any definitions. It provides links to congressional information such as bills, the legislative process, members, federal laws and regulations.

A more sophisticated approach in research guides is the one at Montana State University, Bozeman, entitled "U.S. Legislative Process & Related Publications."[37] This page includes advice on how to follow the legislative process, the library's location for paper sources and indexes and links to other related Web sites such as GPO Access and the Federal Register. Although close in content and style to mine, it does not include links to definitions of individual terms.

A somewhat different style from the ones above are the course outlines being put up on the World Wide Web by instructors and professors. One example is the one done by Dr. Joe Kunkel at Mankato State University.[38] Entitled "P.S. 435/535-01, The Legislative Process" it combines the features of the traditional pathfinders and research guides with the individual requirements of courses. Thus Dr. Kunkel provides links to related Internet sources, an outline of the course purpose, readings, required assignments, grading procedures, the evaluation procedure, and a bibliographic assignment for graduate students.

The final type of presentation for legislative history Web pages that I will discuss to me is also the most fascinating. Some rather creative people have come up with the idea of teaching the legislative process through virtual reality simulations. In other words the participant becomes an active rather than a passive agent in the process. John J. Ulrich of East Central University has developed one called "LegiSim; A Simulation of the Legislative Process in the House of Representatives."[39] Pointing out that doing a simulation is a very enjoyable way of learning about the legislative process he plunges the participant into the position of being a member of the House of Representatives and having to make decisions about various bills, laws, committee participation and debate. In this copyrighted site he provides an enormous number of links including ones to political party pages and instructions on how to write a bill and do legislative research.

A similar page has also been done at the University of San Diego as a Senior Colloquium Project by a current J.D. student, Terence Banich.[40] As he states on the first page, "The goal behind this simulation is to educate people ... about the legislative process in the U.S. Congress in a manner that lifts bland, and sometimes unclear procedures off of the page into real, interactive situations."[41] He then instructs the participant to first read the Congressman's biography, to read the bill BEFORE trying to pass it, to read all the text before making a decision and not to go back if you make a bad decision. I did part of the simulation and found it very personal, enjoyable and realistically frustrating when I made various mistakes and could not pass my bill! The types of exercises experienced in the simulations are particularly interesting because they attempt to reflect the political reality that goes along with the rules and regulations of trying to pass legislation.

IN CONCLUSION

In this paper I have shown my attempt to use the World Wide Web in an innovative manner to teach the federal legislative history process. This experiment was partly a response to a level of frustration at the effectiveness of teaching the subject using traditional bibliographic techniques in a severely limited amount of time. Anyone attempting to learn all the steps involved in doing a federal legislative history can only absorb a certain amount of information at one time. When learning the process myself, I had to go over the material constantly and study it until I understood the different steps, possible approaches and interrelationship of the materials. My hope was to create a more interactive and enjoyable resource to which students could return, according to their own timetables, for definitions, locations, research guidance, and further information when they felt lost in the "web" of legislative confusion. By creating the Web page I hoped to allow the students to find whatever information they needed, work at their own paces, go over the materials as much as they wanted to, make the learning process more interactive and enjoyable, and include extra information that it was not possible to cover within the strictures of the class time. The hypertext feature was particularly appealing because students, by clicking on a certain resource, such as Thomas, could learn more about it if they chose to, be connected to the Internet site for it without having to know its address, if that was their desire, or simply move onto the next step.

Creating the Web page was also a reaction to Congress's clear intention to move toward a much more electronically oriented information system. Although retreating somewhat from its original suggestion that all government documents be converted to online electronic files within two years, the depository library program itself has recommended a five to seven year process for such a conversion. Developing the legislative history Web page is an attempt to deal with this eventual conversion and to introduce students to the new realities of government document availability. Given that the assignments in our undergraduate Political Science courses are often limited to bills introduced within the last ten to fifteen years, I imagine that within a few short years, most of the materials that the students need to use will be available either in both paper and electronic format, or perhaps only via electronic sources.

Both an advantage and a disadvantage of having this information on a Web page is the ability constantly to revise and update its contents. URL (Uniform Resource Locator) addresses tend to change quickly enough that hard copy printouts of Internet resources become rapidly outdated. Updating the addresses and the links within a relatively short period of their changing certainly makes the information we are distributing more accurate and reliable. Our handout of Internet resources from March 1995 consisted mostly of gopher and telnet sources. The handout for 1996 not only had mostly World Wide Web sources, but superseded the previous handout in the accuracy of addresses and resources available. On the other hand, someone has to do the updating and a person or a software program must regularly check that links are not outdated.

The Web page was also a response to and result of the continually decreasing staffing level in our government documents department. Giving students readily available information about and descriptions of the search tools they can use and providing them with the ability to print them out and bring them to the library, may alleviate the librarians' need to repeat simple locational information and reproduce and update lists of resources.

With this paper, I hope I have shown that creating a Web page can be a relatively simple process that does not have to include fancy graphics or Java programming. While developing my own page, I have also discovered the wealth of other legislative history pages that exist or are in the process of creation. I have tried to point out some of the problems that one might encounter and I encourage other people and departments to try their own pages, adapting my ideas and those of others to their particular circumstances. By no means have I exhausted all the possibilities or covered all the variations that are already out on the Web or are being developed.

With the inevitable move toward more electronic access to government information, we should attempt to develop creative bibliographic instruction techniques that will both teach the new skills necessary to access that information and make the process more enjoyable and interesting.

NOTES

1. Trotter Hardy, "Project CLEAR'S Paper Choice: A Hypertext System for Giving Advice About Legal Research," *Law Library Journal* 82:2 (Spring 1990):209-237.

2. Ibid., 209.

3. Ibid., 211.

4. Spry's Mosaic 95. (URL: http://www.spry.com).

5. Microsoft Internet Explorer. (URL: http://www.microsoft.com/windows/ie/ie.htm).

6. Netscape 2.0. (URL: http://home.netscape.com).

7. Hardy, "Project CLEAR'S Paper Choice: A Hypertext System for Giving Advice about Legal Research," 210.

8. Ibid.

9. Ibid., 214.

10. Ibid., 223.

11. I. T. Hardy, "Creating an Expert System for Legislative History Research: Project CLEAR's 'Lexpert'," *Law Library Journal* 85 (Spring 1993):239-273.

12. Ibid., 239.

13. Ibid., 240.

14. Patrick Ragains, "The Legislative/Regulatory Process and BI: A Course-Integrated Unit,"*Research Strategies* 13 (Spring 1995):116-121.

15. Ibid., 116.

16. Ibid., 116-117.

17. Ibid., 120.

18. Ibid., 117.

19. Ibid.

20. Peter Cranshaw, *HTMLed, Version 1.2e* (New Brunswick, Canada: Internet Software Technologies, 1995).

21. Eamonn Sullivan, "Crash Course on Writing Documents for the Web," Micron Electronics Inc., 1995. (URL: http://www.pcweek.com/eamonn/crash_course.html).

22. Ibid.

23. Ibid.

24. "Direct Links to THOMAS Documents," 1996. (URL: http://thomas.loc.gov/home/example.html).

25. Ibid.

26. Gleason Sackman. "Net-Happenings,". (URL: http://www.mid.net:80/net/).

27. "Yahoo". (URL: http://www.yahoo.com).

28. "The Open Text Index". (URL: http://search.opentext.com/omw/compoundsearch).

29. "Alta Vista". (URL: http://www.altavista.digicom/).

30. "Magellan". (URL: http://www.magellan.com/).

31. "Lycos". (URL: http://www.lycos.com/).

32. Dorie Bertram, "Legislative History Research Guide". (URL: http://www.wulaw.wustl.edu/Library/legrg. html).

33. "Legislative History of a U.S. Law". (URL: http://www.wesleyan.edu/libr/pathfind/leghist.htm).

34. U.S. House of Representatives, "The Legislative Process-Tying it All Together". (URL: http://www.house.gov/Tying_it_all.html).

35. Vote-Smart, "How a Bill Becomes a Law". (URL: http://www.vote-smart.org./reference/primer/billlaw.html).

36. "Guide to Congressional Information in Electronic Form," U.C. Davis, General Library. (URL: http://govdoc.ucdavis.edu/GovDoc/congressional.html).

37. "U.S. Legislative Process & Related Publications," Renne Library Government Information Guide #1, Montana State University, Bozeman. (URL: http://www.lib.montana.edu/GOVDOC/bill_law.html).

38. Dr. Joe Kunkel, "P.S. 435/535-01, The Legislative Process." (Mankato State University, 1996). (URL: http://www.mankato.msus.edu/dept/psle/www/facKunkelsy1435.html).

39. John J. Ulrich, "LegiSim; A Simulation of the Legislative Process in the House of Representatives," 1995-96 Version. (Department of Political Science, East Central University, 1995-96). (URL: http://student.ecok.edu/~polsci/faculty/julrich/courses/1113sim.html).

40. Terence Banich, "Virtual Congress." (University of San Diego, 1996). (URL: http://www.acusd.edu/~bookstor/Computers/vc/).

41. Ibid.

Instructional Opportunities
of a Subject-Oriented (Law) Web Page

John A. Lehner
Trudi E. Jacobson

SUMMARY. Library Web pages serve a multitude of purposes, from informing patrons of library hours and class sessions, to providing access to the online catalog, to pointing users towards interest-based resources of particular merit. Web pages can also be used to instruct patrons. In this article, we describe a law Web page that was designed to help teach students and others, as well as to provide access to selected law resources. Some of the benefits of this instructional subject-specific Web page are its user-friendliness, its flexibility, its ability to provide a cognitive structure and to promote critical thinking, and its wide availability. *[Article copies available for a fee from The Haworth Document Delivery Service: 1-800-342-9678. E-mail address: getinfo@haworth.com]*

KEYWORDS. Law resources, legal research, Web page, library instruction, critical thinking, bibliographic instruction

John A. Lehner (lehnerj@asuvm.inre.asu.edu) is Research Support and Liaison Librarian at Fletcher Library, Arizona State University West, Phoenix, AZ 85069. He was formerly the Bibliographer for Business, Law, Economics, and Geography at the University Libraries, University at Albany-SUNY. Trudi E. Jacobson (tj662@cnsvax.albany.edu) is Coordinator for User Education Programs at the University Libraries, University at Albany-SUNY, Albany, NY 12222.

[Haworth co-indexing entry note]: "Instructional Opportunities of a Subject-Oriented (Law) Web Page." Lehner, John A., and Trudi E. Jacobson. Co-published simultaneously in *Internet Reference Services Quarterly* (The Haworth Press, Inc.) Vol. 2, No. 2/3, 1997, pp. 133-142; and: *The Challenge of Internet Literacy: The Instruction-Web Convergence* (ed: Lyn Elizabeth M. Martin) The Haworth Press, Inc., 1997, pp. 133-142. Single or multiple copies of this article are available for a fee from The Haworth Document Delivery Service [1-800-342-9678, 9:00 a.m. - 5:00 p.m. (EST). E-mail address: getinfo@haworth.com].

Public service librarians are constantly looking for ways to make information more accessible to users. Presenting and accessing information through the Internet has become increasingly easy with each new software development. We are light years beyond user-initiated FTP commands, for example, although it was just recently that this clunky capability was new and wondrous. The ease of using Web browsers and hypertext markup language has opened the field to everyone who has information or data to offer, while more and more users have access to computers linked to the Web. Libraries are using this flexible new medium in a number of ways to meet their patrons' needs.

Initially, library Web pages concentrated on providing local information (hours, services, etc.) and on directing users to specific, pre-selected links. As they become increasingly familiar with the Web and HTML, librarians are now using this medium's power to instruct. There is great potential for presenting instructional material and online tutorials using the Web. The Law Page, available through the University Libraries' University at Albany Homepage (http://www.albany.edu/library/), was designed to present discipline-specific material in a manner that would teach students unfamiliar with law research.

LITERATURE REVIEW

Relatively little has been written on designing subject-based WWW pages specifically for instructional purposes. The emphases in the published education and bibliographic instruction literature have been on teaching users to navigate the Internet, using e-mail and other Internet resources in a particular class, and providing lists of resources in various disciplines. Dorothy F. Byers and Lucy Wilson report on an engineering library home page developed to orient incoming engineering freshmen, but the focus is more on orienting users to library services and resources and less on developing the discipline-based section as a teaching tool.[1] Judith M. Pask and Carl E. Snow surveyed undergraduate educational initiatives which incorporate the Internet and Internet resources.[2] Their article touches upon educational and critical thinking issues associated with the Internet. General design guidelines for Web pages are available both in print and mounted on the Internet. Paul G. Shotsberger's article combines suggestions for effective Web page design and caveats about ineffective practices with a list of best WWW instructional sites.[3]

INSTRUCTIONAL WEB PAGES

Some libraries are developing distinct Web pages whose purpose is to teach students how to do research. Two that guide students through the basics of research, either in general or in a particular course, are mounted by Cornell[4] and MIT.[5] Such pages typically consider selecting a paper topic and finding background information on it, understanding controlled vocabulary, finding books, articles, and Internet resources, evaluating information sources and citing them. Esther Grassian, Ann Scholz and others have developed sites that concentrate on evaluating WWW resources.[6] Sites such as these depend upon students accessing them during the course of, or preferably before, doing their research. They are meant to be used in conjunction with subject-specific sites. The Law Page described below was designed to teach through its structure and content, without the need to access a separate document or page.

CONTENT OVERVIEW

The Law Page provides a short guide to selected major primary law sources and secondary materials. The first segment of the page includes a general introduction to the law collections of the two University at Albany libraries. A link to a general description of the collections is provided. The first segment of the Law Page also includes a link leading to a general description of WESTLAW, one of the commercial online legal database systems available for student use.

The second segment of the Law Page directs patrons to sources that would provide assistance with some of the basic questions that arise in undertaking legal research. This segment is entitled "Some Help with the Basics." As seen in Figure 1, it includes three hypertext links. (The hypertext links appear as underlined segments.) The first is a hypertext link to a list of hard copy sources in the University Libraries that address legal abbreviations, citations and definitions. The second link is to online legal citation guide at a remote Internet server. The third link is to a list of legal writing guides in our collections that contain sections on writing case briefs.

The third segment of the page is titled "Law Sources: Hard Copy (Paper) and Electronic." This section cautions users that the sources included in the subsequent segments of the page are not intended to be a complete representation of hard copy or electronic materials available for legal research. A hypertext link is included here to take users to the listing of legal guides included at Michigan's Clearinghouse for Subject-Oriented Internet Resource Guides, with a suggestion that these guides will help users find a broad range of legal materials.

The remaining segments of the Law Page are arranged into federal materials first, with sections for the U.S. Constitution, U.S. Supreme Court

FIGURE 1

Some Help with the Basics

Questions about *legal abbreviations, definitions or citations*? These hard copy (paper) sources in our collections can help:

(Link to hard copy sources list)

And here's a link to a very helpful *online guide to legal citation* at the Legal Information Institute of the Cornell University Law School:

(Link to citation guide)

Questions about *how to brief a case*? These legal writing guides in our collections include sections on case briefing:

(Link to writing guides list)

---

decisions and Federal Statutes. The federal materials are followed by the New York State materials, with sections for the New York Constitution, New York Statutes, and New York Court of Appeals decisions. Each of these sections includes a hypertext link to an Internet source, as well as annotations listing the hard copy sources available in the libraries. For example, the segment titled "The Constitution of the United States of America," includes a link to the section of the (Cornell University Law School) Legal Information Institute's Web site where the full text of the Constitution is available. It also includes a list with call numbers of the hard copy materials where the text of the Constitution can be found. Another example can be seen in Figure 2. This illustration shows the

FIGURE 2

United States
Supreme Court Decisions

Recent decisions of the United States Supreme Court (back to 1990) are available here.

Selected decisions of historical importance (back to 1947) are available here.

Note

The following reporters are available for United States Supreme Court decisions:

At the Dewey Library –

- ☐ The Supreme Court Reporter (abbreviated as in citations as S.Ct.) *LAW KF 101 W4*

- ☐ Cases Argued and Decided in the Supreme Court of the United States [Lawyers' Edition] (abbreviated in citations as L.Ed.) *LAW KF 101 L3*

At the University Library –

- ☐ United States Reports (abbreviated in citations as U.S.) *LAW KF 101*

- ☐ Cases Argued and Decided in the Supreme Court of the United States [Lawyers' Edition] (abbreviated in citations as L.Ed.) *LAW KF 101 L3*

Information on obtaining briefs for cases heard by the U.S. Supreme Court is available here.

segment on U.S. Supreme Court decisions. The hypertext link to a remote site is shown with underlining. The reporters for Supreme Court decisions are listed with locational information in the annotations following the hypertext link. This segment also includes a hypertext link that leads to a local file that explains the sources of briefs for cases heard by the Court.

The local file containing information on briefs for Supreme Court cases includes material of the type that might be included in a library instructional session. This section of the Law Page is included in Figure 3. It is a simple example of how the Web page medium makes practical research instruction available on an on-demand basis. This section of the Law Page sets out multiple sources for the briefs, including a microfilm set, several hard copy sets and one of the commercial online CALR services. It also provides an explanation of where to find a case's docket number and how to retrieve the briefs from the microfilm set using the docket number.

Content decisions were largely driven by impressions of demand from reference desk experience. Students frequently request of copies of the U.S. Constitution and often seek U.S. Supreme Court decisions. The University at Albany's location dictates the inclusion of New York State law materials. State law materials from other states are, of course, often requested by students, but New York State materials are by far the most frequently sought.

RATIONALE

Although the University at Albany is a comprehensive research university supporting a wide range of undergraduate programs and graduate programs, it does not have a law school. Students from a number of academic departments, however, undertake legal research and both of Albany's libraries maintain collections of primary and secondary legal materials. There were a number of reasons for undertaking preparation of the Law Page:

User Friendly Presentation

Legal research is highly specialized with a body of unique finding tools and sources. Students frequently have minimal, if any, background or training in legal research and bibliography. There is a need for presenting basic tools for legal research in an easily understood and user friendly format for users with little familiarity with basic sources.

Additionally, in a general academic library the range of legal research skills of the library faculty may vary considerably. There is a need for a

FIGURE 3

Supreme Court
Records and Briefs

The briefs and records of U.S. Supreme Court cases are available in a microfilm database at the University Library. The database includes docket documents, petitions for writ of certiorari and briefs for cases heard by the Court. Database coverage extends back to the 1974-75 term of the Court. No documents are included in this database for cases that have been denied certiorari, i.e. for cases the Court declined to hear. The documents are arranged by the docket numbers of the cases. (The docket number for a case will appear in the reported decision just after the title of the case. It appears as "No. 89-7376," for example. In this example, "89" indicates the year the item was docketed and "7376" is the case number.)

This microfilm database is available in the Government Documents Reference area of the University Library, where government documents microfilms are kept. The set is titled CIS U.S. Supreme Court Records and Briefs Microform and the call number is *GOVDOC / Ref KF 101.9 L37X.*

There are two sources for records and briefs of selected cases of the Supreme Court at the Dewey Library. They are:

☐ Landmark Briefs and Arguments of the Supreme Court of the United States: Constitutional Law *EXT / LAW KF 101.8 K87*

☐ Criminal Law Series *EXT / LAW KF 9218 U55X*

Finally, the WESTLAW service includes the database "U.S. Supreme Court Briefs." The database identifier is SCT-BRIEF. It provides coverage back to the 1990-91 term of the Court. A general description of the WESTLAW service can be accessed here.

 (Back to main Law Page)

"ready reference" device that permits easy access to frequently-requested legal materials and supports the librarians working at the reference desk.

Web vs. Catalog Capabilities

Limitations of the online catalog and the users' failure to understand the conventions of the catalog suggest an alternative method of supporting user access for a specialized field such as legal research. The Web page format allows great flexibility and easily supports presentation of sources in a subject-based context. The Web and hypertext mark-up language readily support presenting information on wide-ranging sources (electronic and hard copy) in one place. Descriptive text, lists of sources, locational information for hard copy and electronic sources, and hypertext links to other locally mounted documents, as well as to remote Internet sources, can all easily be presented in one place. This can be accomplished without burdensome programming demands. The University Libraries increasingly depend on this wide range of sources in different media for law as well as a number of other subject areas.

Critical Thinking Issues

The structure of the Law Page is designed to encourage critical thinking about the place of Internet resources within the research process, and about the sources and structure of American law. Students and other users "need to place the Internet in their mental model of information retrieval tools and develop proper strategies for fulfilling their information needs. Students must understand not only how to use the Internet, but also when it is appropriate and what problems they need to be prepared to deal with."[7] The Internet is not the only resource for law research, as the information contained in the Law Page makes clear. Students are stimulated to consider the most appropriate source for information, regardless of medium.

Students are also guided in their thinking about law itself. The body of the page represents three essential sources of law, constitutions, statutes, and cases, in a pattern echoed at federal and state levels. By having this model to emulate, students are able to fit their information needs into established categories and are able to better articulate their research problems. It also supports inferences about the nature of the sources. The segment of the page on U.S. Supreme Court decisions, for example, makes clear that there are multiple reporters for U.S. Supreme Court decisions, as well as electronic sources. Seeing these sources in a simple list, with explanations of the abbreviated reporter names, should even help students understand the concept of parallel citations.

The Law Page provides a cognitive structure for users who are unfamiliar with law resources. Without this structure, students have difficulty relating their questions and research problems to the disparate legal resources available.

Remote Access

Off-site access is made possible with the device of the Law Page. Online commercial legal research services (WESTLAW and Lexis) are only available through certain terminals at the University's Dewey Library. The number of simultaneous users is limited and these services can only be used on-site. The hypertext links in the page support student research from any site where Internet access is available. Only Internet traffic and host server capacity limitations would establish some ceiling on simultaneous users.

The Medium Sells the Message

Extensive news coverage of the Internet has stimulated great interest and students frequently express the desire to do their research "on the Internet." The Law Page attempts to exploit student interest in the Internet.

FUTURE DEVELOPMENTS

The Law Page in its current form is quite limited in scope. The range of possible areas for expansion is enormous. Part of the rationale for the page is, however, to provide support to relatively inexperienced researchers. Expanding the page into very specialized areas would not be consistent with this underlying objective. There certainly are some additions to the page which would be consistent with its purposes and rationale.

One possible addition would be to include an international/foreign law segment. This segment might include a link to one of the Internet sources for the constitutions of the nations of the world. Another possibility would be a link to the Fletcher School's server of multilateral treaties at Tufts University. Links could also be included to frequently requested documents such as the North American Free Trade Agreement (NAFTA). This segment would also lend itself to enumeration of some of the important paper sources in our collections for foreign constitutions, treaties and international agreements.

Another possible addition would be a segment providing a telnet hypertext link to one of the computer assisted legal research (CALR) services, such as WestLaw. Such a link would entail password access and require a substantially expanded service contract with one of the CALR services.

CONCLUSION

The creation of such a subject-specific resource should, of course, raise questions about the role of these Web pages in libraries. Is a device such as the Law Page simply a more labor-intensive substitute for a paper handout? The Law Page's annotations, with call numbers and lists of hardcopy sources, in many ways merely reiterate information already available in the online catalog. Can we support this duplication of effort? Such a device may also be seen as competing with the online catalog and further encouraging our patrons' disinclination to become more proficient in their use of that research tool. There is, however, some indication of an increasing awareness that, with the growth of new electronic resources, "the old model of a single, comprehensive catalog containing bibliographic descriptions of the library's resources becomes increasingly outmoded."[8]

The Law Page represents a somewhat experimental approach to supporting and teaching research in a specific subject matter area. Its value and usefulness will ultimately have to be judged by our users.

NOTES

1. Dorothy F. Byers and Lucy Wilson, "Library Instruction Using Mosaic," in *Proceedings of the 16th National Online Meeting*, ed. Martha E. Williams (Medford, NJ: Learned Information, 1995):47-52.

2. Judith M. Pask and Carl E. Snow, "Undergraduate Instruction and the Internet," *Library Trends* 44 (Fall 1959):306-317.

3. Paul G. Shotsberger, "Instructional Uses of the World Wide Web: Exemplars and Precautions,"*Educational Technology* 36 (March-April 1996):47-50.

4. Michael Engle, "Library Research at Cornell: A Hypertext Guide." 1996. [URL: http://urislib.library.cornell.edu/tutorial.html].

5. Jennie Sandberg, "Introduction to Library Research: Psychology 9.00," 1995. [URL: http://nimrod.mit.edu/depts/humanities/bi/900/].

6. Esther Grassian, "Thinking Critically about World Wide Web Resources," 1995. [URL: http://www.ucla.edu/campus/computing/bruinonline/trainers/critical.html]. Ann Scholz, "Evaluating World Wide Web Information," 1996. [URL: http://thorplus.lib.purdue.edu/research/classes/gs175/3gs175/evaluation.html].

7. Pask and Snow, "Undergraduate Instruction and the Internet," 311.

8. Gale M. Daly, "Bibliographic Access to Legal Research Databases Reconsidered," *Law Library Journal* 87, no. 1 (Winter 1995): 199.

The Information Navigation System: A Web-Based Instruction and Reference Tool

Robert F. Skinder

SUMMARY. Today's instruction and reference librarians face new challenges as the gatekeepers to information. The information explosion requires that we create strategies for our customers to navigate through a maze of material. This paper describes a reference tool developed at The Johns Hopkins University Applied Physics Laboratory to meet the information needs of our researchers and offers practical advice to other librarians interested in providing a similar service. *[Article copies available for a fee from The Haworth Document Delivery Service: 1-800-342-9678. E-mail address: getinfo@haworth.com]*

KEYWORDS. Internet, Information Navigation System, INS, Internet Reference System

The fate of reference services in today's libraries is uncertain. Our colleagues at another Johns Hopkins University facility, the Welch Medical Library, offer this thoughtful analysis of the reference function over the past decade:

Robert F. Skinder (rskinder@tcl.sc.edu) is Reference Librarian at the Science Library, Thomas Cooper Library, The University of South Carolina, Columbia, SC 29208. He was previously Reference Librarian at the R.E. Gibson Library and Information Center, The Johns Hopkins University Applied Physics Laboratory.

[Haworth co-indexing entry note]: "The Information Navigation System: A Web-Based Instruction and Reference Tool." Skinder, Robert F. Co-published simultaneously in *Internet Reference Services Quarterly* (The Haworth Press, Inc.) Vol. 2, No. 2/3, 1997, pp. 143-161; and: *The Challenge of Internet Literacy: The Instruction-Web Convergence* (ed: Lyn Elizabeth M. Martin) The Haworth Press, Inc., 1997, pp. 143-161. Single or multiple copies of this article are available for a fee from The Haworth Document Delivery Service [1-800-342-9678, 9:00 a.m. - 5:00 p.m. (EST). E-mail address: getinfo@haworth.com].

Reference as a separate organizational entity will become less and less important. Instead, "Information Services" will include individuals who spend a relatively small percentage of their time on traditional reference tasks, but instead focus on design of new systems, services and educational programs. Such services will increasingly be provided for remote users.[1]

We at The Johns Hopkins University Applied Physics Laboratory (APL) have been affected by the same forces and have come to a similar conclusion (if not similar solutions); namely, end users will be far better served if we help them perform all manner of research by themselves. The staff at the Welch Library have chosen to educate their clientele, whereas APL librarians are more focused on delivering information tools to our researchers' desktops. This paper will examine the reasons behind our approach, describe the large-scale Web-based reference tool we developed to meet the needs of our end users, and detail the implementation of the program at APL.

BACKGROUND

The Applied Physics Laboratory is a separate and distinct entity within The Johns Hopkins University system. For over 50 years, APL has worked with and for the Navy to develop prototype systems and then transition them to private industry. In 1957, while America marveled at Sputnik, scientists at APL observed and timed it, developing the prototype for what we now know as the Global Positioning System. This, along with an earlier focus on captured V-2 rockets, prepared the Laboratory for its work in space. In addition to defense and space work, APL is actively involved in such areas as transportation, bioengineering, and modeling and simulation. At any given time, staff members are working for many different sponsors on about 200 active tasks ranging from acoustics to X rays and on projects spanning deep sea oceanography to experiments being performed by the Hubble Telescope and the Galileo Probe.

About 2700 people work at the Laboratory; 70% are members of the professional staff. Of the professional staff, 18% hold doctorates, 56% have master's degrees, and 21% have bachelor's degrees. Most (52%) staff are concentrated in the engineering field, with others in math and computer science (22%) and physics and chemistry (21%).

The Laboratory is located in a rural setting midway between Washington, DC, and Baltimore, Maryland. More than 140 experimental laboratories are housed in approximately 50 buildings on about 350 acres.

The R. E. Gibson Library and Information Center serves the entire Laboratory as well as the Hopkins evening engineering school, the largest in the nation. In the summer of 1993, the Library underwent a major reorganization based on the findings of various reviews, core studies, and focus groups. Although all library staff were affected, the reference department experienced the most significant changes.

Before the reorganization a professional librarian was always on duty at the reference desk. Under the new organization, trained reference assistants would perform the desk duty all day, including answering staff questions and providing instructional information on the various tools available which, at the time, consisted of connections to our and other online public access catalogs (OPACs) and CD-ROMs.

The professional reference librarians received a new mandate: There is a large amount of information available and there is a lot of information needed by researchers in this Laboratory. Find a better way to bring them together.

Between the summer of 1993 and the fall of 1994 certain drivers were becoming operational.

- The information explosion was starting to rumble; an increasing number of OPACs were becoming interconnected, and CD-ROMs were proliferating.
- Studies clearly indicated that our clients had a strong interest in becoming end users.
- The reference staff sensed an opportunity to contribute, but didn't know quite how.
- In September 1993, NCSA (the National Center for Supercomputer Applications) released working versions of Mosaic browsers for all common platforms: X, PC/Windows, and Macintosh (W3C, 1995[2]). We saw our first copy in 1994.

In retrospect, the introduction of those Mosaic browsers was quite similar to progressing from radio to television overnight.

One idea that did emerge as a result of these forces was a HyperCard stack called the Electronic Librarian, an attempt to develop a scheme using some form of artificial intelligence to guide the users to the appropriate tools to meet their research requirements. (Two previous schemes, called the Personal Reference Information System Manager [PRISM], had the same goal. PRISM was the subject of an unfunded proposal.)

The Electronic Librarian, as well as its previous versions, was intended to be used on the local area network, under the assumption that every Macintosh user at APL could access one of these systems. The HyperCard stack was ideally suited for this type of application. For those not familiar with HyperCard, it was an application that came packaged with earlier Macintosh computers. It worked by building a stack of cards, each of which pointed to at least one other card. It was fairly simple and allowed the users to hide address codes behind words which, when touched, would take them to another card containing additional information. A card asked the user if he or she wanted information from journals, from books, or from technical reports. If journals were chosen, the user would be directed to several CD-ROM titles. If Inspec was selected, the user would then be given the choice of going to the CD-ROM itself or receiving instruction on its use. (Interestingly, Tim Berners-Lee used a similar approach, leading to the invention the World Wide Web.) Incidentally, we never actually implemented any of these systems. The latest version was shelved when we heard that our incoming OPAC would perform many of the same tasks we envisioned for the Electronic Librarian.

Coincidentally, while these HyperCard developments were under way, we were becoming more aware of the Internet. The supervisor of the reference section was already offering several classes and seminars related to it. These typically involved locating a colleague's e-mail address or finding a government program that might provide funding. Tools such as the gophers Archie and Veronica were explained. One could also search for books at several libraries around the world. At this time, however, the potential of the Internet was far from clear to us.

Again, based on the mandate given to the reference staff as well as the information needs of the APL staff, we were anxious to develop a new library tool that would optimize our clients' access to and use of a burgeoning information base. The ability of the library staff to create such a tool was due, in large part, to their adeptness at hyper (nonlinear) thinking.

CREATING ORDER OUT OF CHAOS

Issues

Development of our reference tool was triggered by the creation of the R. E. Gibson Library and Information Center home page. At that time, we had two standard choices. The most common was to use the home page to showcase our many services. Another approach was to use it to point APL staff to some useful sources. We chose a modified version of the second approach; we used the home page as the site to mount pointers to all useful external Internet information. What would make our approach different, however, was our concept of linking many sources of information, an idea that emerged from the design of PRISM and the Electronic Librarian. (Our development process is presented in detail in Note 3.)

From personal experience and conversations with our clientele, we found that we were dealing with two major issues. First, the Internet, even in early 1994, was very large, growing rapidly, and in flux. Second, because of these complexities, our users were adrift and thereby losing interest in the Internet. The Laboratory's busy researchers definitely did not have the time to "surf the 'Net." How could we use our training as librarians to help our colleagues navigate through the maze of information? Kovacs et al.[4] summarize the issue: "Our professional role has traditionally been to identify resources, enhance modes of access to them, and enable users to connect with, and use, appropriate sources. Network resources provide an opportunity for us to extend ourselves professionally within this new medium to provide meaningful service to our users." Based on our earlier experiments, we felt that we had the wherewithal to accomplish exactly that.

We faced several other difficult issues during the design phase.

> Despite the similarity in function and sometimes in form among network resources and traditional information sources, users are often intimidated by this network medium. What is available? Where is it? How do I get to it? Once obtained, the sheer quantity of information that can be, and is, stored in electronic form confronts users with the need to filter and organize it for personal use.[4]

Our solution was to design and introduce a personal Web-based reference tool specifically to point APL staff to tools available on the Internet that would help them to do their daily work, whether they were accountants or nuclear physicists. Because we envisioned this tool as one of guidance, and because of APL's history with navigational devices, we named it the Information Navigation System (INS). (The URL for the INS is http://lib2.jhuapl.edu/APL/ins/ins.html.)

Design

The main purpose of the INS is to segregate our users from everything on the Internet that is not related to their jobs. We do this in the same manner and spirit that we choose technical and scientific titles for the library. In addition to this filtering capability, we carefully select the material that goes into each section of the INS. Again, as librarians, we also provide order to our system, arranging material by subject and/or format and evaluating the material implicitly (by including the information) or explicitly (by appending editorial comments to the pointer).

Our users reach the INS via the APL home page, which points to both internal servers and external resources. The opening page of the INS has evolved from a simple hypertext document to a combination of frames and tables and will continue to evolve as new applications and versions of the html language are introduced. In general, all of the resources available on the Internet to APL staff are broken down into three distinct categories:

1. Useful Information Resources, which are divided in many ways
2. Search Tools, where we list and evaluate a wide range of search engines
3. Communication Tools, which connect to external sources of information dealing primarily with listservs and newsgroups

Each category will be described in more detail and reduced to its components as we proceed.

Useful Information Resources

In many ways, this section is the direct descendant of the Electronic Librarian. It also demanded the most thought and discussion during the planning stages of the INS, since it involved assessing our users' Internet needs, determining how to meet those needs, and finding out what was available on the Internet that related to the mission of APL. Resources are further divided into Library Tools, APL Subjects, and Important Locations.

Library Tools

Of course we were already using OPACs as a result of our previous HyperCard exercises. Although we could easily find and save library sites we had located on the Internet, it was harder to determine the usefulness of a particular site to our researchers and whether our patrons would be able to access the remote collection. We did provide a connection to Hytelnet, a valuable source of information in this regard.

OPACs are arranged in a logical, outward progression: our own server first, then other Hopkins libraries, other technical libraries, followed by all federal and university libraries.

In addition to the OPACs, Library Tools contains two other sections: the Electronic Reference Desk and the Electronic Journal Collection. Originally each section had its own page upon which items were listed as we found them. As the number of entries increased in both categories, organization was at first alphabetical but eventually new categories were formed. This resulted in as many as a dozen new pages being developed at once. It became obvious that standardized pages were critical. We had neither the time nor the inclination to create every page by hand. (We obtained many of these original reference and journal URLs from various library sites with their own electronic reference collections, the University of California at Irvine being one of the most memorable.) We also pointed directly to collections that were already complete such as those found at the University of Michigan's School of Information and Library Science (SILS). The Electronic Reference Desk now contains the following pages (* denotes pages from the SILS Internet Public Library Project):

- Astronomy Ready Reference*

- Chemistry Ready Reference*

- Courses On Line

- Dictionaries, Thesauri, Handbooks, etc.

- Directories

- Economics and Finance

- Internet Information

- Medical Information

- Patent Information

- Physics Ready Reference*

- Politics and Government

- Reference and Interdisciplinary Information

- Scientific Constants from Yahoo

- Travel, Maps and Geography

Although we found no need to examine our electronic reference sources, this was not the case with the Electronic Journal Collection. We soon found that many universities and commercial enterprises had extensive lists, but these were most often URLs to advertise paper copies. We quickly established four criteria for journal inclusion: they had to be relevant to APL's mission, had to be free, had to include some sort of search engine/device, and had to output an abstract at a minimum.

Given the nature of APL's mission, we have been pleased with the availability of various journal preprints, beginning with Physics and its various subsets and expanding into Mathematics as well as the new Oceanographic and Atmospheric preprints. We are looking forward to following the preprint trend along with the entire field of electronic scholarly publishing. These initiatives are extremely important to our researchers, whose technological limits are being pushed while budgets are being reduced.

As mentioned earlier, the original HyperCard Electronic Librarian had at its core connections to our networked CD-ROMs. So far we have been unable to make the connection via the INS. It is not an impossible task but there are more expedient ways to accomplish the same goal. This would certainly have been a particularly nice addition to our Library Tools section. We do, however, include connections to CARL UnCover, which is appreciated and well used.

APL Subjects

This is perhaps the most important portion of the Useful Information Resources section of the INS. Remember, one of our paramount concerns for developing a system such as the INS was that our researchers found the Internet too large and too easy to get lost in. Our original design called for us to construct a filter that would exclude the vast mass of information available. (Initially we felt that this might constitute a benign form of censorship, but no complaints ever materialized.)

Numerous access points to the full Internet reside both within the INS and beyond its scope, and most users seem grateful for the guidance that the system does provide. We explain it as being analogous to our print collection; i.e., no novels, no art history.

We now have about 25 subject categories; 8 are under Science, 9 under Technology, and the remainder under Administration (e.g., business, library science, law, technical writing). All subject pages are not alike; some fields simply have more resources available, we may perceive interest in a particular area and not in another, and certain areas may overlap.

Our Physics page represents our opinion of an optimum application of the INS. The page contains the following sections:

1. Physics reference desk, quick look-up materials
2. Journal collection, pointer to our Physics journals and preprint page
3. Search tools (only those specialized for the subject)
4. Lists and virtual libraries, divided into general and subtopics
5. Societies, pointers to home pages, and collections
6. Government agencies that would be of interest to our researchers
7. Electronic discussion groups, listservs (subscription information), and newsgroups (connections to)

Eventually we hope to standardize all pages to reflect what we consider to be the optimum design.

Important Locations

The Important Locations section evolved again as a filtration device. Beginning as a collection of pointers to companies that have a relationship with APL, the list expanded to include similar laboratories, universities, archives (including software collections), and professional societies in addition to what we have categorized as Government and Military Servers as well as Thrust Areas.

The government has been extremely active in promoting agency home pages. Since APL specializes in solving problems of a national scope, we naturally developed pointers to many federal sites. There are so many, in fact, that we separated the government resources from other locations. This was a fairly easy task, since we are frequently simply pointing to someone else's list. It also eliminates the need to perform continuous updates.

A fairly recent innovation combining subjects and locations (and perhaps other preexisting areas) of the INS is pages dedicated to "Thrust Areas, " i.e., areas of interest to APL and our sponsors as well as cutting-edge technologies. These pages generally do not fall within one or even two subject areas, and the locations that would be of interest could be drawn from a very wide field. Each Thrust Area is handled differently. Whether a Thrust Area is given a page on the INS depends largely on the amount of external information available on the Internet and, of course, the amount of interest we perceive in the particular area.

Search Tools

The second component of the INS is a section dealing with search tools. Whereas the Useful Information Resources section points our users to known sites, libraries, laboratories, etc., Search Tools allows them to query the entire Internet to discover sites that we have not identified.

So many search engines are available that one might look back fondly on the days of Archie and Veronica. Despite their number, however, we have found that none seems able to meet all the needs of our clients. Our approach to meeting those needs has been to collect all tools that present a reasonable set of results. We then break these down into categories: General, Subject, Organizational, and Government. Subject and Organizational, obviously, are peculiar to our situation.

In keeping with our traditions and inclinations, we append editorial comments to each product listed. Our goal in doing so is to educate our users as to the differences among the various search engines. We want them to consider using several search engines, at least until they understand the strengths and weaknesses of each and can make an informed final choice.

In addition to collecting and annotating search engines, the INS attempts to carry the process a step forward by locating tools that are not so well known and then placing the devices in strategic locations where they will be of use. The NASA Tech Report search engine is grouped with Specialized Tools, but can also be found in Space and Aviation Subjects and under Government Agencies. The SPIE search engine will be found under Search Tools as well as Engineering and Photo-Optics.

Communication Tools

In the final section, Communication Tools, we provide our users with ways to interact with their colleagues via the Internet. This section will continue to evolve as long as outside sources continue to improve their compilations. Our goal here is simply to connect information seekers with another resource, with their colleagues, etc., either through listservs or newsgroups. We use Tile.Net/Lists[5] for the listservs and the Clearinghouse for Subject-Oriented Internet Resource Guides for the newsgroups.[6]

We place some Communication Tools in their respective Subject or Thrust Areas as well, particularly if they have achieved prominence or are the only one for a particular subject.

FULFILLING OUR MANDATE

The previous discussion focused on part of our mandate: managing the large amount of information available on the Internet. The second part of that mandate involved finding a better (and implicitly, cheaper) way to bring our customers and the information together.

Although the INS (and the Internet) can recover documents from remote sites, its principal value is as a reference tool and, more particularly, a reference tool intended for the researcher, not the reference librarian. One section of the Electronic Reference Desk, for example, is entitled Travel, Maps and Geography. This section was designed specifically for the APL staff member who is told quite suddenly to prepare for a trip to any place on the globe. Here the user can find travel information, weather forecasts, currency exchange rates, subway maps, train schedules, etc., without the aid of the librarian.

As another example, suppose the researcher is interested in seismic profiles of a portion of the North Atlantic. Very likely he or she could find and download the needed data courtesy of one of the many institutes now attempting to make all such databases universally accessible. With the INS, the user can search for such data by going to the Oceanographic section under Subjects, NOAA, or the U.S. Geological Survey under Government Agencies. Other options are to select Oceanography under Archives or to leave the INS and try one of the several search tools or lists (e.g., Yahoo, Einet). As mentioned earlier, a patron can also quickly connect to a listserv or newsgroup and talk to real experts, who are more than willing to share their knowledge. I can imagine no other forum that offers such capabilities, year long, no matter where the user is located.

We have developed other strategies for helping our clients find the information they need. To meet the growing demand for Internet training, a team of librarians, educators, writers, and computer specialists was formed to develop course material. A fortuitous discovery was made at this point: the INS would provide an excellent framework for teaching the course since we had already filtered out all unnecessary resources, identified valuable sources, and assembled all relevant Internet research tools in one place. (The classroom effort is described in detail in Note 7.)

Two of the reference librarians teach the course entitled Introduction to the Internet. In it, we provide numerous examples and exercises that pose a legitimate research question as well as the answers that the students might not find in any library. For example, we ask: "See what you can find out about the military using modeling and simulation." "Where are the real hot beds of activity?" "What is North Central University doing with M&S?" "Can you find a person there that we can deal with?" Answers to these questions are readily available to our users after only a few hours of instruction.

We demonstrate applications with examples pertinent to numerous departments and employment levels at APL. Most examples use a version of this scenario: You are a new engineer or secretary in the _____depart-ment. Your supervisor wants you to find out about _____technology and what the_____Agency is doing with it. We then take the students to sample sites where they can get a good understanding of an APL-related subject, look at other applications, and find out how to contact personnel with an interest.

The results of our efforts to find ways to bring information and researcher together more effectively have been encouraging. After 17 classes with a maximum of 10 students in each, our usage figures for the INS have at least quadrupled. Most importantly, many students have referred their supervisors and coworkers to the class.

Another benefit derived from our reference setup is the cost savings. Hardly a day passes when we have not discovered a new Internet tool that is comparable to, if not better than, print or CD-ROM products. Numerous Internet-based journals, directories, map products, and search engines are available free of charge. Our application of the Electronic Reference Desk and Electronic Journals Collection, therefore, has allowed us to save several thousands of dollars.

EVOLUTION OF THE INS

Making Refinements to the System

The INS was built upon our experience gained developing the Electronic Librarian using HyperCard. The main categories still exist, but instead of pointing to additional pages that we have created, the earlier pages generally pointed to someone else's work. (Version no. 1 contained only 12 separate pages or files.) The first subject area had 7 pointers, whereas we now have about 25 fully developed pages, each with many pointers. The search tools in the original version would be unrecognizable to many who use the Internet regularly: the appearance of the pages was quite poor, our illustration at the top of the page was little more than a copy of the library's letterhead, and our skill with html was abysmal. It was, however, a start.

We overcame some minor problems as well. For example, the original name of our reference tool, Information Navigation System, was chosen because APL specializes in navigation. We tried to incorporate satellites as part of the system. It was simply too remote an image for most people to grasp. We eventually dropped the satellites and named sections what they actually were; e.g., Navigation Satellites became Useful Information Resources.

We had also planned to update the system once a month, but as the number of pages increased and as the Internet itself expanded, updating was delayed by almost 6 months. Today, with access to the Laboratory server, we can update the INS on a daily basis. I found it easier and faster to keep a working folder on my desktop, make the changes to that folder, and then transfer the information to the server.

Since the INS was introduced, we have occasionally added a page, and updating has been fairly continuous. The biggest changes over time have been (1) the evolution of both the reference pages and the electronic journals into dozens of pages and (2) creation of the thrust areas. The former was a developmental issue; the latter was done in reaction to a perceived need not initially defined.

The INS has recently undergone changes based on the technological advances made possible by Netscape and html 2 and 3. In early 1996, we introduced tables, frames, and colors to our pages. Internet users are very conscious of almost daily advances occurring in this field and can spot dull pages easily.

The first departure from html 1 involved Tables. It allowed us to organize our entire table of contents on one page rather than viewing the five or six broad areas originally shown on our opening page. Our next effort was with Frames, which allowed us to put our table of contents on one-fourth of the page so that the users always know exactly where they are and can navigate quickly to another area. We have used colors primarily to offer an alternative to Internet gray and secondarily to color-code certain areas; i.e., all subject pages are one color, those in the journal section are another, etc. It is also possible for one table of contents to point to another. Our initial table of contents will reveal other subgroups (e.g., subjects) when that category is selected.

Interestingly, all of these innovations evolved from non-INS work. They have instead resulted from our customers' requests and in-house requirements to display technical achievements across the Laboratory.

Our perception of the system has also evolved. The intent of our original design was to use the system as a filtering agent to protect APL staff from a vast wilderness of data. We now have two other images of the system; one views the INS as a physical library offering different services to different levels of user, and the other views it as a corporate bookmark.

As a physical library, users may come to our facility as they would in the fourth grade to write a paper on a given subject. For example, they will look up "boats" in the card catalog or the OPAC and then copy the entry from an encyclopedia. By the time they reach graduate school, they are ready to tackle a design worthy of the America's Cup; they already know that the library has useful materials, but they can now take advantage of a more specialized approach. That strategy is to use search tools, have searches done for them, obtain materials from around the world via interlibrary loan, and perhaps even use the library's computer to talk with international experts. So in this framework, the INS is not merely a repository of sites and resources but also a full set of tools to get more information.

To accomplish our second vision–to use the INS as a corporate bookmark–we are managing bookmarks for our clients by placing them in logical places where they can easily and quickly be located.

Customizing the INS

Many of our sponsors are from the federal sector, and they are very conscious of the Internet. Departments within APL are now becoming involved in supplying some WWW documentation as part of their program deliverables. Although a given department may have its own writers and graphic designers, we have found that an automated reference system such as ours has considerable appeal to the user, particularly where long-distance communication or education is involved. The customized INS uses some parts of the existing design but can be tailored to the client's particular interests and requirements.

Study Rooms

For those unfamiliar with the term, a study room is generally an area set aside to compile information and to examine a particular prospect or idea. A company considering involvement in the electric automobile business, for example, might consider establishing such a tool. A team assigned to the study room would gather all available data and organize, eliminate, replace, and prioritize the information on a series of boards within the facility. As some ideas emerge, experts can be brought in to further refine the results until consensus is reached. This tool has been used successfully at APL. Our goal is to make these study rooms available to the entire staff via Web technology and in addition to link several such facilities together with a cross-indexing capability. Other potential applications include team learning and team teaching, with literally hundreds of documents being interconnected. We envision study rooms as one of the Laboratory's best information tools. As such, the library intends to maintain a leadership role in their application.

Digital Libraries

The term "digital libraries" refers to libraries of digitized material such as databases. At this point we are thinking primarily of populating the INS more completely with book-like materials that become available on the Internet and perhaps ultimately linking our OPAC and the INS to the same resources. Two examples of our foray into digital libraries which we maintain as part of the INS are the Electronic Reference Desk and the Electronic Journal Collection.

IT PAYS TO ADVERTISE

Users throughout the Laboratory, including our own librarians, did not rush to use the INS. We have been involved in a continuous program of publicizing the system and educating all APL staff in its applications.

In the spring of 1994, a committee of librarians was formed to publicize the arrival of our new on-line library system. That committee immediately increased its scope; they decided to hold an open house which would include all of the new library tools and services that would be coming available.

The theme of the open house, Total Access, reflected our goal: to make all (or almost all) library services accessible to every staff person at his or her workstation. Staff members would have access to OPACs (both ours and others), an appropriate suite of CD-ROMs, and search services. We placed 12 display areas throughout the library highlighting the new technologies and services. We also used this occasion to introduce the INS.

Our earliest efforts following the open house promotion involved publication of articles in our Branch newsletter, the Information Exchange. These articles describe innovative library services under titles like "What's New on the Internet?" and "Is There Real Information in the Internet?" We have also printed broadsides giving staff useful information such as points of contact within the library. In addition, we submit copy to publications generated by various APL departments whenever an opportunity presents itself.

As our program has become better known, we are invited to participate in an increasing number of seminars and workshops within the Laboratory. These have been both departmental and subject-related and are well worth our time so far as introducing the Internet and INS. Representing the library as a leader in information technology is also a plus. As more staff become familiar with the Internet and its resources, we will undoubtedly present fewer and fewer introductory-level Internet classes. Instead, future plans are to concentrate our efforts on specific groups (e.g., managers or engineers) and subject matters. These efforts will be much more focused and will certainly require more work on our part.

LESSONS LEARNED

The following section attempts to pass along some useful advice to the reader who may be contemplating developing a reference tool such as the INS. Two fundamental questions relative to undertaking the building of such a system are: (1) how much work is involved in such a project (including upkeep), and (2) how much of an Internet or html background is necessary to construct a similar device. The variables are obvious. The most important part of this undertaking is to win management support and then build a team to do the work. The reference staff of your library might benefit the most from this system, or you may have subject specialists in every section of your library, or you may even be a one-person staff.

If you were to adopt a scheme like the INS, you would find that most of the work has already been done for you. You can normally view or save any document as source which reveals the code and the URLs used. You might want to look at several systems or home pages of various organizations. You will probably find one that will suit your needs after you tailor the wording and the URLs to those needs. The two most difficult tasks are planning what you are going to do and then getting started. After that it's just a matter of librarianship: location, acquisition, organization, and dissemination.

The most important lesson learned is that a system such as ours is a continuously developing effort. Although it has been the work of one person at APL, it could involve several people; for example, one person could serve as coordinator/editor while others could contribute as subject or area specialists.

Once a framework has been established, maintenance should not be prohibitive. Listservs and newsgroups, if wisely selected, can provide a steady flow of resources. There are now emerging commercial and free link checkers. Although one has never been used with the INS, the adoption of such a tool will soon be a necessity.

The following pointers will make your task easier:

- If you believe that your system is going to consist of 1 home page and 5 linked pages, plan on 100 pages. The growth is insidious.
- Standardize everything. Make it easy on yourself and your staff.

- Plan on being your own missionary or salesperson, both to your clients and your supervisors. Do not simply view your work as building an Internet-based reference tool. Look at it as a complete program involving design, development, maintenance, education, and publicity.
- Do not be afraid to attempt a system like this.

The benefits of the INS to our customers are obvious. As reference librarians, we are in a position to make a significant contribution. "What reference librarians should be doing is information systems' design. Reference librarians are the natural designers of the new tools for information organization, access, retrieval and distribution: these are the functions we do best."[8]

CONCLUSION

The intent of this paper was to address several issues under the umbrella of developing a web site as a reference function. We began with the premise that the World Wide Web, in the Spring of 1994, was promising as a reference tool but needed much work to be of use to the scientists and engineers with whom we work. "Surfing the 'Net" was never an option.

Concept and Design of the INS

The librarians at JHU/APL had a distinct advantage because several of us had experimented with hyperlinked documents with prototype reference systems. Making the transition to html and Mosaic was relatively simple. In some cases we merely transferred tools from the prototype. In others we were exercising our training as librarians to determine what was available on the Internet that would be useful to our clientele. Since then we have continued to search for material, evaluate it and place it in useful locations.

The INS as a Reference Tool

This was both the basic idea of the INS as well as the purpose of this paper. My original enthusiasm for the Internet or WWW originated when I discovered that I could answer questions without leaving the Reference Desk. Since developing the INS we have seen a steady stream of new search tools come online but none seem to provide the total answer to every question. The INS provides an other way of looking for answers, particularly in those cases where the question might not be entirely clear, which is often the case in a research institution such as The Applied Physics Laboratory. One way that I think of the INS is as a personal reference collection in the office of each researcher.

The INS as a Training Tool

Some form of education seems to be very important in a program like this one. We were very pleased to discover that our INS made an excellent training device. Not only does it filter out all extraneous resources but includes the resources and tools that are of interest to our users. It is therefore a useful tool and a necessary one. We soon realized that the classes we taught using the INS resulted in an increase in the number of users. In addition to the one-day courses that we have taught, we have been asked to participate in several workshops and seminars, all of which provide increased visibility to our library group.

Spin-Off of the INS

There is something about the potential of html that cries out for new applications. In this paper we have looked at modified or specialized versions of the INS, electronic study rooms and the movement towards a type of digital library. Almost weekly we are consulted on variants of these and soon expect to see others emerge. The major breakthrough at this moment seems to be waiting for the technology that will allow software to perform a function initiated by the browser. Java provides a hint of what that will allow. Equally important is the increase of in-house resources which are now referred to as Intranet.

Evaluation of the System

At the time of this writing the INS has been in development for approximately 18 months. I have questioned its value many times. The one fact that always comes to the fore is that we have taken a new technology that is chaotic in some ways and by applying basic techniques of librarianship have opened up an enormous resource to our clientele. This is particularly telling in a time when budgets are shrinking and the cost of printed resources is increasing. The resources of the Internet are not just growing in number but also in scope. Everyday we see new ways to use and display data, make use of forms and incorporate multi-media into our presentations. Developing this system also provided a bonus in that it put the library into a prominent developmental role, one that will continue to bear fruit for some time. I consider it both important and fortuitous that I was allowed and encouraged to build this system.

NOTES

1. Brandt, K. K., Campbell, J. M., and Bryant, W. F., Jr., "Reflections on Reference Service." *Journal of the American Society for Information Science* 47:3 (March 1996):210-216.

2. W3 Consortium, Laboratory for Computer Science, Massachussetts Institute of Technology, "A Little History." http://www.w3.org/pub/WWW/History. html.

3. Skinder, R. F., and Gresehover, R. S., "An Internet Navigation Tool for the Technical and Scientific Researcher." *Online* 19:4 (July 1995):38-42.

4. Kovacs, D. K., Schloman, B. F., and McDaniel, J. A., "A Model for Planning and Providing Reference Services Using Internet Resources." *Library Trends* 42:4 (Spring 1994):629-647.

5. Walter Shelby Group Ltd., TileNet/Lists, copyright 1995-1996: http://www.tile.net/tile/listserv/index.html.

6. Argus Associates and the University of Michigan, "Clearinghouse for Subject-Oriented Internet Resource Guides." (1996) (online): http://www.lib. umich.edu/chhome.html.

7. DeBrower, A. M., and Skinder, R. F., "Designing an Internet Class for a Scientific and Technical Audience." *Special Libraries* 87:3 (1996):139-146.

8. LaGuardia, C., "Desk Set Revisited: Reference Librarians, Reality, & Research Systems' Design." *The Journal of Academic Librarianship* 21:1 (1995):7-9.

THE CHALLENGE OF SPECIFIC CONVERGENCES: INTERNET USER POPULATIONS

The Trash-Lacan Chat Room . . .

Katharine A. Waugh

The illustrator, Katharine A. Waugh (kawaugh@vaxsar.vassar.edu), is Reference Librarian, Vassar College Library, Poughkeepsie, NY 12601.

[Haworth co-indexing entry note]: "The Trash-Lacan Chat Room . . ." Waugh, Katharine A. Co-published simultaneously in *Internet Reference Services Quarterly* (The Haworth Press, Inc.) Vol. 2, No. 4, 1997, p. 163; and: *The Challenge of Internet Literacy: The Instruction-Web Convergence* (ed: Lyn Elizabeth M. Martin) The Haworth Press, Inc., 1997, p. 163. Single or multiple copies of this article are available for a fee from The Haworth Document Delivery Service [1-800-342-9678, 9:00 a.m. - 5:00 p.m. (EST). E-mail address: getinfo@haworth.com].

Internet Access
in School Library Media Centers

Nancy Everhart

SUMMARY. Internet access in schools should be provided via the school library media center. School library media specialists have sets of skills that allow the connection to the Internet to be made and utilized to its full potential. These skills include technical expertise in establishing and maintaining networks, experience in promoting and integrating new technologies in the educational process, and the ability to identify and evaluate information resources. Additionally, school library media specialists have knowledge and training in dealing with the issues of censorship and equity of access that accompany use of the Internet by school children. *[Article copies available for a fee from The Haworth Document Delivery Service: 1-800-342-9678. E-mail address: getinfo@haworth.com]*

KEYWORDS. Internet, school library media centers, school library media specialists, school children, integration of technology, information technology, instructional consulting, censorship

President Clinton, in his 1996 State of the Union Address, put forth the challenge that all schools be connected to the Internet by the year 2000. But where should this connection reside? The library media center, the

Nancy Everhart (nancye@postoffice.ptd.net) is Assistant Professor in the Division of Library and Information Science, St. John's University, 8000 Utopia Parkway, Jamaica, NY 11439.

[Haworth co-indexing entry note]: "Internet Access in School Library Media Centers." Everhart, Nancy. Co-published simultaneously in *Internet Reference Services Quarterly* (The Haworth Press, Inc.) Vol. 2, No. 4, 1997, pp. 165-184; and: *The Challenge of Internet Literacy: The Instruction-Web Convergence* (ed: Lyn Elizabeth M. Martin) The Haworth Press, Inc., 1997, pp. 165-184. Single or multiple copies of this article are available for a fee from The Haworth Document Delivery Service [1-800-342-9678, 9:00 a.m. - 5:00 p.m. (EST). E-mail address: getinfo@haworth.com].

information hub of the school, is the natural site for two important reasons. The Internet is simply another set of information resources that can complement those found in books and media already located there and school library media specialists have sets of skills that allow the connection to the Internet to be made and utilized to its full potential. These skills include technical expertise in establishing and maintaining networks whether they be local area networks or access to networks outside of the school, experience in promoting and integrating new technologies in the educational process to faculty and students via formal and informal training and the ability to identify and evaluate information resources, as well as teach these skills to students.

Many school library media centers today are fully automated. That is, they have automated circulation systems, OPACs, CD-ROMs, and perhaps access to online databases.[1] Some school library media centers may be hard to distinguish from small academic libraries. It is not unusual to find dozens of terminals in school library media centers as part of a local area network with access to an online catalog, magazine index, electronic encyclopedia, and other products. A natural extension of these networks is to have a menu option for the Internet whereby simultaneous use for students is possible, following the academic model and often referred to as a "supercatalog."[2]

To manage these supercatalogs and networks takes the technical expertise of the school library media specialist. In addition, technicians may be available at the media center, via county-wide support centers that provide on-call service through their technology office to maintain the network.

School library media specialists can provide support for teachers who want to use the Internet in their teaching much like they have in the past with other technologies. Using their skills in curriculum and instructional development, school library media specialists can provide inservice training, one-on-one consultation, instructional support materials, and help with locating beneficial Internet resources to teachers. Teachers can then further implement the Internet in the classroom with their students.

This third skill, that of identifying and evaluating information resources, is of particular importance. Even though children, in many cases, can be more technically proficient in navigating the Internet than adults, they may lack the ability to determine the quality of information they find. Indeed, as the Internet grows rapidly on a daily basis, this ability is one that is difficult even for adults to manage. Children will need the assistance of school library media specialists to guide them in the selection and evaluation of information available on the Internet much as they do with more traditional print sources.

This article will deal with Internet resources available for children, how these resources can be integrated into the total educational program and current and future concerns regarding this information technology all in relation to the school library media center.

EXAMPLES OF HOW TO USE INTERNET RESOURCES IN SCHOOLS

There are resources on the Internet that are specifically geared to children. Because children vary widely in their range of interests and abilities, there are also resources geared to adults that may be of use to children.

Electronic Mail

Electronic mail, or e-mail, is often a starting point for Internet users. Children can send and receive messages literally around the world. Some sample projects using electronic mail in the curriculum have been posted on the LM_NET listserv,[3] a discussion group for school library media specialists.

Science

Weather

Have students from all over e-mail the high and low temperature in their town for a certain day. Compile, post, and share.

Nutrition

Collect regional nutritious recipes that would be easy for kids to prepare. Find a class who would be interested in recording what each kid eats for dinner on one certain date. Both classes exchange results.

Social Studies

U.S. Facts

Collect greetings and one interesting fact from all the states and post on a U.S. map or bulletin board.

Planning Summer Vacations–Working on Map Skills and States

Collect information from a native's point of view. Ask them to tell you what we would like to see and do in their state. Also ask about interesting facts, places or events in their state that would not be found in an atlas, encyclopedia or almanac.

Newspaper

Publish a 4th grade global newspaper. Solicit articles from 4th graders in about 8 countries. Edit, assemble it, and e-mail it to numerous schools around the world.

Language Arts

Story Problem Book from Around the World

Collect story problems written by different classes. Story problems should be written to reflect the native character of the area the author(s) is from. An example would be: Many years ago Mr. Sharp planted 6 cotton-wood trees along the Green River in the town of Green River, Wyoming. Mr. Smith also planted 7 trees along the river. How many trees were planted by both men?

Newsgroups and Listservs

Newsgroups are electronic worldwide discussions about topics of common interest. There are thousands of newsgroups about almost any subject. They are ideal for browsing and reading at leisure.

Like newsgroups, listservs are also electronic groups that center around a common item of interest. The difference is that each electronic mail message sent to the listserv is automatically distributed to all of its members whereas a message to a newsgroup is posted only to a common bulletin board. Membership on listservs is free but if a child is interested in joining a listserv they must have an individual e-mail account. Newsgroups don't require individual accounts. Some newsgroups and listservs are quite active, generating over 100 separate messages per day.

Children can subscribe to appropriate listservs and read newsgroups for pleasure or research. By reading posted correspondence they can identify experts in their field of interest and later contact them individually if desired.

Some newsgroups cater directly to children such as k12.chat.elementary and alt.kids-talk. There are newsgroups for collectors of Barbie dolls, Lego sets, baseball cards, and coins. Teens can access newsgroups that keep them up to date on their favorite rock star or college sports team.

Gopher

Internet Gophers allow users to browse for resources using menus. They are ideal for children because they do not have to remember addresses of sites or utilize a list of commands to get what they want. Gophers can lead to all types of resources: online catalogs, WWW sites, publications, telnet sites, and mailing lists.

An interesting example of a Gopher for children (and educators) is "Best of K-12 on the Internet."[4] Virtually every subject area is covered in such links as: "Blind Children's Center," "Children's Literature Web Guide," "E-mail Pen Pal Connection," "Franklin Institute Science Museum," "Kid's Web–Digital Library for Schoolchildren," "KidPub–Children's Stories Published on the Web," "NASA SuperQuest Home Page," "The Homework Page," "Wild Geometry Page" and much, much, more. Many of these sites have links taking children to other sites, ad infinitium.

World Wide Web (WWW)

One of the simplest, and most exciting, ways for children to access information over the Internet is through the World Wide Web. Johnson provides a colorful description of the World Wide Web in the classroom:

> Imagine your class having access to the world's largest HyperCard or Linkway stack. Click on a highlighted word and hear F.D.R. intone, "We have nothing to fear but fear itself." See a satellite fly by Saturn. Watch as a high-resolution graphic slowly reveals the eyes of a huge gray wolf staring back at you. . . . Now imagine those "cards" being on computers scattered throughout the world. A click takes you to the White House in Washington, DC. The next click takes you to the Paleontology Museum in Berkeley, California. Next, you'll go to the Louvre in Paris, France. Virtual field trips like these and a host of other educational activities are possible with an Internet connection to the World Wide Web (WWW) and browsing software like Mosaic.[5]

Web sites are constantly changing. A good way to keep on top of the changes for schools is to check lists of updated pages such as *Classroom*

Connect's home page of "links to more than 300 of the Net's hottest, most useful educational World Wide Web sites"[6] which is updated twice weekly. Some examples cited in the September 1995 issue are:

Volcano World

http://volcano.und.nodak.edu

NASA's Volcano World contains timely updates about volcanic activity worldwide, historical eruption reports, information on how volcanoes work, and guidance on becoming a volcanologist. Also of interest is an online Web form you can use to sign up for the popular, year 'round Ask a Volcanologist Project.

The Tele-Garden

http://www.usc.edu/dept/garden/

This tele-robotic art site allows visitors to view and interact with a California garden filled with living plants. Children can plant, water, and monitor the progress of seedlings via the tender movements of an industrial robot arm. A class can plant a seed in September and watch it grow over the course of the school year via the Net!

Pathfinder

http://www.pathfinder.com

Pathfinder is an interactive link to Time Incorporated's publications including the latest week's issue of *Time*, *Sports Illustrated*, *Money*, and *Vibe*. There are full-text stories (and a searchable database of past articles) from more than a dozen other publications.

Big Dog Math

http://fedida.ini.cmu.edu:5550/bdf.html

Blue Dog is a friendly, intelligent dog on the World Wide Web. Fill in any basic math equation (such as $1 + 1$ or $12 - 10$) and Blue will bark the result through the computer's speaker.

Civil War Photograph Collection

http://rs6.loc.gov/cwphome.html

For students studying the Civil War, the Library of Congress-sponsored Civil War Photographs Collection contains more than 1,000 images, most of which include scenes of military personnel, preparations for battle, and battle after-effects. The collection also includes portraits of Confederate and Union officers and enlisted men.

The World Wide Web can be integrated into the curriculum as in the examples that follow.[7] Students can access these resources via the school library media center's Internet connection:

Science

Weather Prediction

Use a national weather service site on the Internet. Choose some different localities, and compare the predictions of the Internet site with the actual weather for a certain date.

Creating an Ecosystem

Students searching the Internet often locate names of scientific researchers who have offered their expertise to those needing specific information. A group of students studying global science were searching for information on the rain forests, in order to build their own ecosystem for a class project. Just completing a subject search using the webcrawling searching option on Netscape, found them a scientist researching the rain forests, who also happened to have an e-mail address. The students listed particular questions, and sent their message directly to the researcher. His responses were sent the next day to the one of the students' e-mail address.

Social Studies

Current Events

Have students access the new CNN, and Casper Star web site to download articles for daily national, international, state, and regional current events to share at the beginning of each class session.

The Sixties

After determining a list of major events that reflected the time period between 1960 and 1970, students completed subject searches on the Internet. They found information on the Cold War, Kennedy's assassination, and Woodstock. They also found information on Woodstock's 25th anniversary festival, and were able to compare the two events through photos and film clips.

Wyoming Government

One requirement of Bill Thompson's senior government students at Green River High School, is to complete a search using the state server, Ferret. Students can find a list of state legislators, the governor and other state officials, to whom they can send e-mail messages. They are also able to follow the legislature, and the status of bills.

Language Arts

CARL

Access to the Colorado Alliance of Research Libraries allows students to search the library collection and the University of Wyoming, CARL, as well as many other major universities. Students can research the card catalog, as well as a periodical collection, and borrow materials for any subject via library loan.

Foreign Language

I have a student print out Spanish daily newspapers from Mexico, Costa Rica, Ecuador, and Madrid. The teacher loves it, the kids love reading about "El Bulls," y Miguel Jordan. It lets advanced students move ahead alone. It's a major hit, and not possible any other way.

Student Designed Web Pages

An almost natural evolution on the Internet is student produced materials. Hotlist, Kids Did This! is a starting point for links to student produced Web Pages and school servers.[8] Students as young as fourth graders have designed their own Web Pages using HTML programming. These projects have included student newspapers, art exhibitions, stories, curriculum projects, and electronic portfolios.

If students make Web pages as part of school projects and cannot put them online because their school does not have a Net-connected computer or the money to place them online, they can submit them to the Classroom Web Project.[9] Over 150 schools have mounted pages at the site. *Classroom Connect* is a K-12 educator's guide to using the Internet and other online services with children.

A CASE STUDY

Brandon Taylor is an eight-year-old third grader. He takes a seat at the family's Macintosh II si and prepares to log-on the World Wide Web. The system he is using is equipped with a color monitor, 28,800 baud FAX modem, scanner, laser printer, external CD-ROM, and Sony speakers. When he turns the computer on, a photo of himself pops on the screen, along with that of his four year-old brother, Michael. Brandon clicks on his photo and the computer asks him for his password. He enters it correctly and his father's voice rewards him with, "Welcome to the computer, Brandon!"

Next to the computer sits an elementary school composition book with a black and white marbleized cover containing directions on how to access the commercial service to which his family subscribes. (See Figure 1.) Brandon doesn't need to use it, as he is very adept at pulling down the correct menu bars, pointing, and clicking to get where he wants to go. With some pride he announces, "My mom doesn't know how to use this yet." Utilizing the Netscape program he clicks on the "Bookmarks" portion of the menu bar. Up pops a listing of Brandon's favorite Web sites giving hint to his interests—monsters, oceanography, exploration, movies, and reading. There are Bookmarks for The Great White Shark, Mummies, the Bermuda Triangle, Disney, Jurassic Park, Dinosaurs, Batman, R.L. Stine-Goosebumps, Godzilla, Alien, Seaquest, Congo, Star Wars, Indiana Jones, National Geographic Society, Discovery Channel, MMPR, the White House, and Apollo 13.

Perhaps his favorite Web site is the JASON Project. The JASON Project chronicles the underwater exploration activities of Dr. Robert Ballard, discoverer of the Titanic and Bismarck. Brandon developed an interest in the Titanic when he was about six years old. Reading voraciously on the subject, he found out about Ballard. Research in the library uncovered information about the JASON Project, including Ballard's address. All this led to a personal response from Ballard to Brandon's letter and a visit to the project site by the Taylor family.

FIGURE 1. Third Grader's "Favorite Web Site" Listing with Directions for Access

Pacman: up-8 down-2 over 6 over 4 To Stop Shift 🔲 A

Encyclopedia: Hindenburg, titanic, the ark, Sharks, Dinosaurs, Lochness monster, Mummy, egypt, Bermuda triangle.

World Wide Web: the ark, titanic, Jason Project, Bismarck, Great white Shark mummies, Bermuda triangle, Disney, Jurassic Park, Dinosaurs, Batman, R.L. Stine's Goosebumps, Nessie, Godzilla, Alien, Aliens, Alien³, Seaquest, The chase, Carmen Sandiago: Name, enter, to stop push power Yes.

More WWW Go on apple and pull down to Prolog and let go. When your on Prolog push icon. Go back and pull it down to Netscape and let go. Here ars some more sights, Congo, Godzilla, Atlantis, Star Wars, and X-files.

Another example of how Web sites can fuel a child's interest is the Apollo 13 page. Brandon went to the movie and began accessing the page. He found out there that the Discovery Channel would be airing, "Crisis in Space," the true story of Apollo 13. He has replayed the video of that show again and again. Brandon's next step is developing his own Web Page that will include his favorite book and movie lists, among other things.

Luckily for Brandon he has parents that have both the knowledge and financial resources to get him onto the Information Superhighway. His father is a newspaper editor who uses the Internet in his work, and his mother is a teacher. The family values educational opportunities and because they do Brandon has access to something most of his classmates do not. The Internet is not available in his school or public library. The only access in the town is through the commercial provider, which has been installed for about six months.

EQUITY OF ACCESS

There are issues of equity of access when some children, like Brandon, arrive at school already skilled in obtaining and using information, and other children have no access to this information:

> Another serious question related to the assumption that students arrive at school already skilled in obtaining and using information is, Who actually has access to the database? In a democratic society, will everyone in all walks of life be able to use any database? Or will there be an information elite who have all the information they want and others who are locked out? In discussions of national and international information networks, the illustration is sometimes made of the child who will use electronic information for learning at home. Do we actually expect that all children will be able learn in this way? Will there not be children who lack the necessary equipment and others who lack the necessary skills? A librarian must assume the responsibility of guarding the right to know for those who are likely to be "locked out" of the database.[10]

School library media specialists are challenged in the latest guidelines for school media programs, *Information Power,* "to ensure equity and freedom of access to information and ideas, unimpeded by social, cultural, economic, geographic, or technologic constraints."[11] This is quite a formidable task given the socioeconomic range that exists in the United States today both in and out of the schoolhouse. A recent *Time* magazine issue, devoted to cyberspace, reports: "wealthier school districts naturally tend to have equipment that is unavailable to poorer ones, and schools in the more affluent suburbs have twice as many computers per student than their less-well-funded urban counterparts."[12]

A case in point is the Dalton School in New York City, one of the nation's wealthiest private schools. They provide their students with a wide array of Internet curriculum related activities. Almost routinely, students in classes access online text and visual databases, work in collaborative learning groups around a computer, send e-mail to friends and teachers, and participate in online discussions and conferences. For example, one 10th-grade English class compares various images of Lady Macbeth by artists and in films via an online database while a senior-class seminar debates civil rights in an online discussion group. Contrast this to a neighboring school in Queens where 60 percent of teachers had no access to telecommunications within their schools.[13]

CENSORSHIP

The Telecommunications Law of 1996 contains a provision called the Communications Decency Act (CDA) stating children should not have access to "indecent" or "patently offensive by contemporary community standards" materials via the Internet. This is currently being challenged in court by ALA and other groups as a form of censorship and violation of First Amendment Rights.[14]

Newsgroups and discussion lists that deal with sexually explicit topics are the most obvious targets for censorship efforts. But there are other examples:

> The School Stopper's Textbook, for instance, tells how to short-circuit electrical wiring, set off explosives in school plumbing and break into your school at night and burn it down. The Big Book of Mischief features bombmaking instructions. Suicide Methods, based in part on Derek Humphry's book, Final Exit, comprehensively analyzes various ways of killing oneself. A drug archive offers recipes for marijuana brownies and a guide to constructing "bongs, pipes and other wonderful contraptions." Or, several archives and Usenet discussion groups hackers provide tips on breaking into computer networks, telephone systems and cash machines. Some Usenet groups contain pornographic stories, other have photos of naked men, women, and occasionally children.[15]

Software filtering programs, like SurfWatch, claim to screen out Web, gopher, and FTP sites that carry sexually explicit materials as well as some newsgroups and chat channels.[16] Even if there is only one resource at that site, everything at that site is blocked. The filter may also be used as a positive one, whereby only those sites specifically chosen can be accessed.

A concern of some school library media specialists is that these types of programs, "give adults a false sense of security."[17] The Internet is growing so quickly that it is possible there will be sexually oriented pages available within hours after an update is done. SurfWatch updates its software, revising its list of blocked sites, once a month.

> There are technical reasons why censorship will not work. Any system of denying access to certain parts of the Internet can be defeated. Major corporations and governmental entities such as the Department of Defense have had expensive and sophisticated computer security systems violated by children and other hackers. One of the major problems with trying to deny portions of the Internet to children is that there are multiple routes to almost everything. Closing all possible routes is usually impossible short of completely shutting down use of the Internet, or continually monitoring every child's every telecommunications act. It may be possible to make it more difficult to access the most clearly objectionable material such as pornography or other obscene material, but an ingenious and determined child will probably find ways around such measures.[18]

Judith Krug, executive director of the American Library Association's Office for Intellectual Freedom, agrees with this view. She also comments on SurfWatch.

> I probably would not buy a mechanism like SurfWatch. I don't need a SurfWatch determining that certain materials, certain programs, certain music, certain whatever, is not appropriate for my children . . . The other thing that bothers me: You understand, of course, that at this point SurfWatch is not willing to tell us what groups they have eliminated. They consider this proprietary information. Now, [SurfWatch is] working out, from what I understand, some kind of give-and-take that will allow people to request some particular bulletin board, newsgroup, etc. to be unlocked. The reason I'm concerned about that is that at one point, [access to] anything dealing with gays or lesbians was also being eliminated [by SurfWatch] because that deals with sex. I mean, nobody who considers himself or herself part

of the gay community does anything except engage in sex, right? So that's one problem.[19]

Another censorship problem is that what is acceptable or objectionable is not usually a matter on which we can all agree. "For example, hunting may be objectionable to animal rights groups, and liberal ideas may be objectionable to conservatives, or vice versa. Should we therefore censor Internet interest groups on hunting or fishing, cooking groups that feature recipes that list meat as an ingredient, and those that deal with liberal or conservative causes?"[20]

Perhaps the most dangerous problem with censorship, is that parents may interpret censorship programs as an "implicit guarantee that their children will not be able to gain access to inappropriate material."[21] When the children do gain access they view this as a failure of the school rather than a failure of their own children to behave responsibly.

Issues of access and censorship have been addressed by Flanders[22] who surveyed school library media specialists regarding possible solutions. Strategies in place in some schools include training students using only those Internet resources with menus such as gopher servers, supervising all dial-in sessions with the Internet, parental permission forms, and signing contracts with technology codes of conduct. (See Figure 2.) Other solutions are forms students must fill out describing each on-line session, and using "smartcards" which record students' online movements for subsequent review by teachers.[23]

INTEGRATING INTERNET RESOURCES IN THE CURRICULUM

Simply having the Internet available in schools does not guarantee that it will be used in educationally appropriate ways. Teachers must be provided with curriculum support to maximize students' use of the Internet. "Those providing curriculum support should produce teaching materials such as documentation for both teachers and students; locate Internet resources of potential benefit; make suggestions about integrating these resources into the curriculum in various subjects at various grade levels; and provide inservice training aimed at facilitating this integration."[24]

Integrating the Internet with class projects allows teachers and media specialists to teach electronic information skills within the context of filling information needs. This need, along with teaching the skills within an overall process model, has been confirmed in the studies of Eisenberg and Berkowitz[25] and Kuhlthau[26] as being one of the most effective methods of information skills instruction. Eisenberg[27] provides suggestions in

FIGURE 2. Sample Technology Code of Conduct for Internet Usage

INTERNET USAGE GUIDELINES

Rights

Students have the right to access the Internet to facilitate diversity and personal growth in technology, information gathering skills, and communication skills.

Students have the right to use the following methods for retrieving information: File Transfer Protocol (FTP), Telnet, and Electronic Mail (e-mail).

Students have a conditional right to request newsgroups from the Internet in order to facilitate real-time learning with members of the network. Students have the conditional right to sign-up for Lists on the Internet.

Students have the unconditional right to send e-mail to any member on the network. This right does not require prior approval.

Responsibilities

The student exercising his/her right to use the Internet as an educational resource shall also accept the responsibility for all materials received under his/her user account. Only those students with prior experience or instruction shall be authorized to use the Internet.

Students have the responsibility to monitor all material received via the Internet under his/her user account.

Students will accept the responsibility of keeping all pornographic material, inappropriate text files, or files dangerous to the integrity of the network from entering the school via the Internet.

It is a student's responsibility to make all subscriptions to newsgroups and Lists known to the technology facilitator. Approval is required by the technology facilitator prior to requesting a newsgroup and/or List from the network.

It is a facilitator's responsibility to maintain the privacy of students' electronic mail. The faculty has the responsibility to include a student in all acts of viewing, modifying, or removing that student's electronic mailbox.

It is a student's responsibility to maintain the integrity of the private electronic mail system. The student has the responsibility to report all violations of privacy. Students are responsible for all mail received under his/her user account. Students have the responsibility to make only those contacts leading to some justifiable personal growth on the Internet. The student is responsible for making sure all e-mail is received by him/her does not contain pornographic material, inappropriate information, or text-encoded files that are potentially dangerous to the integrity of the hardware on school premises.

The student is responsible for adhering to the Full Value Contract and using the Core Competency Guidelines while on-line with the Internet.

(Reprinted with permission of Roger Ashley, Media and Technology Specialist, Bloomfield Hills Model High School, Bloomfield Hills, MI.)

Figure 3 for using Internet capabilities in his process model, *The Big Six Skills Approach* for library skills instruction.

LM_NET recently contained this post listing locations on the Internet where lessons plans could be obtained on-line that integrate the Internet into the curriculum:[28]

- BBN National School Network Testbed: Gopher to: copernicus. bbn.com
  Look in National School Network Testbed, Community of Explorers Lesson Plans.

- Columbia Online Information Network: Gopher to: bigcat.missouri. edu
  Look in School House, Columbia Public Schools, Resource Library, WISE-Columbia School Resource Library.

- ERIC-Educational Resource Information Center: Gopher to: ericir. syr.edu

- The Explorer Database: http:/ /unite.ukans.edu

- Internet for Minnesota Schools: Gopher to: informns.k12.mn.us

- KIDLINK: Gopher to: kids.ccit.duq.edu

- NASA's K-12 Gopher Site: Gopher to:quest.arc.nasa.gov

- National Consortium for Environmental Education: Gopher to: nceet.snre.umich.edu

- Outreach and Technical Assistance Network: Gopher to: gopher.scoe. otan.dni.us

- PeachNet: Gopher to: gsl.gac.peachnet.edu
  Look in Libraries alias, Curriculum Library, Lesson Plans & Ideas

- San Diego City Schools: Gopher to: ec.sdcs.kl 2.ca.us

- Scholastic Net: Gopher to: scholastic.com:2003
  Look in Scholastic Internet Libraries, Integrating Technology Library, Lesson Plans

- SchoolNet: Gopher to: schoolnet.carleton.ca
  Look in Schoolnet gopher, Classroom & Academic Projects, Classroom Lessons and Projects

- STEM-Net: Gopher to: info.stemnet.nf.ca
  Look in STEM-NetHelp and training

- Big Sky: telnet: / /bigsky.bigsky.dillon.mt.us Login:bbs

- Curricular Infusion: gopher://rain.psg.com:70/00/schools/IRDinfusion-ideas.txt

- Curriculum Projects gopher://gopher.pps.pgh.pa.us:70/11/net

- Curriculum Repository gopher://k12.colostate.edu:70/11/Curriculum

- Lesson Plan Goldmines gopher://pps.pgh.pa.us

- Science Lesson Plans gopher://ec.sdcs.k12.ca.us

IDENTIFICATION AND EVALUATION
OF INTERNET RESOURCES

Choosing among thousands of information resources in electronic library environments presents challenges to students. Oberman[29] likens these choices to those consumers encounter in a shopping mall and cites studies of consumer tolerance indicating that consumers faced with an overwhelming supply of competing goods tend to suffer increased anxiety. School library media specialists can assist students in choosing correctly from a profusion of electronic sources.

Studies of college students use of databases indicate areas that may be correlated to school students' use of the Internet.[30] Students often have a false sense of confidence regarding the understanding of an online catalog's content and knowledge of how to use it effectively.[31] They are unable to match even basic subject needs with the appropriate database[32] and they do not fully comprehend the large array of available search options and rarely apply the correct ones even when they are cognizant of them.[33]

Adding even more to this confusion is that the Internet is unregulated. Anyone can "publish" information and make it available. Prior models and standards used for evaluating authority of print sources are obsolete

FIGURE 3. Internet Capabilities in an Information Problem-Solving Context

THE BIG SIX SKILLS	INTERNET CAPABILITY	APPLICATION
1. Task Definition 1.1 Define the problem 1.2 Identify information requirements of the problem	E-Mail E-Mail Discussion/Interest Groups (listservs, newsgroups)	to seek clarification from teachers to consult with group/team members to share and discuss concerns/questions/problems with persons in similar settings or with experts
2. Information Seeking Strategies 2.1 Determine the range of possible sources 2.2 Evaluate to determine priority sources	electronic libraries, data centers, resources WA IS, Gopher, various Internet resource guides use of AskERIC, NICs E-Mail Electronic discussion Groups (listservs, newsgroups)	to he aware of options, to determine possible and priority sources to determine possible resources to search for types of files and databases available to consult on resources, files, databases to consult with group/team members to request recommendations from persons in similar settings or from experts
3. Location and Access 3.1 Locate sources (intellectually, physically) 3.2 Find information within sources	Archie, Veronica WAIS, Gopher Telnet, Remote login, ftp	to search for the location of specific files or databases to search by subject within/across sites for remote access to computers and electronic libraries
4. Use of Information 4.1 Engage (read, view, listen) 4.2 Extract relevant information	download and file transfer, ftp	to get the relevant information from a remote computer to your own
5. Synthesis 5.1 Organize information from multiple sources 5.2 Present information	E-Mail Listservs, newsgroups Electronic Journals Ftp and Gopher sites	to share drafts and final communications to share papers, reports, and other communications to present papers and reports to archive reports, papers, products
6. Evaluation 6.1 Judge the product (effectiveness) 6.2 Judge the process (efficiency)	E-Mail Listservs, newsgroups	to gain feedback to gain feedback

(Reprinted with permission of Dr. Michael B. Eisenberg.)

182

but have not yet been replaced by any new standards for evaluating Web pages, gophers, and other Internet products. So not only do students need help in identifying these resources, but they will need skills in determining if the information they found is trustworthy. There are no easy answers here as this process is still evolving. School library media specialists and librarians will need to keep abreast of developments in this area and relay them to patrons on a continuing basis.

NOTES

1. Nancy Everhart, "An Analysis of the Work Activities of High School Library Media Specialists in Automated and Non-Automated Library Media Centers," *School Library Media Quarterly* 20 (Spring 1992): 86-99.

2. Kathleen Craver, *School Library Media Centers in the 21st Century* (Westport, CT: Greenwood Press, 1994), 116.

3. *LM_NET*, listserv, 15 October 1995.

4. "Best of K-12 on the Internet," [URL: gopher://gopher.cic.net:3005/].

5. Doug Johnson, "Captured by the Web: K-12 Schools and The World-Wide Web," *Multimedia Schools.* 2 (March/April 1995): 25-35.

6. "World Wide Web Gallery," *Classroom Connect* 9 (September 1995): 6-7.

7. Ibid.

8. The McKinley Group, Inc., "Hotlist, Kids Did This!," 1995. [URL: http://sln.fi.edu/tfi/hotlists/kids.html].

9. Classroom Connect, "Classroom Web Project," 1996. [URL: http: / /www. wentworth.com/ classweb].

10. Carol C. Kuthlthau, "Response 2 to Ann Irving" in *School Library Media Annual 1992* eds. Jane Bandy Smith and J. Gordon Coleman, Jr. (Englewood, CO: Libraries Unlimited, 1992), 48-51.

11. American Association of School Librarians (AASL) and Association for Educational Communications and Technology (AECT), *Information Power: Guidelines for School Library Media Programs* (Chicago, IL: American Library Association, 1988).

12. Suneel Ratan, "A New Divide Between Haves and Have-Nots?," *Time* 145 (Special Issue, Spring 1995),: 25-26.

13. Brian Murfin, "A Survey of Telecommunications Use by Secondary School Science Teachers in New York City" (paper presented at the Annual Meeting of the National Association for Research in Science Teaching, San Francisco, CA, 22-25 April 1995).

14. "ALA-led Coalition Challenges Communications Decency Act," *American Libraries.* 27 (April 1996): 13-14.

15. Stephen Bates, "The Next Front in the Book Wars," *New York Times* (6 November 1994): 4A, 22.

16. "New Software Blocks Sex on the Internet," *School Library Journal* 41 (July 1995): 11-12.

17. Ibid.

18. Cleborne D. Maddux, "The Internet: Educational Prospects-and Problems," *Educational Technology* 34 (September 1994): 37-42.

19. Beverly Goldberg, "On the Line for the First Amendment," *American Libraries* 26 (September 1995): 774-778.

20. Maddux, "The Internet: Educational Prospects-and Problems," 37-42.

21. Ibid.

22. Bruce Flanders, "A Delicate Balance," *School Library Journal* 40 (October 1994): 32-35.

23. Bates, "The Next Front in the Book Wars,"4A, 22.

24. Jan Summers, "Beyond the School Walls," *Computers in Libraries* 15 (March 1995): 48-50.

25. Michael B. Eisenberg and Robert E. Berkowitz, *Information Problem-Solving: The Big Six Skills Approach to Library and Information Skills Instruction* (Norwood, NJ: Ablex, 1990).

26. Carol C. Kuthlau, *Seeking Meaning: A Process Approach to Library and Information Services* (Norwood, NJ: Ablex, 1993).

27. Michael B. Eisenberg, "Free from the Constraints of Space and Time: Considering the Opportunities and Challenges for Electronic Publishing," *Educational Technology* 34 (September 1994): 59-64.

28. *L M NET* listserv, 23 September 1995.

29. Cerise Oberman, "Avoiding the Cereal Snydrome, or Critical Thinking in the Electronic Environment," *Library Trends* 39 (Winter 1991): 191-192.

30. Craver, *School Library Media Centers in the 21st Century:* 117.

31. Betsy Baker, "A New Direction for Online Catalog Instruction," *Information Technology and Libraries* 5 (March 1986): 36.

32. Oberman, "Avoiding the Cereal Syndrome, or Critical Thinking in the Electronic Environment," 191.

33. Betsy, H. Baker and Maureen Pastine, "Making Connections: Teaching Information Retrieval," *Library Trends* 39 (Winter 1991): 210-222.

Designing Internet Instruction for Latinos

Lori S. Mestre

SUMMARY. It is becoming increasingly important to provide appropriate library instruction for the rising number of Latino students enrolling in higher education. Of particular concern is how librarians can provide effective Internet instruction to Latinos. Latino students' needs and learning styles tend to differ from those of the mainstream population from which the majority of librarians come. These differences have implications for the ways that librarians offer instruction. This paper will discuss cultural issues and varying learning styles that librarians need to be cognizant of when working with a Latino population, and will provide guidelines for shaping instruction for Latinos within an Internet environment. *[Article copies available for a fee from The Haworth Document Delivery Service: 1-800-342-9678. E-mail address: getinfo@haworth.com]*

KEYWORDS. Latinos, Hispanic Americans, cognitive style(s) or learning styles, computer literacy, training methods, equal education, teaching-learning process, educational technology, bibliographic instruction

As the library expands its technological role and incorporates the Internet as one of its services, there is a growing need to become familiar with techniques that will enable the librarian to assist all cultural groups in using this medium to access library and worldwide resources. The Latino

Lori S. Mestre (lori.mestre@library.umass.edu) is Education Reference Librarian at the W.E.B. Du Bois Library, University of Massachusetts, Amherst, MA 01003.

[Haworth co-indexing entry note]: "Designing Internet Instruction for Latinos." Mestre, Lori S. Co-published simultaneously in *Internet Reference Services Quarterly* (The Haworth Press, Inc.) Vol. 2, No. 4, 1997, pp. 185-199; and: *The Challenge of Internet Literacy: The Instruction-Web Convergence* (ed: Lyn Elizabeth M. Martin) The Haworth Press, Inc., 1997, pp. 185-199. Single or multiple copies of this article are available for a fee from The Haworth Document Delivery Service [1-800-342-9678, 9:00 a.m. - 5:00 p.m. (EST). E-mail address: getinfo@haworth.com].

185

community, the second largest cultural group in the United States, is growing dramatically: between 1980-1990, there was a 53% increase in the Latino population.[1] It is becoming increasingly important to provide appropriate library instruction for the rising number of Latino students enrolling in higher education.[2] However, Latino students' needs and learning styles tend to differ from those of the mainstream population from which the majority of librarians come. These differences have implications for the ways that librarians offer instruction. In addition to different learning styles, Latinos come to the library with different experiences in using technology, not always having the same access to technology as does the mainstream population. To fill this chasm, the library can take the initiative in providing Internet instruction to Latinos. In doing so, however, librarians need to be aware of different learning styles, cultural aspects and expectations, in order to provide effective instruction to Latinos in using this powerful tool. This paper will discuss the reasons for using the Internet with students, present issues that librarians need to be cognizant of when working with a Latino population, and provide guidelines for shaping instruction for Latinos within a library session or an Internet workshop environment.

The term Latino will be used in this paper to describe any group of people from Latin American countries or those identifying with ties from a Latin American country. Of that group I will more specifically be referring to those whose first language is Spanish or who were raised in a Spanish-speaking environment. The purpose of combining all Spanish-speaking groups under one term is for ease in generalizing among commonly shared cultural and linguistic experiences. It is by no means intended to classify all Latinos as being the same. Having immigrated over generations from many different countries, America's Spanish-speaking population is educationally, politically, and economically diverse. Major differences exist between various Latino groups, such as the varying and diversifying influence of their native traditions.[3] There are differences that also depend upon whether or not the Latino individuals in question have "developed a conscious ethnic pride about Hispanic cultural traditions."[4] However, since Latinos tend to share a similar cultural heritage and language, I will use the term Latinos in the broad sense.

THE IMPORTANCE OF USING THE INTERNET WITH LATINOS

Computer Literacy Inequalities

Members of minority groups come to college with varying levels of computer experience, but generally speaking, their experience is not as extensive as that brought by non-minority students. In 1993 the U.S.

National Center for Education reported that 35 percent of whites were using computers at home in comparison to only 9.8 percent of Hispanics.[5] This initial imbalance has both immediate and long-range effects on minority students' academic success and their eventual career opportunities. Librarians are in a position to develop programs to address some of these initial disparities by encouraging these students' use of libraries, including the effective use of computers to access computerized information.

Although the Internet can serve to level the playing field for all students, there are still inequalities in who has access to computers. Researchers have identified a number of social and economic reasons why minority students leave secondary schools with less computer experience than nonminority students, with issues of access being a primary factor.[6] For example, computer usage by mainstream students is usually for enrichment purposes whereas for minority students it is for remedial purposes. Mainstream students also tend to attend more affluent schools that frequently have access to more sophisticated programs and more extensive resources like the Internet. Often instruction in computing is linked to math and science instruction; if minority students proceed more slowly in these content areas, they will also proceed more slowly in developing computer skills.[7]

There are other concerns. In most computer labs, few mentors and role models exist for Latino students. In addition, advanced students usually fare better than others in competition for computer time, thus widening the knowledge gap between majority and minority students. Students whose parents are affluent or well-educated are far more likely to have computers at home than other students. Some analysts warn that unless disadvantaged students are introduced to the more exciting uses of computers, they may be consigned to a new technological underclass.[8]

African Americans and Hispanics will account for more than one-fourth of all entrants to the labor force between 1996 and 2005.[9] These groups will need computer literacy skills if they are to compete in the future labor force. Students with well-developed computer skills know how to use various productivity tools like spreadsheets, databases, and word processors, and recognize their benefits. In addition, they may have the advantage of knowing how to use the Internet to retrieve and evaluate up-to-date or obscure information. Those who don't have prior experience using the tools may spend their available time doing tasks manually, running out of time (and energy) before they get to more intellectually rewarding activities.[10] Lack of computer experience, especially with networked resources, may hinder minority students when they encounter technologically-rich educational activities. In addition to inhibiting stu-

dents' academic success, lack of computer experience can cripple opportunities for career development, and thus restrict minority students' chances
of long-term economic success.[11] In a paper presented at a conference
entitled: "The New Information Technology and Hispanics," Henry T.
Ingle states:

> The issue of equitable access to the new information media and
> technology by Hispanics and other groups . . . has far-reaching
> implications for our nation as a whole. It is a particularly significant
> issue for minorities because of the majority role envisioned by His-
> panics and other minority population groups in society and the future
> work force. With the existing and continuing spread of the new
> information technology at work, school, and in the home, we all
> need to learn more about the technology to assume positions of
> leadership and expertise in guiding its evolution and service for the
> best benefit of the society. Numerous scholars and researchers . . .
> are warning us of the dangers inherent in widening the existing gap
> between the so-called "information rich" and "information poor"
> segments of our society unless constructive and systematic interven-
> tion approaches are implemented to curb and reorient the current
> trends.[12]

The Internet as a Motivating Influence

Computer networks are becoming an integral part of college campuses.
Students can take courses, compose and submit work, register for classes,
browse the library, find pertinent worldwide information or query or consult with people from around the world from their computer. The Internet
is providing more and more possibilities for librarians and teachers in
stimulating students to find alternate ways to access information.

Finding information through networked computers is one way to create
enthusiasm in learning. By altering the way information is presented to
students, librarians and educators can be an important influence in motivating students to learn. It is also a way to allow students to access
information that is relevant to them. Upon discovering the intriguing scope
of the Internet, a new world is opened up to them. They can travel almost
anywhere, speak with anyone else who is online (authors, presidents,
researchers, librarians, students from other countries) and read and see
exhibits and information from a variety of sources. Using technology in
the classroom is a way in which all students can participate. By allowing
students to be creative and to find information that is relevant to their

needs and interests, they will usually have a more positive outlook on what they are doing.

As students gain proficiency in collecting, organizing, analyzing, evaluating, constructing and publishing knowledge, they become active learners. They also acquire skills and attitudes that will help prepare them for lifelong learning. Networked learning naturally tends towards a collaborative process as it accommodates and reflects different, individual learning styles and orientations. In this manner the learning styles of most students are accommodated.

A Tool for Broadening One's World View

The Internet holds great potential to link classrooms and people to exchange cultural information and address common problems. Books only provide an established body of facts which is of limited value since knowledge is changing so rapidly. The Internet, however, provides links to resources that are updated continuously, thus allowing for the creation of a curriculum that is current and exciting. Linking computers also increases social interaction and collaboration. It is possible to find experts on almost any topic who are usually willing to share their expertise. Students who are reluctant to converse with those outside their racial, ethnic, or cultural group may find greater ease in communicating via the Internet as differences based on age, ethnicity, race, gender and disability are generally not noticeable. Through Internet communication, students learn more about the cultures, languages and perspectives of those with whom they communicate. They develop critical literacy skills as they discuss problems and potential solutions to those problems with others in class and with others from around the world. Librarians and educators can help foster these skills with appropriate lesson plans and guidance.

Working on projects through the Internet is an exciting way for students to learn and explore what is happening in the world. The computer can be a tremendous amplifier of social issues that are real to students. The student can take on all kinds of roles: world traveler, foreign correspondent, explorer, intelligence analyst, scientist, artist, musician, published author and respected commentator. Latin America is becoming very active in providing Web sites, which give us first hand information about culture, politics, history and geography, including through some daily newspapers. To supplement textbooks, the class can use the Internet to visit the city or country being studied and access timely information about virtually any topic. One way for students to be appraised of current events is for them to write to computer "keypals" or through listservs or news groups. In this way they can communicate with others around the world and find out about specifics in culture, politics, geography, or even practice another language. If, for example, there is an earthquake or hurricane in a Latin American country, students can learn via the Internet what is happening, sometimes as it happens. They can become investigative reporters of a sort and cull other information about the country. Students are more motivated when they know they are communicating with people beyond the school. In the global classroom the curriculum is a *living curriculum* with real people, not textbooks.

While broadening their world view, students may also encounter primary and secondary sources related to their own ethnicity. It is common for Latinos to go through school rarely seeing their ethnic group portrayed as achievers.[13] The Internet provides them an opportunity to learn about their history, culture and achievements, which can help validate their own ethnicity. This, in turn, may provide incentives for Latino students to stay in school and learn about themselves, while allowing them to see how they are not only a part of their own cultural or ethnic group, but also a part of the community as a whole.

Cummins and Sayers[14] believe that global networking through telecommunications can play a key role helping teachers adopt a more transformative approach in their classrooms. They suggest that collaborative projects in which classrooms in different parts of the nation and world discuss, research, and comment on common problems can help give students a better sense not only of people who are different from them, but of their own identities as well. Moreover, such connections give students the ability to undertake social action that goes beyond their own classroom and links up with others around the country or globe, and can thus potentially take on broader significance.

CREATING OPTIMUM LEARNING ENVIRONMENTS FOR LATINOS

Learning Potential and Learning Styles

Instructing students to use technology is occurring at a very young age. Because not all students have the same access to computers, the level of facility will differ among students. Librarians must take not only that into account when demonstrating the use of the Internet or other computer accessed information, but also that learning styles among people may differ.

Librarians need to be aware that there is a cultural difference model between groups. Cognitive, learning and motivational styles of many students may be different from those most often expected by teachers and librarians who represent the majority culture. Researchers suggest that individuals *tend* to fall in distinct categories with the manner in which they prefer to learn and, to a large degree, that these preferences are culturally determined.[15] Two different characterizations of learners are field-independent learners and field-dependent learners. The majority culture usually falls into the category of field-independent learners who are parts-specific, can isolate facts as needed, are rather linear in their thinking and problem solving and tend to test well. On the contrary, field-dependent learners, such as Latinos, must see the big picture, seek to find personal relevance in the task at hand, and require that some sort of personal relationship is established between the instructor and the student. Examples of the above may be reflected in the difference between the lecture, teacher-centered classroom that encourages competition as opposed to the cooperative learning environment that encourages peer interaction and support.[16]

Differences in value systems may also have an impact on how individuals learn. European Americans value independence as the basis of their own identity and their relationship with others, while Latinos build relationships of interdependence, especially within family. European Americans are also more independent and expect to do things for themselves through self reliance and competence, whereas Latinos identify with a group and emphasize cooperation and loyalty.[17]

Learning Styles of Latinos: Some General Characteristics

This section will discuss various learning style characteristics of Latinos, but it is important to remember that Latinos have different backgrounds and experiences and may or may not demonstrate the same characteristics. Applying these characteristics to all Latinos could result in stereotyping or ineffective instruction if the librarian is not sensitive to subtleties. Learning to be flexible and open to different approaches is a great step in improving instruction. The following are some general observations.

Hispanic students may not be able to demonstrate what they have learned or what they can do on tests which: are not in their native language; are timed; contain items to which they have not been exposed; are too thing rather than people oriented; do not allow for feedback from the assessor.[18]

These characteristics are also present in a computer workshop session in that the information provided will probably not be in the Latinos' native language; there is a set time element for accomplishing each task; there are many new items to which they have not been exposed; the workshop is usually object-oriented and there is little opportunity for feedback from the workshop presenter.

In a session hands-on time is important because students tend to learn well by doing.[19] Some Latino students learn more by touching, seeing, and manipulating concrete objects than by discussing or reading about them.[20] Hands-on sessions which provide a lot of individual instruction work well with most, but provide a much needed chance for Latinos to become acquainted to the world of computers. Latino students may relate better to a person-centered rather than an object or idea-centered session, so this individual attention may facilitate learning for them. They also tend to like to work in groups or with others whom they know. Planning sessions so that there is a type of camaraderie can be useful for the success in a workshop and in class. If possible the librarian should team up with a Latino assistant when conducting library sessions with Latinos, not only to assist with the language, but also because this individual can more readily identify with the culture and serve as a role model.

Taking this into consideration, in order to create the most optimum environment, librarians need to alter the ways in which they typically present material to Latinos. Facilitator should set them at ease, maintain an involved and supportive posture with them and actively determine that they understand the directions. Both oral and written directions should be provided, if possible in Spanish. It may be helpful to realize that Latino students tend to have cognitive and learning styles that may differ from that of the facilitator. In a computer workshop setting this may be evidenced by the Latino student needing to finish a task and process what has been presented before proceeding to the next task. Many times a facilitator will begin to demonstrate a function and then speak about how that function or task can be applied globally, rather than allowing all students to master the function first. Only after the students feel comfortable with the task at hand should the facilitator proceed. Latinos tend to be more concerned with doing a job well regardless of the amount of time required than they are in finishing rapidly just so they will have more time for the next task. They tend to work at a relaxed pace, even if it means taking longer to finish something.

When offering training sessions it is important to keep in mind that Latinos may come to a session with a view that it is somewhat a social affair, possibly anticipating refreshments if it is a session that lasts longer than an hour. After a welcome and a short introduction of what will be covered, the librarian might provide a brief online demonstration to the whole group, preferably using a computer with overhead projection capability. The librarian could then distribute a handout with step by step instructions (bilingual if possible) and allow participants the majority of the session to complete the desired tasks, thus providing optimum hands-on time. Once the session begins, the librarian may notice digressions from the topic at hand. These digressions can make for a more personal, relaxed atmosphere. It may also allow the librarian to learn concerns, priorities or views from people from other backgrounds, which may in turn help to improve the instruction for others.

Of major importance is the issue of language, not only that of English versus Spanish, but also terminology used to explain how to move around in a computer, database, or the Internet. It is advisable to assume nothing, not even that students know terms such as *Space Bar* or *Enter.* Assessing students prior to the sessions makes it possible to arrange the sessions to best accommodate the beginning, the intermediate and the advanced users of technology. By having a written step-by-step guide of what will occur in the session, it is possible for those who are more experienced to move at a faster pace. It may be necessary to have a few facilitators on hand to move around the group and answer questions.

Below are other specific ideas that may be useful for working with Latinos.

- Do not maintain an impersonal, aloof or distant relationship with the students. Some suggestions for personalizing interaction might be to utilize physical contact when expressing approval and acceptance, stand close to them when talking or relating to them, provide more guidance and feedback, and maintain close personal relationships.[21]
- When communicating avoid using slang, library jargon and unfamiliar references. Repeat and define important words and concepts. Check for comprehension and use synonyms for difficult words.
- Allow them to arrive at a consensus in whatever way is most comfortable.
- Be sensitive to the subtle and indirect ways in which they communicate that they do not know something or cannot do something, including nonverbal communication.[22]
- De-emphasize competition and utilize group participation.
- Include more community projects, group projects, group work and peer tutoring.
- Do not rush them if they do not answer quickly or work rapidly.

- De-emphasize the lecture approach in favor of an active learning approach.
- Utilize bilingual methods with limited English-proficient students.

IMPLICATIONS FOR LIBRARIANS

Keeping Up with Technology

Assuming that librarians have access to the technology needed to bring the Internet to the students, there are still other considerations and barriers to confront. Librarians must master computer technology and learn new ways of conducting their classes. They will need to use open-ended inquiry and learn techniques for guiding student research. It is not enough to just find interesting and exciting information. Students, teachers, and librarians will need to work together to decide what to do with the information, such as synthesizing it into a relevant research project. It will also be necessary for librarians to learn to evaluate group performance and to be able to pinpoint problems that individual students may be having. Their role will evolve into one of being a "guide on the side" or a "coach."

Training is often a barrier to the effective integration of the Internet into the classroom. If librarians are to learn how to use technology and how to make use of that technology in their classrooms, they will need hands-on training and staff development workshops. There is a feeling of continual pressure to keep current, a need to constantly learn, and a feeling that whatever one knows, it is not sufficient. Instructional librarians may defer to others for technical problems or advancements with software, hardware and design, but they need to be aware of the broader sense of technology in order to know what questions to ask when confronted with technology problems. Another important component in forging ahead with the Internet is for librarians to have the time to explore the Internet for new connections, enough time to process and evaluate what they have found, and time to develop appropriate lesson plans, assess sites and student performance, maintain contact with teachers and students and keep pace with the advances in teaching and other academic subjects. If librarians are not allocated the time necessary to learn and keep up with this technology, there will continue to be barriers.

Becoming More Proactive

The librarian's role, more than ever, needs to be one of providing public service. College and university libraries affect students at all levels and cultures and across all academic disciplines. Sooner or later most students pass through the library's doors. The library is in a singular position to have an impact on a large segment of the campus population. Here is an opportunity for librarians to take a proactive stance and to help set the pace, not only for other libraries, but also for the larger institutions they serve. Within the multicultural society all students need to have access to library services, including technology. That access means instruction as well as the materials or equipment. When designing projects, creating publicity, establishing evaluation, and presenting workshops, librarians should keep in mind that their targeted audience extends beyond the mainstream population.

In order to understand the needs of Latinos, librarians need to reach out to that community on campus. They may begin by offering workshops geared for Latinos and publicize the workshops in Spanish and English. By contacting the various departments and student organizations around campus with interest in Latin America and Spain, the librarian may develop strong contacts. Examples of departments to contact may be the Spanish and Portuguese departments, the bilingual programs, the Latin American studies center, the school of education's bilingual and ESL departments and the student organizations with Latino interests. These contacts can help in wording flyers and with scheduling. Arranging to have a representative from one of the programs attend and help facilitate at the workshop can help foster a more amiable environment.

CONCLUSION

All around us there are references to being online, using the Web and getting on the Information Superhighway. This is revolutionizing the way we all acquire information. Librarians are increasingly asked to provide leadership, instruction and consulting assistance in the use of educational technology. They need to be trained in all of the possibilities that technology and a tool like the Internet can create for their classrooms. Rather than conducting library instruction sessions based mainly on print material, the OPAC, CD-ROMS and the LAN, librarians need to be innovative and demonstrate to their users alternate ways to access information by exploring the Internet. However, in doing so, they will need to keep in mind that students do not all learn in the same way and they will have to be open to varying the way they assist students from diverse cultural backgrounds in acquiring information technologically.

NOTES

1. Bureau of the Census, *We the Hispanic Americans* (Washington, DC: U.S. Department of Commerce, 1993).

2. Lori Mestre and Sonia Nieto, "Puerto Rican Children's Literature and Culture in the Public Library," in *Multicultural Review* 5:2 (June 1996); Rebecca R. Martin, *Libraries and the Changing Face of Academia: Responses to Growing Multicultural Populations* (Metuchen, NJ, and London, 1994); Otis A. Chadley, "Addressing Cultural Diversity in Academic and Research Libraries" *College and Research Libraries* 53:3 (May 1992): 206-214; Robert Trujillo and David D. Weber, "Academic Library Responses to Cultural Diversity: A Position Paper for the 1990's," *Journal of Academic Librarianship* 17:3 (1991): 157-161; Lorraine M. Gutierrez, and Cindy Poore, "Retaining Latino Undergraduates: Lessons from the University of Michigan," paper presented at the Annual Meeting of the American Association for Higher Education (San Francisco, CA, April 3, 1990). ERIC Reproduction Number ED 367 745; Salvador Güereña, ed. *Latino Librarianship: A Handbook for Professionals* (Jefferson, NC: McFarland & Co., Inc.) 1990.

3. By native traditions I am referring to the cultural, religious, and linguistic influences of an ancestry comprised not only of European people, but also of distinct indigenous groups and African people. These factors make for unique experiences among many Latin American regions.

4. D. Bryan Stansfield, "Serving Hispanic Persons: The Cross-Cultural Border Library Experience at Fabens," *RQ* 27:4 (Summer 1988): 549.

5. United States Department of Education, "Student Use of Computers 1984 and 1993," in *Digest of Education Statistics* (Washington, DC: United States Department of Education, National Center for Education Statistics 1994).

6. Delia Neuman, "Technology and Equity" in *Educational Media and Technology Yearbook* eds. Donald P. Ely & B.B. Minor, 18 (Englewood, CO: Libraries Unlimited, 1992): 100-103.

7. Bernadette Martin, and J. Dixon Hearne, "Computer Equity in Education," *Educational Technology* 29:11(1989): 47-51.

8. Charles Pillar, "Separate Realities," *Macworld* 9:9 (September 1992): 230.

9. General Accounting Office, *The Changing Workforce. Demographic Issues Facing the Federal Government* (Government Printing Office: Washington, DC 1992).

10. Karen T. Schwalm, "Providing Computer Conferencing Opportunities for Minority Students and Measuring Results," in *Proceedings of the 1995 Annual National Convention of the Association for Educational Communications and Technology* (AECT) (17th, Anaheim, CA 1995): ERIC Reproduction Number ED 383335.

11. Joanne M. Badagliacco, "Gender and Race Differences in Computing Attitudes and Experience," *Social Science Computer Review* 8:1(1990): 42-63.

12. Henry T. Ingle, *Sharpening the Issues and Shaping the Policies: The Role of the New Information Media and Technology Within the U.S. Hispanic Community* (Claremont, CA: Tomas Rivera Center, March 1988): 19.

13. See for example: Edward Fiske, "The Undergraduate Hispanic Experience," *Change* 20:3 (May/June, 1988): 29-33.

14. Jim Cummins, and Dennis Sayers, *Brave New Schools: Challenging Cultural Literacy Through Global Learning* (New York: St. Martin's Press, 1995).

15. James A. Anderson and Maurianne Adams, "Acknowledging the Learning Styles of Diverse Student Populations: Implications for Instructional Design," in *Teaching for Diversity: New Directions for Teaching and Learning* 49 (Spring 1992): 19-33; Kenneth Cushner, "Preparing Teachers for Intercultural Context," in *Improving Intercultural Interactions: Modules for Cross-Cultural Training Programs,* eds. Richard W. Brislin and Tomoko Yoshida. Multicultural Aspects of Counseling Series; 3. (Thousand Oaks, CA: Sage Publications): 113-125.

16. For descriptions of several learning styles and research summaries see: Robert E. Slavin, "Cooperative Learning and Intergroup Relations" in *Handbook of Research on Multicultural Education,* James A. Banks and Cherry A. McGee Banks, eds. (New York: Macmillan Pub., 1995): 628-634; John Ogbu, "Understanding Cultural Diversity and Learning," *Educational Researcher* 21:8 (November 1992): 5-14; Bette C. Erickson and Diane W. Strommer, "Learning Style and Intellectual Development," in *Teaching College Freshman* (San Francisco, CA: Jossey-Bass, 1991): 46-62; Roger T. Johnson and others, "Effects of Cooperative, Competitive, and Individualistic Goal Structures on Computer-Assisted Instruction," *Journal of Educational Psychology* 77:6 (December 1985): 668-77; Roger T. Johnson and David W. Johnson, "Student-Student Interaction: Ignored but Powerful," *Journal of Teacher Education* 36:4 (July/August 1985): 22-26; Bruce R. Hare and Daniel U. Levine, Effective Schooling in Desegregated Settings: What Do We Know About Learning Style and Linguistic Differences?," *Equity and Choice* 1:2 (Winter 1985): 13-18.

17. Virginia Vogel Zanger, *Exploración Intercultural: Una Guia Para el Estudiante* (Rowley, MA: Newbury House Publishers, Inc., 1984).

18. Herbert Grossman, *Educating Hispanic Students: Implications for Instruction, Classroom Management, Counseling, and Assessment* (Springfield, IL: C.C. Thomas, 1995): 205.

19. For a classic study see Yuichiro Anzai, and Herber A. Simon (1979). "The Theory of Learning by Doing," *Psychological Review* 86:2 (March 1979): 124-140.

20. See Grossman, *Educating Hispanic Students: Implications for Instruction, Classroom Management, Counseling, and Assessment* for findings from surveys administered to Latinos and non-Latinos.

21. Differences in the use of space often cause problems in interactions. Edward T. Hall, *The Hidden Dimension.* (New York: Doubleday and Co., 1966) has described the distances which North Americans choose for interactions. These distances differ from those preferred by most Latinos. Carmen Judith Nine-Curt, *Non-Verbal Communication in Puerto Rico* (Cambridge, MA: National Assessment and Dissemination Center for Bilingual/Bicultural Education 1976) also discusses these issues in relation to working with Latinos and the importance of non-verbal behavior and touching for Latin Americans.

22. See for example Suzanne Irujo, "Do You Know Why They All Talk at Once? Thoughts on Cultural Differences Between Hispanics and Anglos" *Equity and Choice* (May 1989): 14-17; Marynelle DeVore-Chew, Brian Roberts and Nathan M. Smith "The Effects of Reference Librarian's Nonverbal Communications on the Patrons' Perceptions of the Library, Librarians and Themselves" *Library and Information Science Research* 10:4 (October 1988): 389-400; Carmen Judith Nine-Curt, *Non-Verbal Communication in Puerto Rico* (Cambridge, MA: National Assessment and Dissemination Center for Bilingual/Bicultural Education 1976); Annette Lopez, "Did I See You Do What I Think You Did: The Pitfalls of Nonverbal Communication," *New Jersey Libraries* 27 (Winter 1993/94): 18-22; and Aaron Wolfgang, *Nonverbal Behavior: Perspectives, Applications, Intercultural Insights* (Lewiston, NY: C.J. Hogrefe, 1984).

BIBLIOGRAPHY

Arp, Lori, "Reflecting on Reflecting: Views on Teaching and the Internet," *RQ* 34 (Summer 1995): 453-457.

General Accounting Office, *School Facilities: America's Schools Not Designed or Equipped for the 21st Century* (Government Printing Office: Washington, DC, April, 1995): 39-42.

Hall, Patrick A., "The Role of Affectivity in Instructing People of Color: Some Implications for Bibliographic Instruction," *Library Trends* 39 (Winter 1991): 316-326.

Johnson, Douglas A., "Student Access to Internet: Librarians and Teachers Working Together to Teach Higher Level Survival Skills," *Emergency Librarian* 22:3 (January/February 1995): 8-12.

Lucas, Tamara, and Sandra R. Schecter, "Literacy Education and Diversity: Toward Equity in the Teaching of Reading and Writing" *Urban Review* 24:2 (June 1992): 85-104.

Macias, Robert. and David. J. Rose, "Wired for Knowledge: Advanced Technology Keeps Students Stimulated and in School," *Hispanic* 7:7 (August 1994): 17-22.

McKenna, Teresa and Flora Ida Ortiz, *The Broken Web: The Educational Experience of Hispanic American Women* (Berkeley, CA: The Tomas Rivera Center and Floricanto Press, 1988).

McLaughlin, Pamela Whiteley, "Embracing the Internet: The Changing Role of Library Staff," *Bulletin of the American Society for Information Science* 20 (February/March 1994): 16-17.

Office of Technology Assessment, *Teachers and Technology: Making the Connection* (Washington, DC: Congress of the United States, 1995).

Olivier, Terry A., and Faye Shapiro, "Self-Efficacy and Computers," Journal of Computer-Based Instruction 10:3(1993): 81-85.

Pask, Judith M. and Carl E. Snow, "Undergraduate Instruction and the Internet," *Library Trends* 44 (Fall 1995): 306-317.

Resnick, Rosalind, "Olé: Latin America's Net Presence is Growing," *Internet World* 6:4 (April 1995): 86-90.

Resta, Paul, "Organizing Education for Minorities: Enhancing Minority Access and Use of the New Information Technologies in Higher Education," *Education & Computing* 8:1-2 (1992): 119-127.

Rodriguez, Clara, *Puerto Ricans: Born in the U.S.A.* (Boulder, CO: Westview Press. 1991).

Tijerina, Derly, "Exploring the Internet: Why Hispanics Need to Get on the Information Superhighway." *Hispanic* 8:2 (March 1995): 58-64.

One Thing Leads to Another:
Faculty Outreach Through
Internet Instruction

Kate Borowske
Karen Campbell

SUMMARY. Establishing meaningful connections to faculty is a continuing challenge for academic librarians. One library's efforts at faculty outreach received unexpected assistance from the Internet, when faculty and student curiosity about this resource created opportunities for new library staff to build connections to faculty and establish their credibility on campus. In the process, the library made progress towards meeting another challenge: determining the role of the Internet in the library. Internet instruction is now integrated with library instruction and is available to faculty and students in a variety of formats. *[Article copies available for a fee from The Haworth Document Delivery Service: 1-800-342-9678. E-mail address: getinfo@haworth.com]*

KEYWORDS. Library instruction, Internet instruction, faculty outreach, bibliographic instruction

Bush Library supports the undergraduate and graduate programs of Hamline University, a small, private university in St. Paul, Minnesota. In a

Kate Borowske (kmborows@piper.hamline.edu) is Graduate School Librarian and Karen Campbell (kmcampbe@piper.hamline.edu) is Technology Librarian, Bush Library, Hamline University, 1536 Hewitt Ave., St. Paul, MN 55104.

[Haworth co-indexing entry note]: "One Thing Leads to Another: Faculty Outreach Through Internet Instruction." Borowske, Kate, and Karen Campbell. Co-published simultaneously in *Internet Reference Services Quarterly* (The Haworth Press, Inc.) Vol. 2, No. 4, 1997, pp. 201-210; and: *The Challenge of Internet Literacy: The Instruction-Web Convergence* (ed: Lyn Elizabeth M. Martin) The Haworth Press, Inc., 1997, pp. 201-210. Single or multiple copies of this article are available for a fee from The Haworth Document Delivery Service [1-800-342-9678, 9:00 a.m. - 5:00 p.m. (EST). E-mail address: getinfo@haworth.com].

year of organizational and personnel change within the library, the staff was organized into functional teams. With most staff either new or in new positions, a lot of energy developed; a little healthy competition was coupled with an unusual sense of urgency. New staff were constantly looking for opportunities, anxious to establish departmental liaisons, and combat a poor image resulting from several years of inadequate funding.

To smooth the transition, the library staff decided to try a "bonding activity." The resulting workshop on the Myers-Briggs Type Indicators enabled two staff in particular, the graduate school librarian and the technology librarian, to effectively build on their strengths, pairing a "thinker" and a "doer." Their adventures follow.

THE LIBRARY, THE CAMPUS, AND TECHNOLOGY

The undergraduate dean charged librarians to lead faculty in learning and applying new technology. A long standing technology literacy requirement had recently been abolished; instead e-mail and Internet training were inserted into the Introductory English curriculum, to be taught by computing staff and library staff cooperatively. The faculty Library Task Force established a Technology Subcommittee; the technology librarian served on this committee, drafting a "Technology Blue Sky Vision" for Bush Library.

The Academic Computing Center was undergoing its own changes, including a move to a newly equipped and ethernetted building with good teaching facilities, wiring of the library building with fiber-optic cable, installation of networked computers with direct Internet access (including Mosaic), and reassignment of the former in-library computer lab to a Library Bibliographic Instruction room.

These events served as catalysts to a series of opportunities for librarians at Bush Library. Two local professional organizations provided additional stimuli: a Minnesota Library Association conference session on Internet instruction provided information and inspiration in its discussion of faculty seminars; discussions within our local consortium, CLIC (Cooperating Libraries in Consortium), provided additional models of outreach. Many opportunities flowed from these catalysts; the first appeared in the graduate school.

OPPORTUNITIES IN THE GRADUATE SCHOOL

Hamline has four graduate degree programs. The majority of students are part-time, the majority of faculty adjunct. Faculty outreach in the best of situations is difficult; the difficulties increase when most are adjunct. While the library's liaison to the graduate school was able to establish contact with many of the school's administrative staff, her initial attempts at outreach to the faculty failed to capture their interest.

INTERNET SEMINARS

An invitation to the graduate school librarian to teach part of a half-day Internet seminar for Graduate Public Administration students was an encouraging first step. A staff member from Academic Computing was scheduled to teach the basic Internet protocols; the graduate school librarian was to speak briefly about the library's online catalog and databases. Two sessions of this seminar were scheduled for January.

Shortly after the session was scheduled, and just after the brochures went out, the co-presenter from Academic Computing left Hamline. Asked whether she would consider teaching the entire seminar, both the Internet protocols and the library databases, the graduate school librarian agreed. This was in spite of the fact that she was just learning gopher, had little experience with Mosaic, and didn't understand how everything fit together to make up "the Internet." When told of this upcoming seminar, the technology librarian offered her assistance. When the magnitude of the task–designing a half-day seminar for twenty people, not to mention learning more about the Internet–sank in, her offer for assistance was gratefully accepted.

One of the most useful resources used in the development of the seminar was the listserv, NETTRAIN, where experienced Internet trainers share advice and training materials. A previous experience at a poorly-designed Internet workshop provided inspiration of a different sort: how not to do it. The seminar was broken down into modules, primarily as a way of dividing up the work for this large project. Four modules were developed: an Internet overview, e-mail and listservs, gopher, and the World Wide Web. The gopher module included a demonstration of the library's gopher and a brief introduction to the library's OPAC and FirstSearch. A "script" was developed for the seminar, with each of the demonstration sites mapped out in advance. This enabled the instructors to work as a team, one working at the keyboard while the other spoke. An added benefit was the record of the session that this script provided; subsequent seminars are based on the script of the session preceding it.

An informal title for the seminar was used as a guide for the overall instructional goal: "Getting a Foot in the Internet Door." The seminar was designed to include several short hands-on periods. Tutorials were developed for each of the Internet protocols, and for CLICnet and FirstSearch. Tutorials would create a structure for students' first attempts at the Internet during the hands-on periods as well as providing a safety net for their earliest independent efforts following the seminar. Additional materials designed included: an "Emergency Road Kit," a guide to solving common problems such as hung connections; a glossary of Internet jargon; and a resource list of print and online information for further study. After the seminar these guides and tutorials were made available on our library display rack and World Wide Web homepage (www.hamline.edu/library/index.html).

While in the process of planning this seminar, the graduate school librarian received a note from Graduate Liberal Studies administration asking who on campus might be able to provide Internet training to students in this program; enclosed with the note was a newsletter from a similar liberal studies program describing their training opportunities. When told about the January Internet seminars being developed for Graduate Public Administration, she asked whether a seminar could be scheduled for her students; two seminars were ultimately scheduled. There were now four half-day seminars scheduled in January for graduate students.

The day of the first of these January seminars it became quickly apparent that there was enough material for a two-day seminar; during students' hands-on time the instructors met to make the adjustments necessary to cover the most important information in the scheduled four hours. More adjustments were made before the second seminar; the last two seminars ran comfortably within the time allotted.

Three additional seminars were scheduled for Graduate Public Administration the following semester. Because these particular seminars were to be open to the general public it was decided it would be more appropriate to teach them as a teaching overload rather than part of the librarians' regular duties. These seminars have further raised the credibility of library staff as resources and trainers on campus.

An invitation was also extended to teach the Internet section of a Public Administration Computer Skills course, a summer semester course in which students would learn to use spreadsheets, presentation software, and asynchronous conferencing in addition to the Internet. The technology and graduate school librarians taught five half-day class sessions and participated in the "listserv with training wheels" established for the course, answering students' questions as they practiced their newly-acquired skills.

ONE-ON-ONE SESSIONS

As the first of the Internet seminars were being developed and taught, a number of graduate students, faculty, and administrative staff expressed curiosity about the Internet and the library's other online resources to their library liaison. Anxious not to miss an opportunity, she offered to meet with them in one-on-one sessions. These were intensive sessions, each lasting nearly two hours. The immediacy of this format provided instant feedback on the most effective approach, and the most effective metaphors, for teaching the Internet. Most importantly, these sessions demonstrated the tremendous need among graduate school students, faculty, and staff for very basic instruction in using the library's online resources. An interesting discovery was that, while most of them said they wanted to "learn the Internet," they were especially interested in the library's online catalog and databases.

The success of these informal one-on-one sessions, and the previously mentioned discussions within our consortium regarding faculty outreach and training, inspired the library's departmental liaisons to extend official invitations to faculty for one-on-one sessions. This was not the success hoped for: there were only three responses. The session with the single graduate faculty respondent, however, led to an opportunity to meet with her class, one of the graduate school's first off-campus groups, for a library instruction session. This session, in turn, led to the opportunity to meet with each of the off-campus groups for instruction. Library instruction is now scheduled regularly for these students.

COLUMNS

Following her one-on-one session, another graduate school administrator expressed interest in helping students in her creative writing program learn about writing and literature related listservs. Seeing another opportunity, the liaison offered to write an article about listservs for writers. She had been exploring ways to reach graduate students with library information and had been considering starting a library newsletter. An offer to write a regular column in the monthly departmental newsletter was enthusiastically accepted. This column on listservs for writers led to a series of columns on Internet protocols. After the first of these columns appeared, the other graduate programs requested similar columns for their newsletters. The library column in each of these graduate program newsletters provides yet another means of reaching students and faculty with library and Internet news, information, and instruction.

MOVING INTO THE COLLEGE OF LIBERAL ARTS

Spurred by the increased demand for bibliographic and Internet instruction in the graduate school, we became convinced that our success could be marketed to our undergraduate campus, the College of Liberal Arts (CLA). A proposal was made to the Library Reference Team to conduct seminars for CLA based on those done for the graduate school. The time-consuming development work was already done; all we needed was a way to "hook" CLA. It was clear that the seminars would be a very effective way to begin to meet the Dean's charge to be leaders in technology and to justify the university's expenditures on the library.

The Reference Team decided that, given the lack of response to our offer for one-on-one faculty Internet instruction, we should host a faculty Internet seminar. Such a seminar would help establish librarians' credibility with faculty in general. A faculty Internet seminar would also give us the opportunity to work toward another goal: that of building on the seminar's modular structure to divide up the work of teaching the Internet among librarians and begin to insert more traditional bibliographic instruction into the mix.

To lend credibility to the library's offering, the Dean's office was asked to sponsor a Faculty Development Workshop featuring our "Getting a Foot in the Internet Door" seminar. This raised the relevance of the workshop in faculty eyes, as well as providing another incentive: free box lunches.

In planning the Faculty Development Seminar, new World Wide Web sites were researched to use as examples of Internet relevance to research and teaching. Otherwise, the content was unchanged from that presented to the graduate school. Utilizing the modular nature of the original design, this seminar was offered as a series of ninety minute sessions, as opposed to a single four hour session. The entire reference staff participated; those who had not been involved in the original workshop served as "lab assistants." This gave them an opportunity to see the work that had already been done and to consider becoming a part of such training in the future.

Response to the announcement was skeptical in some quarters; one faculty member even paid a special visit to express her fear that this would be another jargon-filled lecture and a waste of her time. Library staff worried whether any faculty would return for the second session of the seminar. Instead we found dedicated participation, extremely positive feedback and a sudden increase in the library's relevance on campus. The box lunches provided a wonderful opportunity to strengthen faculty-library communication. Comments on evaluations and those received by the Dean's office were very encouraging. Perhaps most rewarding were two things: the demand for more workshops and the increased incidence of faculty posting to the campus faculty listserv items from listservs introduced in the seminar. To have faculty who had previously questioned technology begin to embrace its use for scholarly communication was very gratifying indeed. In response to demand, the workshop has been offered repeatedly, in both one day and modular formats.

DIVIDING THE TURF

A rising demand for Internet training on campus combined with a desire to keep the library relevant in the increasingly electronic information world fueled the desire of at least one librarian to see the library become the primary campus Internet trainer. Furthermore, the addition of the title "Internet trainer" seems to have a positive effect on the way "librarians" are perceived.

The reference staff had some reservations about the staff's ability to provide an all-campus program of Internet instruction. The head of Campus Computing was invited to assist us in dividing the instructional turf. As librarians, our goal was to keep training focused on the undergraduate curriculum and our primary clientele, students and faculty. The library should teach the "substance" of the Internet, its use in meeting information needs, rather than the technical details of performing Internet functions. Expecting some resistance on the part of the Computing Center–after all, the World Wide Web is hot and everyone wants to be viewed as an expert–librarians were prepared to defend their instructional role. In fact, the Computing Center was overwhelmed with work without doing any training at all and welcomed library participation; we could have taken over all campus computer training. Instead, it was agreed that the library would focus on teaching the informational use of the Internet to faculty and students, while the Computing Center would focus on non-academic staff and those Internet tools that require some technical instruction, such as e-mail, ftp and html.

The Library and Computing Center staffs also agreed to share more of the instruction and planning processes. Efforts in the past year have helped build a largely cooperative relationship, which seems to be somewhat unusual. Teaching partnerships have evolved; a Computing Center staff member teaches e-mail and a librarian teaches the online catalog and the World Wide Web. The technology librarian's role as liaison to the Computing Center has been strengthened by involvement in Internet teaching. At an off-campus multimedia class attended by members of both departments, she was introduced by Computing Center staff to other class members as "our campus World Wide Web expert." While this is an overstatement, it does evidence an unusual level of trust between Campus Computing and the library.

There are still frustrations, though. Librarians are often confronted with technical support questions from unhappy students who have not found answers in the Computer Lab. The library must assert that it is not the help desk for e-mail and SLIP connections. But the relationship has generally continued to thrive; one Friday afternoon a Computing Center staff person voluntarily left his home number in case of network problems during a Saturday library Internet class.

THE MOD SQUAD

The modular nature of the original Internet seminar eventually evolved into a series of stand-alone modules, taught by the Mod Squad. This is both the logical and the desired outcome of the past year's work. It had become obvious that the graduate librarian could not continue to hold one-on-one instructional sessions in either Internet or library resources for all graduate faculty and students. At the same time, there was a growing demand from undergraduates for some formal instruction in the increasing plethora of online sources. The popularity of the Windows-based Pacs, all running Netscape, made clear an increased need for Web based instructional support. Success with the faculty seminars compelled us to find a way to share Internet instruction with the undergraduate community. Finally, we wanted to share the responsibilities and rewards of Internet instruction among all library staff.

A series of modular classes in online information sources, both Internet and library related, was proposed to the library's Administrative Team. They would be offered to the campus community at large, in two formats: the original four-hour seminar, and a series of stand-alone one-hour sessions. Included in the one-hour sessions were the most popular parts of the four-hour seminar, and some new "Mods," such as "CLICnet: basics and beyond" and "Introduction to hyper-research" to meet the increasing demand for instruction in finding useful information on the Internet.

Response to the Mods has been very positive. Some have filled beyond capacity. The concept needs refining; meeting demand while balancing librarians' workloads is a challenge. Currently offered are daytime, evening and weekend sessions, with one librarian teaching one session of each Mod. A well-balanced attendance by undergraduate and graduate students has demonstrated that their respective attention span and "need to know" is quite different. Future plans include refining the "Mod Squad" offerings, perhaps even to the point of a credit course.

In addition to the Mods, our librarians have been overwhelmed with requests for in-class instruction in both traditional online library resources and in the Web as an informational resource. Positive feedback has ranged from the Dean informing the Library Director that he "hears good things about the Library" these days, to individual faculty and graduate program directors informing librarians that they are very excited about the changes and the energy coming from the library.

CRISIS = OPPORTUNITY

A series of opportunities, starting with a staff change in the Computing Center, led to librarians' involvement in Internet instruction. Involvement in Internet instruction, from seminars to one-on-one sessions and columns, provided a "hook" where several other attempts at faculty outreach had not succeeded. Finally, while information on library databases such as CLICnet and FirstSearch was "snuck" in with Internet information, the way a parent might hide a pill in a spoonful of pudding, people listened equally intently to the library instruction. For many, this was what they wanted most: information on using the library and doing research.

It was their curiosity about the Internet, though, that first led them to library staff and gave us the opportunity to establish our credibility on campus. It was likely easier for students and, especially, faculty, to ask librarians about the Internet–new and unfamiliar territory–than to admit to needing help with the OPAC or the Library's online databases. Furthermore, librarians, already experienced teachers of online skills, were readily able to develop effective Internet teaching methods. This expertise has been recognized and affirmed by students, faculty, and administrators; librarians are increasingly involved in the integration of technology into the curriculum on the Hamline campus. Not only are librarians regularly asked to teach Internet skills within the classroom context; they are also involved in campus wide planning and policy initiatives, such as Technology Task Forces. The success of our instructional program recently led to a much-needed upgrade of the hardware in our bibliographic instruction room, which doubles as a Web access lab for students. Most gratifying of all is the increased relevance of the Library in student eyes. Undergraduates crowd the public access terminals; as often to search online bibliographic and fulltext databases as to surf the Web. Graduate students regularly seek out librarians for in-depth consultations on effective searching methods. Far from fading into a virtual electronic realm, Bush Library is busier than ever!

It is hoped that this story will help illustrate how technology's increasing role in librarians' professional lives can be a blessing as well as a challenge. While the graduate school librarian's initial motivation was to make connections to her faculty, and the technology librarian's to establish the library's relevance in a changing context, the library's overall vitality was greatly strengthened in the process. One thing truly did lead to another and another and another, in a very domino-like pattern. This indicates one way in which librarians can assert their "pathfinder" role in the changing world of information.

BIBLIOGRAPHY

Diaz, Karen R. and Helena M. VonVille, "Internet Training at the Ohio State University: The Process, the Product, the Potential," in *The Internet Library,* ed. Julie Still (Westport, CT: Mecklermedia, 1994): 85-96.

Farber, Evan Ira, "Teachers as Learners–The Application of BI," in *Working with Faculty in the New Electronic Library: Papers and Session Materials Presented at the Nineteenth National LOEX Library Instruction Conference,* ed. Linda Shirato (Ann Arbor: Pieran Press, 1992): 1-5.

Fishel, Terri and Jeanne Stevens, "Teaching the Internet: An Undergraduate Liberal Arts College Experience," in *The Internet Library,* ed. Julie Still (Westport, CT: Mecklermedia, 1994): 109-126.

Miller, Donna and Michael C. Zeigler, "An Internet Workshop for Lebanon Valley College Faculty and Staff: 'Striking it Rich with the Internet,'" in *The Internet Library,* ed. Julie Still (Westport, CT: Mecklermedia, 1994): 167-179.

Page, Mary and Martin Kesselman, "Teaching the Internet: Challenges and Opportunities," *Research Strategies* 12:3 (Summer 1994): 157-167.

Silva, Marcos and Glenn F. Cartwright, "The Internet and Reference Librarians: A Question of Leadership," *The Reference Librarian* 41/42 (1994): 159-172.

Thomas, Joy, "Faculty Attitudes and Habits Concerning Library Instruction: How Much Has Changed Since 1982?," *Research Strategies* 12:4 (Fall 1994): 209-223.

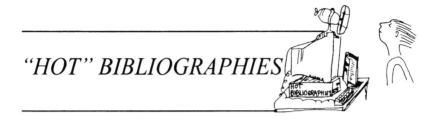

"HOT" BIBLIOGRAPHIES

Internet Resources for Tests
and Measurements

Brian Quinn

SUMMARY. The reference collections of most research libraries contain a readily identifiable collection of standard paper sources used in locating tests and test-related materials for education and psychology. Yet currently there is no electronic equivalent, no set of Internet resources that has been identified as constituting an online literature on tests and measurements. This study attempts to investigate what resources are now available on the Internet for tests and measurements, and identifies the most useful ones. In order to keep the study manageable, the emphasis is on resources for psychologi-

Brian Quinn (libaq@ttacs.ttu.edu) is Social Sciences Librarian at Texas Tech University, Box 40002, Lubbock, TX 79409.

The illustrator, Katherine A. Waugh (kawaugh@vaxsar.vassar.edu), is Reference Librarian, Vassar College Library, Poughkeepsie, NY 12601.

[Haworth co-indexing entry note]: "Internet Resources for Tests and Measurements." Quinn, Brian. Co-published simultaneously in *Internet Reference Services Quarterly* (The Haworth Press, Inc.) Vol. 2, No. 4, 1997, pp. 211-235; and: *The Challenge of Internet Literacy: The Instruction-Web Convergence* (ed: Lyn Elizabeth M. Martin) The Haworth Press, Inc., 1997, pp. 211-235. Single or multiple copies of this article are available for a fee from The Haworth Document Delivery Service [1-800-342-9678, 9:00 a.m. - 5:00 p.m. (EST). E-mail address: getinfo@haworth.com].

cal testing, with some educational psychology materials included as well. Whenever possible, evaluative summaries of these resources have been included. *[Article copies available for a fee from The Haworth Document Delivery Service: 1-800-342-9678. E-mail address: getinfo@ haworth. com]*

KEYWORDS. Internet, resources, tests, measurements, assessment, psychology, education, evaluation

There is a remarkable amount of information about tests and measurements to be found on the Internet, if one is willing to spend long hours online tracking it down. Hopefully, this study should eliminate the need for extended searches, as I have tried to include as many worthwhile resources as I have been able to find. Admittedly, it is difficult to offer a comprehensive collection of anything on the Internet, given the rapidity with which it is growing and changing.[1] Because of the large volume of resources available, it has been necessary to limit this study primarily to psychological tests and measurements. There are undoubtedly many valuable test resources available on the Internet that are specific to education that could not be included in this study.

For easier reference, the resources have been organized into broad categories that give one a clue to their purpose. This study begins with a list of Comprehensive Web Sites that could logically serve as a starting point for any basic search for test information. In order to be considered comprehensive, a resource had to contain many links to other sites specific to tests and measurements. It is the richness and variety of resources that these sites have to offer that make them such a good place to start. Indeed, one site, the ERIC Clearinghouse on Assessment and Evaluation, has so much to offer that it even comes with its own site-specific search engine.

The next category of Internet resources, Research and Reference, features factual information about particular tests, test terms, and the science of testing as well. There is also information in this section regarding research strategies for finding test information. Many of the standard reference works used in finding test information are complex and difficult to use,[2] and this section includes pointers on how to use these works and how they are organized. There is also considerable information in this section about the effectiveness of particular tests, and sources of funding. Both the librarian needing information about a test or testing, and the student needing help in locating test information will find this section of value.

The following section covers journals and newsletters related to tests and measurements. Currently, only a few journals cover this area, and some, like Rasch Measurement Transactions, are quite specialized. Several of these publications are available online, so that the searcher can access the actual full text of the article. Scanning these publications is a good way to obtain an overview of some of the current issues involved in the field of testing. Since many of the articles include bibliographies, monitoring these publications can be a way of finding related sources.

The next group of resources that will prove useful to researchers in the field is that of electronic discussion lists, or "listservs." There are several that particularly emphasize tests and measurements, and most seem to be for specialists with considerable background in assessment. They can be a valuable resource for the researcher who is searching for esoteric or technical information regarding tests and needs the advice of a forum of experts who might be willing to share their expertise in response to a particular query from a searcher.[3] However, they will also prove to be of interest to the person seeking more background regarding a particular aspect or technique of testing, as much can be learned from reading the electronic dialogue of experts conversing about topics of importance to them. One unfortunate disadvantage of listservs is that a few are relatively inactive, making them less fruitful sources of information.

The field of testing is rather poorly represented in the category of usenets. The one usenet that does have bearing on the subject is mentioned in this next category, and the searcher will find much here of interest related to personality testing. Of course, other usenets in the field of psychology make occasional mention of testing topics, but none with enough frequency to merit mention here as a bona fide test resource.

In the category that follows, the reader will find Internet resources devoted to specific organizations that are prominent in the field of tests and measurements. Organizations such as the APA and the Buros Institute are very influential and active in the field,[4] and the searcher who needs to find test-related information will find much here of interest. The material to be found at these sites ranges widely in its sophistication, and one can find everything from very basic test information, to cutting-edge research. Presumably, these organizations might also serve as reference points for inquiries about a particular topic related to their interests.

The final category, Test-Specific Resources, contains more in-depth material about particular tests. Included here are a wide range of personality tests, many of which are offshoots of the well-known Myers Briggs Type Indicator,[5] which attempts to determine the personality type of the test subject. Other tests try to measure the intelligence quotient, or "IQ" of the subject. There are even tests that are available to measure a person's style of learning or spending personality. Many of these tests are available in online interactive format, allowing the subject to actually take the test online, usually by clicking on one of several possible responses to a multiple choice question. Several of the tests also feature online scoring, which allows the subject to click on a submit button after completing all the questions. The questionnaire is then scored on a computer and returned electronically to the subject. These tests should prove valuable not only to those seeking to learn more about their personality or IQ, but also to those seeking to learn more about test design and construction. Given the ease of administration and scoring that these online tests offer, it is likely that many more will appear in the near future, and perhaps someday even established tests like the SAT and the GRE will be routinely administered online.

COMPREHENSIVE WEB SITES

Assessment and Evaluation on the Internet

http://www.cua.edu/www/eric_ae/intass.html

This Web site may have the best collection of resources for tests and measurements currently available on the World Wide Web. It was created to help professionals quickly identify Internet resources of special interest to researchers in the assessment field. AEI has divided these resources into two categories: gopher sites and listservs. Each category is prefaced by a helpful definition and description of the type of resource and how to use it. Resources are arranged alphabetically by title within each category. Many of the resources are accompanied by a paragraph-length abstract describing the resource. These abstracts are primarily of a descriptive nature and do not attempt to evaluate a given resource to any significant degree.[6]

The first category of resources covers gopher sites, and features links to dozens of useful sites, including professional associations like the American Educational Research Association, and the American Evaluation Association. Oddly, some of the most valuable resources, like the Clearinghouse for Subject-Oriented Internet Resource Guides, do not have abstracts. A few of the links, such as the MMPI link, appear to be inactive. There is nonetheless much valuable information, including links to online journals and newsletters, research centers, and statistics software. The second category is devoted to listserv discussion groups. Most of the listservs are accompanied by a brief description of the list. There are many education and social sciences research listservs in this category, and some of the listservs appear to be relevant to psychology.

Assessment and Evaluation on the Internet should be one of the first stops on the Web for anyone interested in getting an overview of the wide variety of resources available to anyone interested in tests and measurements. Few other sites on the Internet offer as many resources for tests and measurements in a single location as this one.

Eric Clearinghouse on Assessment and Evaluation

http://www.cua.edu/www/eric_ae/

This Web site offers a huge amount of information related to tests and measurements. The site opens with a series of links to ERIC (Educational Resources Information Center). There is a list of known Web, gopher, and telnet sites that are valuable for searching ERIC, RIE, and CIJE.

Even more useful for research on tests and measurements is the ERIC/AE Test Locator. It is jointly sponsored by ERIC, the Educational Testing Service, the Buros Institute of Mental Measurements, the University of Nebraska, and Pro-Ed Test Publishers. The ERIC/AE Test Locator provides links for searching the ETS Test Collection database,[7] which now contains over 10,000 records on tests and research instruments. The records describe the tests and provide information about their availability. There is also a link to the Buros Test Review Locator, which tells you which publications of the Buros Institute contain reviews and descriptions of the test you are searching for. A similar test review locator for Pro-Ed publications is also available, as well as a test publisher locator.

Other useful links that are available at this site include a searchable database of over 1,700 full-text articles posted at the ERIC/AE gopher site. Another helpful link provides access to a searchable database of the 1996 annual meeting of the American Educational Research Association. There is also a link to the Language Tester's Guide to Cyberspace, which itself provides numerous links to resources related to applied linguistics and language testing sites.

The ERIC Clearinghouse on Assessment and Evaluation has a separate gopher for news about testing, and one that features essays, bibliographies, and resources about testing. It has a collection of online guides and FAQ's on assessment, evaluation and learning theory. There is information about testing projects, a directory of educational researchers, and links to assessment resources for K-12 students. All of these resources make The ERIC Clearinghouse on Assessment and Evaluation one of the most useful sites for tests and measurements available on the World Wide Web.

Mental Health Net-Assessment Resources

http://www.cmhc.com/guide/pro01.htm#other

This is a Web site that offers numerous links to assessment information. The emphasis is primarily on psychological tests, particularly personality assessment instruments. Tests are arranged alphabetically by title, and several tests are accompanied by brief descriptions of what the test is about. Sixteen links to tests resources are featured at this site.

Among the test resources to be found here is a link to the Child Behavior Checklist gopher site. The Child Behavior Checklist is a questionnaire used by psychologists to help assess children's problems.[8] The site describes the test, offers bibliographic information about studies performed on the test, and describes information manuals that provide instructions about how to use the test.

Also featured at this site is an online version of The Ennegram Test, which is a test designed to categorize personality into one of nine types. There is a link to the Kiersey Temperament Sorter, which is a test that measures personality types in the same vein as Meyers-Briggs, and a link to a series of neurological rating scales. A link has also been provided to a downloadable version of the Personality Diagnostic Questionnaire for DSM-IV, which is useful for detecting the presence of personality disorders using the framework of DSM-IV, Axis II.

One can find here reviews and excerpts of tests such as the White Sands Personality Test 1.4 and the Meyers-Briggs personality test. There are also links to Wada testing, a neurological test used to assess cerebral functioning in the postoperative phase of epilepsy surgery, and the Zang Personality Test, which uses shapes to measure personality types. With such a wide variety of links to tests and test information, Mental Health Net-Assessment Resources is an excellent source for someone searching for a particular scale, as well as for someone who just wants to get an overview of what is available in this area.

Neuropsychology Central-Neuropsychological Assessment

http://www.premier.net/~cogito/neurocen/neuroass/neuroass.html

Neuropsychological Assessment is a comprehensive Web site offering numerous links to sources of information related to the measurement of the neurologically impaired. The site begins with links to behavior analysis and geriatric assessment resources at New York University. It was created to provide psychiatrists with a site to test their understanding by offering a series of board-style questions and annotated answers online. Access to the material is limited to NYU students, however.

For those interested in the measurement of children, there is a link that provides information about a test used in the neurological assessment of pediatric patients. The test is used for conditions like coma and acute neurological deterioration. There is another link that treats the whole subject of neurological assessment and treatment in more general terms and gives useful definitions of such key concepts as diagnostics, assessment of treatment efficacy, delineation of functional capabilities, and cognitive remediation.

Also featured at this site is a course description for Patient Oriented Neuropsychiatric Assessment, and a link to the APA journal *Psychological Assessment*. There is a study of the relationship between two well-known severity scoring systems for brain-injured patients, and a set of links to the Web sites of some leading neuropsychological tests. These include the Ackerman-Banks Neuropsychological Rehabilitation Battery and the MBTI Identification Checklist. There is also a link to a site that features a list of important neurological rating scales, complete with descriptions and actual scale samples.

Yahoo-Education: Educational Standards and Testing

http://www.yahoo.com/Education/Educational_Standards_and_Testing/

Yahoo offers a very useful and well-chosen set of links related to Educational Standards and Testing. It begins with a list of companies that offer test preparation services to candidates in a variety of fields, including law, medicine, business, liberal arts, and English as a foreign language. This is followed by a dozen links to established sites such as the Buros Institute, the ETS Gopher and the ERIC/AE Test Locator.

A number of interesting sites that are less well known can be found here as well. There is a link to CRESST, the National Center for Research on Evaluation, Standards, and Student Testing at UCLA, which provides information about assessment alternatives in American schools. Information about ICAP, the Inventory for Client and Agency Planning, is listed here too. This measure assesses adaptive and maladaptive behavior in children and adults with developmental disabilities.[9]

Along with these links, one can also find a connection to Immex, the Interactive Multi-Media Exercises project at the UCLA School. This project involves using a software program that analyzes student performance in problem solving activities as an alternative to traditional multiple-choice questionnaires. There is a link to the National Association of Test Directors, an organization that shares information about testing in education, particularly at the elementary and secondary levels. This site offers a particularly good array of links to other ed psych resources on the Web.

Other interesting links that can be explored at Yahoo are Question Mark, a company that provides software that enables the user to create, administer, and analyze tests using a computer, and Roc Research. The latter is a company that writes test questions for teachers and textbooks. Overall, Yahoo may not be as large as some of the mega-sites mentioned previously, but it offers a useful and substantial collection of links that are not easily found elsewhere. Anyone interested in educational testing should find this a valuable site.

RESEARCH AND REFERENCE

A Glossary of Measurement Terms

gopher://vmsgopher.cua.edu/00GOPHER_ROOT_ERIC_AE%3A%56B_EDIR.GUIDE%5D1AAJGUIDE.txt

This is an excellent site for anyone seeking definitions of technical terms used in testing research. Approximately 30 terms are featured at this site. Terms are arranged alphabetically in a dictionary-style format. Each definition is brief and averages two to four lines. The definitions are clear and succinct.

There is a wide range of material represented, ranging from basic test terms to more technical ones. Basic terms include items like "achievement test," "age norms," "average," and "battery." Among the more technical terms that can be found here are "criterion-referenced test," "normal curve equivalent," and "stanine." This site should prove to be particularly valuable to those who are new to the field of testing and are not very familiar with the specialized terminology. One wishes that more terms could be included, so that this resource could be more comprehensive.

Assessment Digests Table of Contents

http://www.uncg.edu/~ericcas2/assessment/toc_assessment.html

This site, which is co-sponsored by the ERIC Counseling and Student Services Clearinghouse and the University of North Carolina, Greensboro, features over 30 scholarly articles or digests on a wide variety of topics on assessment. Each article averages 10-12 pages in length, and most of the authors have academic affiliations. Some of the topics covered include understanding client concerns in mental health counseling, assessment of abilities, interests, self-concept, and temperament, gender and multicultural differences in testing, ethics in assessment, computer-assisted testing, and evaluating career assessment instruments. This site is an excellent resource for the researcher who wants to get a brief overview of a particular aspect of testing by a specialist in that area.

Cresst/UCLA Research on Evaluation and Testing

gopher://gopher.cse.ucla.edu/1

This gopher server is sponsored by the National Center for Research on Evaluation, Standards, and Student Testing (CRESST) at UCLA. It provides information about K-12 assessment research conducted by the Center. Researchers will find an extensive collection of technical reports on test effectiveness, assessment procedures, test construction, and related topics. CRESST also provides access to articles from its newsletter on performance assessment and a huge database on alternative assessment research.[10] There is information about upcoming CRESST conferences and proceedings of recent conferences. Information about various CRESST products such as videotapes and books related to assessment is provided. A list of research and funding sources in the field of education is another valuable feature of this site. The server also includes a link to the ERIC database. There is an enormous amount of research available at this server, which will be of particular interest to those working in the field of educational psychology and related areas.

Frequently Asked Questions (FAQ) on Psychological Tests

http://www.apa.org/science/test.html

The American Psychological Association receives many queries about psychological tests and measurements each year. This site contains answers to the most frequently asked questions posed by those trying to locate a certain test or find more information about psychological tests. It is divided into two sections, one answering questions about published tests and another for questions about unpublished instruments. The section on published tests offers suggestions for locating tests on a given subject, where to locate test publishers, and how to obtain computerized testing material. The second section on unpublished tests gives information on locating unpublished tests and discusses some of the responsibilities of users of unpublished tests in relation to copyright issues. Taken as a whole, the many questions answered at this site give the reader an excellent general strategy for locating both published and unpublished tests. It reviews basic test directories and review sources and discusses how to use them, and how to obtain copies from the publisher or author. Of particular value is the section on computerized testing materials used in administering, scoring and interpreting test results. Librarians who want a detailed strategy for locating test information will find this site invaluable.

Job Analysis/Classification and Personality Research

http://harvey.psyc.vt.edu/

A wide variety of information regarding various aspects of testing in the fields of industrial and organizational psychology can be found here. Considerable data is also provided on the subject of personality testing and research. Some of the material focuses on task-inventory methods[11] and the Common-Metric Questionnaire, a standardized scale for job analysis. Other topics covered include testing and the Americans with Disabilities Act, and software programs used in job analysis and classification. In the area of personality assessment, some of the information focuses on personality tests used in employment-related settings, especially the Myers-Briggs Type Indicator. There are lengthy files on topics such as using item response theory to score the Myers-Briggs, improving the measurement precision of the MBTI, and a discussion of its dimensionality. Those working in the area of industrial/organizational psychology will find this a useful site, as will human resource professionals and students of business and commerce.

The Mental Measurements Yearbook

http://library.uwaterloo.ca/howto/howto22.html

The Mental MeasurementsYearbooks are such an important and complex set of tools for finding information about tests and measurements that the University of Waterloo library has set aside a special section of its Web page to explain them. This site begins with a basic description of the *Yearbook*. It describes the rather complicated cumulative structure of this series of volumes, and then goes on to describe exactly what test information can be found using the *MMY*. Each of the *MMY*'s six indexes are explained briefly. There is a particularly lucid explanation of the potentially confusing score index, which if understood correctly, can prove more useful than searching the title index. The explanation of the name index is equally clear, and is careful to distinguish between persons designated as authors or as reviewers. Overall, this resource gives a valuable summary of how to get the most out of one of the most important sources in testing literature.

Social Sciences Review Sources for Tests in Psychology

http://www.colostate.edu/Depts/LTS/research/socsci/ps.html

This resource offers a brief overview of some of the key reference sources used in locating tests and measurements. Eight titles are listed, including standard sources like *The Mental Measurements Yearbook, Tests in Print*, and *The ETS Test Collection Catalog*. Each citation is accompanied by a brief abstract describing the contents of the work and how it is arranged. The site includes works covering both published and unpublished tests. This can be useful for researchers desiring a quick snapshot of some of the key sources available. The list is not comprehensive, however, and some of the entries need to be updated with the latest editions.

Tests and Measurements: A Guide to Resources and Their Use

http:// luna.cc.lehigh.edu/BIBLIO:/home/inref/tests.txt

Anyone seeking a detailed online guide to a variety of reference sources used in searching for tests and measurements will find this a worthwhile site to visit. It was created by librarians at Lehigh University, and it provides the user with a fairly complete search strategy for locating test materials. Not only does it provide citations and abstracts describing seminal reference works like *Tests in Print*, *Test Critiques*, and *The Mental Measurements Yearbook*, it also describes many secondary sources for test material. One particularly valuable feature of this site is that the descriptions of reference works on tests include sample entries which help make these works easier to use. This site also gives suggestions about which subject headings to use in searching, describes how to use social sciences indexes for finding test information, and tells how to use the ERIC gopher site on tests and measurements. It also shows how to search for a test when one has only partial information. This resource guide should prove useful to the librarian who is not familiar with how to search for test information, and it might also serve as an excellent online tutorial for students in psychology or education.[12] A bit more material on unpublished tests and a listing of sources containing actual test samples would make this site even stronger.

JOURNALS AND NEWLETTERS

About Psychological Assessment

http://www.apa.org/journals/ass.html

Psychological Assessment is a relatively new journal sponsored by the American Psychological Association. It contains articles, case studies and reviews on the construction, validation and evaluation of tests, with particular attention paid to issues of testing in cross-cultural and gender-related contexts. This site contains detailed information about the journal, which is currently issued in paper format. In addition to describing *Psychological Assessment*, it contains the table of contents of current and past issues, information about how to submit manuscripts for review, and particulars about prices and subscriptions. The site even features an order form that can be printed and mailed by someone wishing to subscribe. Anyone interested in tests and measurements will want to know more about this promising new journal, and this site is an excellent starting point.

Rasch Measurement Transactions

gopher://vmsgopher.cua.edu/11gopher_root_eric_ae%3a%5b_rasch%5d

Rasch Measurement Transactions is an online journal of current information about Rasch measurement, which utilizes quantitative techniques to analyze qualitative data.[13] It is published quarterly by the American Educational Research Association. The content consists of abstracts, reviews and brief articles on both the theoretical and applied aspects of Rasch measurement, especially in relation to multiple choice testing, questionnaire analysis, computer adaptive testing and performance assessment. This site features an introduction to Rasch modeling, a membership form for the Rasch SIG of the AERA, and the tables of contents and actual full text of articles appearing in the last ten issues. Most of these articles are highly technical in nature, and will be of interest primarily to educational psychologists and psychometricians. Many of the articles are accompanied by a bibliography and the database is searchable by keyword.

TIP: The Industrial-Organizational Psychologist

http://cmit.unomaha.edu/TIP/TIPOct95/schneide.html

An important part of industrial/organizational psychology is testing,[14] and *TIP* is an electronic newsletter that includes full-text articles about tests and measurements in many of its issues. *TIP* is the official quarterly of the Society for Industrial-Organizational Psychology. It was created to provide subscribers with the latest research findings in industrial and organizational psychology. The latest issue features an article on testing for integrity, and back issues are also available at this site. Previous issues include articles about the Office of Personnel Management updating its guide for testing persons with disabilities, and about the changes in educational and psychological testing being proposed by the AERA, APA, NCME Joint Committee on the Standards for Educational and Psychological Testing. *TIP* is a very valuable site for those doing research in I/O psychology, at both the undergraduate and graduate levels.

LISTSERVS

Idanet

mailbase@mailbase.ac.uk

Idanet (Individual Differences and Assessment Net) is a moderately active discussion group whose members are interested in the testing of individual differences. Specifically, the focus is on using multivariate analysis to measure intrapsychic variables such as personality and cognitive ability and attempting to explain the variance among different individuals. The broad theme of the discussion makes it appealing to a wide variety of researchers from different specialties in the social sciences, including both clinical, experimental, industrial, and educational psychology. The discussion is therefore wide ranging and can include anything that falls within the realm of individual differences. Some recent topics of discussion among this group include the use of Rasch models in ability testing, whether intelligence is different from personality, the posting of a

Web page by the Personnel Testing Council of Metropolitan Washington, D.C. and news about an upcoming conference on the rights and responsibilities of test takers. Much of the list discussion can be fairly technical, so it appears more appropriate for graduate students and professionals.

Personality Type Mailing Lists

http://www.brad.ac.uk/~mdavarle/e-lists.html

This site provides a listing of listservs, each of which is dedicated to the discussion of a different personality type. All of these lists stem from sixteen possible personality types measured by the Myers-Briggs Type Indicator, a test which measures personality along four basic dimensions: extroversion, introversion, sensing, and intuition.[15] This theory of personality assumes that one function is always dominant, and the result is 16 possible personality combinations. There are nine listservs to be found at this site, each of which focuses on a dominant personality type. The list is annotated, and includes a brief description of the list, the name of the list administrator, the number of subscribers, and information about how to subscribe. Subscription to some of the lists is limited to members who have that particular personality type.

Rorschach

LISTSERV@sjuvm.stjohns.edu

Rorschach is a highly active discussion list that covers a variety of topics related to the technique of Rorschach testing, which is used to test personality. The technique consists of ten cards containing ink blots, which the subject is asked to interpret freely.[16] The interpretations are then encoded with the aid of a system of interpretation, which allows one to arrive at an assessment. Subscribers to this list include practicing psychologists as well as many graduate students in the area of clinical psychology. Because the language used is often technical, this is not an appropriate list for laypersons. In addition to discussion of Rorschach testing, other projective tests are occasionally mentioned on the list. Some of the postings to the list that have appeared recently include a discussion of inter-rater reliability, a new book recommendation, using the Rorschach with children, Rorschach training workshops, determining the amount of time necessary to administer, score, and interpret the test, and the overinterpretation of color shading blends in certain cards. This list should be of interest to anyone interested in projective tests and how to use them effectively.

Validata

LISTSERV@UA1VM.UA.EDU

The subject of this discussion list is the development, testing, and validation of psychological measures. It was established to serve as a forum for discussion of topics related to tests of personality, particularly multiple choice tests. Topics of particular interest to the list include methods of improving tests, psychometric flaws in existing instruments, face validity issues, the use of confirmatory factor analysis techniques to purify measures, and constructs that require measurement improvement. The list should prove to be of interest to researchers interested in improving test measurement and developing new scales. The list is unmoderated, and at the time the author subscribed to it, largely inactive.

USENET NEWSGROUPS

alt.psychology.personality

news:alt.psychology.personality

The alt.psychology.personality newsgroup is based on the same personality typology that is used in the Myers-Briggs Type Inventory. Indeed, many of the postings are from people who have taken the MBTI and whose test results have indicated they are one of the 16 personality types measured. So one will find postings speculating about what Hitler's personality type might have been, whether introverted personality types need to be around others, whether gifted introvert-type children are more likely to pursue scholarly occupations, etc. There are also postings about people seeking more information about a particular personality type (usually their own) or about the test itself. Despite the heavy emphasis on Myers-Briggs, it appears that the group is unmoderated, and there are many messages about topics unrelated to testing that span a wide range of psychology topics. This newsgroup is nonetheless valuable for those interested in Myers-Briggs testing and the concept of personality typing.

ORGANIZATIONS/INSTITUTIONS

American Psychological Association

http://www.apa.org/

The Web site of the American Psychological Association is a good source of information about recent research and trends in testing. There is a link here that allows the viewer to search the PsycINFO database, which is an excellent source of data about tests and measurements. Reviews, both pro and con, can be found here about the most controversial book recently published on the subject of testing, *The Bell Curve*.[17] A copy of the Code of Fair Testing Practices is also available. The best way to locate test information is to use the search link located at the end of the site. Typing in a simple search term like "tests," will bring up instructions for how to find test information in libraries, information about graduate study in educational and psychological measurement, an abstract describing the APA publication *Psychological Testing of Hispanics*, and other resources related to testing. The APA site is thus a valuable resource for anyone seeking general information about testing.

Association for Psychological Type

http://www.aptcentral.org/

The APT is an association of persons interested in the study of psychological types. It attempts to promote the theory and application of psychological typing through education and research, and also advocates the ethical use of test instruments based on psychological typing. This site gives information about the benefits of membership, such as staying current with the latest developments in the Meyers-Briggs Type Indicator. The APT also offers continuing education for psychologists in administering and interpreting the MBTI. The association holds meetings and conferences and publishes the *Bulletin of Psychological Type* and the *Journal of Psychological Type*, as well as biennial conference proceedings. The site includes an online membership application that can be printed out and mailed.

The Buros Institute

http://www.unl.edu/buros/home.html

This is very useful site that is sponsored by The Buros Institute of Mental Measurements at the University of Nebraska. It opens with a description of the Institute and an explanation of its goals and purposes, and how it goes about accomplishing them.[18] This introduction is followed by a series of links to other test resources. There is a link to the Buros Test Review Locator, which indexes Buros publications like the *Mental Measurements Yearbook* and *Tests in Print*. The Locator enables a searcher to quickly identify which Buros publication a review of the test can be found in, by typing in key words and clicking on the "Submit Query" option. This site also includes detailed online guides to using the *Mental Measurements Yearbook* and *Tests in Print*. Another link features a list of Buros publications complete with ordering information. Other information available includes details about *MMY* on Silverplatter, free user's guides, a schedule of forthcoming publications, articles and reviews about Buros publications, and more. This is the best site for information about Buros publications and the Buros Institute. It will appeal to anyone who uses tests and measurements, from undergraduates to post-doctoral researchers.

Jefferson Psychometric Lab

http://kiptron.psyc.virginia.edu/

This resource not only includes information about tests and measurements, it also includes data regarding the use of quantitative methods in psychological research. The lab, which is affiliated with the Psychology Department at the University of Virginia, specializes in researching new methods for experimental design and the computerized analysis of data. This site features summaries of recent research that the lab's researchers have been involved in. Some of the lab's current research topics include decision validity methods applied to the assessment of brain disorders with the WAIS, and an investigation of the measurement properties of the WAIS using novel structural equation modeling techniques. The research available at this site is highly technical in nature, making this site more appropriate for graduate students and professionals working in the area of quantitative research methods and psychometrics.

TEST-SPECIFIC RESOURCES

Belbin Self-Perception Inventory

http://www.brad.ac.uk/~mdavarle/other.html

Technically this site is called "Other Personality Tests," but since it only features one test, the Belbin Team-Role Self-Perception Inventory, it might be more accurate to refer to it by that name. The Belbin Self-Perception Inventory was created to measure a subject's strongest and weakest team roles.[19] This site does not feature the actual test, but it does include a form that can be automatically e-mailed for a copy of the test. An online version of the test will then be e-mailed back to the requester, who can then complete it and return it online. This test should be especially valuable to researchers working in the area of industrial and organizational psychology.

The Comar IQ Tests

http://www.euronet.nl/users/cor/iq.html

The Comar IQ tests consists of four separate tests representing four levels of increasing difficulty. Each test features 10 questions designed to measure a subject's level of intelligence. The nature of the questions precludes the use of reference works such as dictionaries or encyclopedias, since most of the questions cannot be answered by consulting them. The test can be completed online, and submitted electronically for scoring. Tests are scored and a person's ranking is posted electronically to a list at the site. Subjects have the option of remaining anonymous if they do not wish to have their e-mail address published. This site should prove useful for anyone interested in measuring their IQ, as well as those interested in studying how an IQ test is constructed. The site could use more introductory background material about how the test was developed.

The DDLI Page

http://sunsite.unc.edu/pub/academic/psychology/alt.psychology.personality/
html/ddli.html

The DDLI Page is home to the Duniho and Duniho Life Pattern Indicator, an extension of the well-known Myers-Briggs personality test. It measures the same 16 personality types, by posing a series of questions in order to determine the subject's life pattern. The DDLI is still an experimental measure, so there is no published paper version, only a digital one. This web site offers links to Amiga, PC, Unix, Macintosh, and Acorn versions of the test. There is a lengthy introduction of life patterns theory, which is based on Carl Jung's concept of psychological types. This site also includes an extensive series of FAQ's that go into much detail regarding the finer points of the test and what it is supposed to measure.

Emotional Intelligence Quotient

http://www.utne.com/cgi-bin/eq

Those familiar with the best selling book *Emotional Intelligence*[20] by Daniel Goleman will find this site of interest. It begins with Goleman explaining the concept of emotional intelligence, and his belief that it can be measured. This is followed by ten multiple-choice questions that ask a subject how s/he would respond emotionally in a particular hypothetical situation. The questions are followed by a chart for interpreting one's score on the test. An outline of the basics of emotional intelligence is also included, along with an answer key with detailed explanations of why a given response is considered appropriate. This is a fascinating site, but it could be better organized (e.g., the answer key should immediately follow the questions rather than be separated by other material).

European IQ Test

http://oscar.teclink.net/~tektite/iq/html

This is a intelligence test designed to measure IQ scores up to 174. The test consists of 25 questions, which are of the sequence-completion type. For example, many of the test questions ask the subject to complete sequences of numbers or letters or pictures (Netscape or Mosaic are necessary to complete the test). The test is designed to be completed in twenty minutes, but because the questions are all of a similar format, it might be completed in less time. Once the test is completed online, it can be submitted electronically and is then scored automatically. The test seems poorly designed given the monotony of the question format and the fact that most of the questions seem designed to measure logical reasoning, which is only one measure of intelligence.[21] Nonetheless, those curious about the subject of IQ will find this site worth investigating.

The Keirsey Temperament Sorter

http://sunsite.unc.edu/personality/keirsey.html

This site is concerned with a personality test developed by Daniel Keirsey, who has adopted elements of Jung's and Myers' approaches to measuring personality types. Keirsey differs from his predecessors in proposing that four temperaments are more basic and deserve greater emphasis than the eight types posited by Jung or the 16 types utilized by Myers. Another difference is that the Meyers-Briggs test is a professional instrument and may only be administered by a trained practitioner, while the Keirsey test is available at this site. A viewer can take the test online, and it will be scored automatically. The test itself is a lengthy questionnaire taken from Keirsey's book *Please Understand Me: Character and Temperament Types*,[22] and consists of 70 randomized multiple choice questions. This site also includes a solid introduction to the theory underlying the test, as well as a helpful bibliography of reference materials on personality typing.

Learning Style

http://www.gse.rmit.edu.au/~rsedc/learn.html

Learning Style is a somewhat cryptic site because it contains a complete psychological test whose author and source are unknown. The only information provided is that the questionnaire has been converted to digital form by David Chia, who is affiliated with the Graduate School of Engineering at RMIT University in Australia. The test itself is a brief nine-question instrument requiring multiple choice responses. The questionnaire can be completed online, and is automatically scored by computer once it has been completed and the viewer has clicked on the submit button. The questions probe the subject's preferred learning style in a number of different situations, such as decision making, learning a foreign language, and making major purchases. Despite the lack of introductory background material, the test itself is thought-provoking and can be instructive. This test will be particularly interesting to those working in the area of educational psychology.

Meyers-Briggs FAQ—A Summary of Personality Typing

http://sunsite.unc.edu/personality/faq-mbti.html

Anyone wishing to get a quick grasp of the Myers-Briggs test and the psychological theories upon which it is based[23] will find this site quite useful. It is also helpful for understanding other tests that are based on Myers-Briggs and the concept of personality typing, such as the the DDLI and the Keirsey Temperament Sorter. This site is actually mistitled in the sense that the information does not appear in standard FAQ question and answer format. It begins with a detailed summary of personality typing from a broad historical and theoretical perspective. This is followed by detailed descriptions of the four scales used and the 16 personality types measured, preferred vocabulary for the scales, and a bibliography of books, periodicals, and other resources on personality typing. This is likely the best general source of information on personality typing currently on the Web.

Personality Diagnostic Questionnaire-4

http://www.travel-net.com/~alphalog/

The PDQ-4 is a test used for detecting the presence of personality disorders, based on Axis II of the DSM-IV. It is intended for use by practicing professionals in the mental health field. The predecessor of the PDQ-4, the PDQ-R, has been widely used and extensively researched.[24] This version, the PDQ-4, evaluates several different types of personality disorders—the schizoid, depressive, and histrionic-narcissistic, as well as the avoidant-dependent, obsessive-compulsive, and negativistic-depressive disorders. By clicking on a link at the site, one is able to download a copy of the paper and pencil version of the test, which is free for unlimited use. A hard copy can also be obtained from the publisher, whose e-mail address is included. The test is only sent to addresses that indicate an academic or professional affiliation. This site also contains links to other services that the publisher provides, such as questionnaire design and evaluation. PDQ-4 provides links to several other Internet resources for psychology and psychiatry as well.

The Personality Index

http://www.astro.washington.edu/ingram/mbti/index.html

The Personality Index is another Web site based on the Jungian concept of personality types.[25] It includes a number of links to personality type resources, which have all been mentioned elsewhere in this study. Its particular contribution is to provide a listing of links to home pages organized by personality type. Doug Ingram, who maintains the site, sees the page as a test of the validity of the concept of personality typing. Specifically, it appears to be an application of the Meyers-Briggs Type Inventory. The typing at this site corresponds to the 16 personality types used in the MBTI. Each type has two links. One link connects to a set of links to home pages of people whose test results suggest that they are that type. The other link provides an explanation of that particular type along with examples of famous people through history who have exemplified that type. Those interested in testing based on personality types will find this page interesting, and anyone who is uncertain about what their personality type is can get an idea by trying the Keirsey Temperament Sorter, mentioned earlier in this study.

Rorschach Inkblot Test

http://www-students.biola.edu/~markm.rorsch.html

This site contains several links to Rorschach-related material. It begins with a rather ingenious and entertaining online version of the Rorschach called "cyber-blots." This consists of ten Rorschach-like patterns created by using the symbol keys on the computer keyboard. Another link is titled "The Exner Bible" a reference to John E. Exner, who pioneered one of the most significant advances in the development of the Rorschach by devising a comprehensive system for scoring and interpreting the test in the 1970s.[26] There is also a link to a proposed Internet relay chat group for Rorschach issues (at the time of this writing the channel had been applied for). Another useful feature of this site is a history of the Rorschach test, and a link to a bibliography of non-Exnerian interpretive schemas. This is an important site for anyone interested in projective testing, particularly faculty and students working in the areas of clinical and counseling psychology.

Spending Personality Assessment

http://www.ns.net/cash/selftest//selftest.html

This is an online interactive test that is designed to help a subject understand his or her subconscious spending patterns or "spending personality." The author of the test, a certified financial planner, believes that errors in money management stem from seven unconscious patterns, and that most people have a dominant spending personality. The test consists of 26 Likert-scale type questions that are divided into seven categories: fanatical shopping, impulsive buying, passive buying, avoidance shopping, esteem buying, overdone buying, and hot potato buying. Each category of question is followed by a set of links corresponding to one's score range, which connect to explanations of what that score means. This test may prove useful to those in applied areas of psychology, especially counseling psychology.

VALS Questionnaire

http://future.sri.com/VALS/survey.html

This is a test created by SRI Consulting, a marketing research firm interested in measuring consumer values and lifestyles (VALS). The test is designed to measure consumer self-orientation,[27] based on the theory that consumers are motivated to purchase products by one of three basic self-orientations: principle, status, or action. Principle-oriented consumers purchase on the basis of ideas, while status-oriented purchasers attempt to demonstrate their success to peers. Action-oriented consumers are motivated to purchase products by a desire for physical or social activity. The VALS questionnaire attempts to measure a subject's VALS type based on online responses to 42 multiple-choice questions. Once completed, the questionnaire can be submitted online, and upon receipt is processed in a matter of minutes. This site should prove especially interesting to anyone working in the area of industrial and organizational psychology.

CONCLUSION

This study represents one of the first attempts to explore the rapidly growing body of resources that now exist for tests and measurements on the Internet. It can be seen that there is a surprisingly large amount of information available having to do with tests and measurements. Much of this material is education-related, but there is a large and growing literature related to psychological tests and measurements. Within the field of psychology, it is personality testing that is most predominant on the Internet. Tests measuring personality type are by far the most prevalent, and several of the major test instruments are represented by one and in some cases several sites.

Many of these Internet resources complement or supplement the existing paper resources covering tests and measurements that are typically found in the reference section of most research libraries. These include valuable electronic guides to classic reference works such as *Tests in Print* and *The Mental Measurements Yearbook*. Some sites even feature overviews of the reference literature on testing and have been clearly designed as aids to students in search of information about a particular test. But perhaps the most exciting discovery is that there are not just test resources, but the actual tests themselves to be found on the Internet. Some of these exist as online interactive versions that can be completed, submitted, and scored electronically, without the need for paper or pencil. This suggests that the Internet may now serve as a testing ground for a form of "virtual testing" that may one day become standard practice.[28] For now though, it can be safely said that the Internet has much to offer anyone searching for information about tests, how to find tests, or even the tests themselves.

NOTES

1. Richard W. Wiggins, "The Unfolding Net: The Internet's Massive Growth Continues to Drive Commerce and Innovation," *Internet World* 6 (November, 1995):42-45.

2. Robert P. Jordan, "Searching for Information on Tests," *The Reference Librarian* 48 (1995): 199-221.

3. Deborah C. Sawyer, "A Matter of Confidence: Asking Reference Questions Over the Internet," *Online* 17 (July, 1993):8-9.

4. James V. Mitchell, "A Potent Triumvirate: Librarian, Buros Institute, and Test User," *RQ* 26 (Spring, 1987):338-34.

5. David J. Pittenger, "The Utility of the Myers-Briggs Type Indicator," *Review of Educational Research* 63 (Winter, 1993):467-488.

6. Thomas Childers, "Evaluative Research in the Library and Information Field," *Library Trends* 38 (Fall, 1989):250-67.

7. Susan Klingberg, "Online Access to Tests: the ETSF and MMYD," *Reference Services Review* 12 (Winter, 1984):15-19.

8. Gregg M. Macmann, David W. Barnett, Steffani A. Burd, Trina Jones et al., "Construct Validity of the Child Behavior Checklist: Effects of Item Overlap on Second-Order Factor Structure," *Psychological Assessment* 4 (March, 1992):113-116.

9. Kevin S. McGrew, Robert H. Bruininks, Martha L. Thurlow, "Relationship Between Measures of Adaptive Functioning and Community Adjustment for Adults With Mental Retardation," *Exceptional Children* 58 (May, 1992):517-529.

10. Ana Huerta-Macias, "Alternative Assessment: Responses to Commonly Asked Questions," *TESOL Journal* 5 (Autumn, 1995):8-11.

11. Richard D. Arvey, Eduardo Salas, Kathleen A. Gialluca, "Using Task Inventories to Forecast Skills and Abilities," *Human Performance* 5:3 (1992):171-190.

12. Josey Y.M. Chu, William L. Palya, Donald E. Walter, "Creating a Hypertext Markup Language Document for an Information Server," *Behavior Research Methods, Instruments and Computers* 27 (May, 1995):200-205.

13. Scott Snyder and Robert Sheehan, "The Rasch Measurement Model: An Introduction," *Journal of Early Intervention* 16 (Winter, 1992):87-95.

14. Thomas K. Fagan and Gary R. VandenBos eds., *Exploring Applied Psychology: Origins and Critical Analyses* (Washington, D.C.: American Psychological Association, 1993):83-118.

15. David M. Karesh, Walter A. Pieper, Clarence L. Holland, "Comparing the MBTI, the Jungian Type Survey, and the Singer-Loomis Inventory of Personality," *Journal of Psychological Type* 30 (1994):30-38.

16. Andrew M. Colman ed., *Companion Encyclopedia of Psychology* (London: Routledge, 1994):1301.

17. Richard J. Herrnstein and Charles Murray, *The Bell Curve: Intelligence and Class Structure in American Life* (New York: Free Press, 1994).

18. Barbara S. Plake, Jane C. Conoley, Jack J. Kramer, Linda U. Murphy, "The Buros Institute of Mental Measurements: Commitment to the Tradition of Excellence," *Journal of Counseling and Development* 69 (May/June, 1991):449-455.

19. Adrian Furnham, Howard Steele, David Pendleton, "A Psychometric Assessment of the Belbin Team-Role Self-Perception Inventory," *Journal of Occupational and Organizational Psychology* 66 (September, 1993):245-257.

20. Daniel Goleman, *Emotional Intelligence* (New York: Bantam Books, 1995).

21. Robert J. Sternberg, Richard K. Wagner, Wendy M. Williams, Joseph A. Horvath et al., "Testing Common Sense," *American Psychologist* 50 (November, 1995):912-927.

22. David Keirsey, *Please Understand Me: Character and Temperament Types* (Del Mar, California: Prometheus Nemesis, 1984).

23. Mary H. McCaulley, "The Myers-Briggs Type Indicator: A Measure for Individuals and Groups," *Measurement and Evaluation in Counseling and Development* 22 (January, 1990):181-195.

24. Jayne Patrick, Paul Links, Rob Van Reekum, Janice E.M. Mitten et al. "Using the PDQ-R BPD Scale As a Brief Screening Measure in the Differential Diagnosis of Personality Disorder," *Journal of Personality Disorders* 9 (Fall, 1995): 266-274.

25. C.G. Jung, *Psychological Types* (Princeton University Press, 1971).

26. John E. Exner, Leon S. Martin, "The Rorschach: A History and Description of the Comprehensive System," *School Psychology Review* 12 (Fall, 1983):407-413.

27. Thomas P. Novak, Bruce MacEvoy, "On Comparing Alternative Segmentation Schemes: The List of Values (LOV) and Values and Life Styles (VALS)," *Journal of Consumer Research* 17 (June, 1990):105-109.

28. Georg Warzecha, "The Challenge to Psychological Assessment from Modern Computer Technology," *European Review of Applied Psychology* 41:3 (1991):213-220.

Select Bibliography
of Resources for Internet Trainers

Hollis Near

SUMMARY. This article presents selected bibliography listing resources for Internet trainers with an emphasis on training the trainer. It includes print and electronic formats. *[Article copies available for a fee from The Haworth Document Delivery Service: 1-800-342-9678. E-mail address: getinfo@haworth.com]*

KEYWORDS. Internet trainer, Internet training

SCOPE

This bibliography highlights print and electronic resources for Internet trainers, with an emphasis on educational materials for training the trainer. Typical resources include: model training sessions, shared training materials, as well as books, articles, conference papers and discussion lists that address issues related to Internet training. In the interest of currency, titles published between 1994 and 1996 were given priority.

INTRODUCTION

To complement this volume I've compiled a bibliography of Internet training resources suitable to a range of skill levels. This range includes

---

Hollis Near (hnear@seattleu.edu) is Acquisitions Librarian, A.A. Lemieux Library, Seattle University, Seattle, WA 98122.

[Haworth co-indexing entry note]: "Select Bibliography of Resources for Internet Trainers." Near, Hollis. Co-published simultaneously in *Internet Reference Services Quarterly* (The Haworth Press, Inc.) Vol. 2, No. 4, 1997, pp. 237-242; and: *The Challenge of Internet Literacy: The Instruction-Web Convergence* (ed: Lyn Elizabeth M. Martin) The Haworth Press, Inc., 1997, pp. 237-242. Single or multiple copies of this article are available for a fee from The Haworth Document Delivery Service [1-800-342-9678, 9:00 a.m. - 5:00 p.m. (EST). E-mail address: getinfo@haworth.com].

237

beginning trainers with little preparation time, as well as trainers with some experience who are now able to concentrate on broader training issues and resources.

On October 31, 1996 I attended a statewide video teleconference, sponsored by the Washington State Library, entitled *Training Others to Use the Internet.* Informative and concise presentations, by Cindy Cunningham and Joan Johnson, focused on training the trainer. Of the participants, the level of actual training experience appeared to range from beginner to expert. A few people were in the early planning stage of preparing a training program. During comment periods and afterwards, I heard attendees express a common need for practical training resources: educational resources for improving their training skills as well as sources of presentation materials and model training sessions. As I read and reviewed material for this bibliography, I encountered similar needs for training resources expressed repeatedly among Internet trainers from a variety of institutions and backgrounds.

Even though commercial providers of Internet training are proliferating, not every institution chooses, or is able, to contract for outside training services. In such cases Internet training, for both staff and patrons, will likely fall to in-house trainers. Depending on staffing levels, ability to create new positions, and any prior establishment of bibliographic instruction or staff development training programs, there may be a robust pool of experienced trainers or none at all. When developing an in-house Internet training program, especially in cases where training expertise may be scarce, materials for training the trainer become as vital as any Internet tutorial.

Recognition of varied backgrounds among Internet trainers is conveyed in the mission statement for NETTRAIN, an established discussion list for Internet trainers. The list audience is described as "network managers at large research universities" along with "others . . . who have found themselves assigned the job of training others to use BITNET and Internet because they have shown the initiative to learn a little on their own." These "others," among whom I count myself, have been foremost in my mind while researching this bibliography.

Writing in November 1996, I anticipate that by the time this volume goes to press, some of the electronic citations may have changed. For this reason I've tried to choose electronic resources which, because of organizational sponsorship or prior track record of stability and maintenance, appear likely to have some staying power and therefore longer utility.

BOOKS ON TRAINING

Barron, Ann E., Karen S. Ivers, *The Internet and Instruction: Activities and Ideas* (Englewood, CO: Libraries Unlimited, 1996).

Kovacs, Diane, *The Internet Trainers Guide* (New York: Van Nostrand Reinhold, 1995).

Tennant, Roy, John Ober, and Anne G. Lipow, *Crossing the Internet Threshold-2nd ed.* (Berkeley, CA: Library Solutions Press, 1994).

INTERNET TRAINING SERIES

The *Internet Workshop Series* (Berkeley, CA: Library Solutions Press), coordinated by Anne G. Lipow, includes model workshops developed by experienced Internet trainers. Most titles are available in two editions. The learner's editions are text-based, self-paced tutorials. PLUS editions, for trainers, add presentation notes and text files of the complete lecture. Overheads are provided in print (full-page copies for making transparencies) and electronic format (Macintosh and Windows diskettes containing PowerPoint presentation slides in color, and a PowerPoint Viewer file for displaying them). For training purposes, all titles in this series are recommended in PLUS edition when available.

Jaffe, Lee David, *Introducing the Internet PLUS: A Model Presentation for Trainers-2nd ed.* Internet Workshop Series no. 1 (Berkeley, CA: Library Solutions Press, 1996).

Robison, David F.W., *All About Internet FTP: Learning and Teaching to Transfer Files on the Internet.* Internet Workshop Series no. 2 (Berkeley, CA: Library Solutions Press, 1994).

Peete, Gary R., *Business Resources on the Internet: A Hands on Workshop* Internet Workshop Series no. 3 (Berkeley, CA: Library Solutions Press, 1995).

Clement, Gail P., *Science and Technology on the Internet: An Instructional Guide.* Internet Workshop Series no. 4 (Berkeley, CA: Library Solutions Press, 1996).

Junion-Metz, Gail, *K-12 Resources on the Internet: An Instructional Guide* Internet Workshop Series no. 5 (Berkeley, CA: Library Solutions Press, 1996).

Tennant, Roy, *Practical HTML: A Self-Paced Tutorial* Internet Workshop Series No. 6 (Berkeley, CA: Library Solutions Press, 1996).

Jaffe, Lee David, *All About Internet Mail: An Instructional Handbook* (Berkeley, CA: Library Solutions Press, in press).

Ober, John and Anne Lipow, *How to Teach the Internet* (Berkeley, CA: Library Solutions Press, in press).

JOURNAL ARTICLES ON TRAINING

DeBrower, A.M., R.F. Skinner, "Designing an Internet Class for a Scientific and Technical Audience," *Special Libraries* 87:3 (Summer 1996):139-146. [Describes one day introductory course for Applied Physics Lab, Johns Hopkins University.]

Gold, Etta D., "Do Spiders Live on the Web?" *School Library Journal* 42 (July 1996):34. [Using a metaphor to teach children the Internet at the Coral Gables Branch of Miami-Dade Public Library.]

Greenfield, Louise and Others, "A Model for Teaching the Internet: Preparation and Practice," *Computers in Libraries* 16:3 (March 1996):22.

Kohut, Dave and Joel Sternberg, "Using the Internet to Study the Internet: An Active Learning Component," *Research Strategies* 13:3 (Summer 1995):176-181. [Undergraduate course at the Dept. of Mass Communications, Saint Xavier University, Chicago.]

Konrad, Lee and James Stemper, "Same Game, Different Name: Demystifying Internet Instruction," *Research Strategies* 14:1 (Win 1996):4-21.

Pask, Judith M. and Carl E. Snow, "Undergraduate Instruction and the Internet," *Library Trends* 44:2 (Fall 1995):306-317.

CONFERENCE PAPERS ON TRAINING ISSUES

Hert, C. A., H. Rosenbaum, S.C. Skutnik, and S.M. Backs, "Information Needs and Uses During Internet Training," *ASIS '95: Proceedings of the 58th ASIS Annual Meeting, Chicago, Illinois,* 32 (October 9-12 1995):61-76.

Miller, D. L., M.C. Zeigler, "Striking It Rich with the Internet: An Interactive Workshop for Teaching Faculty the Internet," *The Impact of Technology on Library Instruction: Library Orientation Series* 25 (1995):85-91. [Presented at 21st National library instruction conference–1993 May: Racine, WI.]

Makulowich, John, "Training the Internet Trainer: Toward a Systematic Approach," *INET'96, 6th Annual Conference of the Internet Society, 28 June 1996,* <http://www.cais.com/makulow/t3.html>.

Scott, J. F., "Training the Trainers–An Introduction to Teaching Other People About the Internet," *Online information-International Meeting-1994, Issue 18.*

INTERNET TRAINING RESOURCE LISTS

IETF/Training Materials Catalogue <http://www.trainmat.ietf.org/catalogue. html> [Select, yet extensive, list of network training materials for Internet trainers from Internet Engineering Task Force and Trans-European Research and Education Networking Association. Each resource is described in concise detail using a consistent template for all entries.]

WITR World Internet Training Registry <http://granite.sentex. net/~witr> [Frequently updated list of training events, seminars, and courses. Covers training and consulting services.]

ELECTRONIC DISCUSSION LISTS

C-TRAIN, SchoolNet Community Access Net Trainers Forum, <mailto:listserv@unbvm1.csd.unb.ca>.

COMPINST-L, A Computer Instructor Listserv for teachers in San Francisco and Sacramento, CA-USA <e-mail:listserv@netcom.com> [Local in focus but open to all interested. COMPINST-L information at <http://www.mother.com/~osherry/compinst-l.html>.]

NETTRAIN, Network Trainers <usenet:bit.listserv.nettrain> [NETTRAIN information at <http://www.fau.edu/rinaldi/nettrain/listinfo.html>. Primarily a list for Internet trainers, not beginning Internet users.]

TRDEV-L, Listserv Discussion Group for Training & Development <e-mail:listserv@psuvm.psu.edu> [TRDEV-L information at <http:// milkman.cac.psu.edu/~dlp/TRDEV/trdev-l.html>.]

INTERNET TRAINING MATERIALS

15-Minute Series: Tools for the Internet Trainer <http://www.rs.internic. net/nic-support/15min/> [Internet training materials provided for the research and education community by InterNIC Information and Education Services and the Library and Information Technology Association (LITA), a division of the American Library Association (ALA). This is the site if your preparation time is limited! Truly modular and ready-to-use slide presentations on a variety of Internet topics. The series has a consistent outline and visual style which enables modules to be used alone or in combination. Modules can be adapted using templates to modify or create additional slides. Modules are reviewed and updated regularly by the InterNIC/LITA editorial board. Available in HTML and MS PowerPoint files. Copyright 1996 Network Solutions, Inc. Permission is granted to quote, copy, or otherwise reproduce the materials in the *15 Minute Series*, provided that appropriate credit is given and the copyright notice is retained.]

Larson, Laura, *University of Washington Internet Training* <gopher://nisp. ncl.ac.uk:7070/11/OtherMat/GeneralTrainMats/Washington/> [Full series of MS PowerPoint presentation files on Internet tools. File 10-train.ppt is a useful how-to presentation on training. No restrictions on downloading other than usual acknowledgments.]

Netskills Training Kits © Netskills 1996, University of Newcastle <http://www.netskills.ac.uk/> [Supersedes the much cited Network Training Materials gopher. Copyrighted material developed for UK Higher Education community only. Superbly organized site, worth the look even though files may not be downloaded by non-UK sites without explicit prior permission from copyright owner.]

Teaching Critical Evaluation Skills for World Wide Web Resources <http:/www. science.widener.edu/~withers/webeval.htm> [Prepared by Jan Alexander and Marsha Tate of Widener University. Comprehensive and essential website for this topic. Includes checklists for evaluating Web resources. Adapts five traditional print evaluation criteria to Web resources: accuracy, authority, objectivity, currency, and coverage. Includes MS PowerPoint slide presentation.]

Warren-Wenk, Peggy, "Internet Training: Program Planning, Curriculum Content and Leading a Session," *Internet World Canada '96: Internet & World Wide Web Conference and Exhibition* <http://www.library.yorku. ca/staff2.pwarren/> [Presentation given as part of half day tutorial: *A Blueprint for Internet Training*. Lots of content here. Not just how-to but why. Focuses on using a "process-based approach" which teaches the usual navigational skills while emphasizing trouble-shooting skills, critical evaluation of sources, and the position of Internet resources within the broader context of information resources in general.]

Index